Female Genital Mutilation

Female Genital Mutilation

When Culture and Law Clash

CHARLOTTE PROUDMAN

Great Clarendon Street, Oxford, OX2 6DP,
United Kingdom

Oxford University Press is a department of the University of Oxford.
It furthers the University's objective of excellence in research, scholarship,
and education by publishing worldwide. Oxford is a registered trade mark of
Oxford University Press in the UK and in certain other countries

Published in the United States of America by Oxford University Press
198 Madison Avenue, New York, NY 10016, United States of America

British Library Cataloguing in Publication Data

Data available

Library of Congress Control Number: 2021946951

ISBN 978–0–19–886460–8

DOI: 10.1093/oso/9780198864608.001.0001

Printed and bound in Great Britain by
Clays Ltd, Elcograf S.p.A.

I dedicate this book to all of the girls and women who dare to speak out,
Speak the unspeakable,
Change the world.

Foreword

Patriarchy and the Pandemic of FGM

We are mere footnotes to the future. If we are lucky.

If we are not completely forgotten.

Future generations will, I am convinced, look back in astonishment that in this time of viral infection and fear, silently and surreptitiously 2 to 3 million more young women and girls every year were being genitally cut.

It is an unimaginable amount. I choose not to imagine it. Because I have met one, and two, and groups of three and four, during my human rights work in Sub-Saharan Africa. I have seen their pain and it wounds me.

But why am I, a lawyer in the inconceivably privileged Global North, and a male, concerned about FGM? That's a question I am often asked. What's it to you? It is a question that I know the author of this ground-breaking book Dr Charlotte Proudman – Charlotte – is often asked too.

It's because Charlotte and I share a moral conviction and an unqualified belief that FGM is one of the most egregious human rights abuses in the world.

It is a pandemic inflicted on the powerless.

It is a pet project of patriarchy.

Of course it is.

The social control and policing of women through the pain-induced regulation of their sexuality and reproduction has subsisted for centuries. It endures because on an insidious, despicable level, it works. It is alive. It evolves. Harmful practices are like that. They mutate.

How are we to understand the current mutations, even as variants of other contagions spread across the globe – how, if we are to better protect at-risk women and girls? We can read Charlotte Proudman's book.

I have. It is a game-changer. Charlotte has devoted years of her life to researching and fighting FGM. This book is her accounting.

Read it.

I am convinced that Charlotte's work already has and will continue to spare countless entirely innocent girls from unfathomable suffering. It has and will save lives.

But here's the thing I put in front of you today: we can all be part of the fight in the assault on abomination. I know no better word to describe the mutilation of the genitalia of children.

Accordingly, it is an honour for this privileged male in the cool northern latitudes of the globe to be invited to jointly contribute to the Preface with my good friend and fellow anti-FGM activist Leyla Hussein. Leyla, you are an inspiration.

Charlotte, in court and in the academy and in your writing you are too.

I am proud to have worked with both of you to bring our vision, our fever dream, closer: the end of FGM. We have worked on the Parliamentary Inquiry, we have worked on reports to the Special Rapporteur, we have worked in courts and out of them. And still it is not enough.

For I return to the girls I have come across. I was in a displaced persons camp in Central Africa on the fringe of a war zone. We were discussing FGM and one of them asked me in French, 'But how can it change?' There was silence in the DP camp, an impromptu village of billowing bone-white sheets and tent posts under an equatorial sun that had no idea that so many of the children around me had been cut. Yes, silence, until another girl said, 'But how can it not?'

Dr Charlotte Proudman's book will explain to you what FGM is, why it is, and how together we can change it. For how can we, mere footnotes to the future, not?

Dexter Dias QC
8 August 2021

Foreword

Confronting Uncomfortable Realities

The uncomfortable reality is that in 2021, we are still being forced to collectively navigate an overtly patriarchal, racist, violent, and oppressive global system. Charlotte Proudman is doing everything in her power to change that and I have complete faith in her ability to touch minds, hearts, and lives with this book. In my 19 years as an anti-FGM campaigner, psychotherapist, and consultant, I have met so many impressive individuals fighting for gender equality, human rights, and global safety. However, Charlotte stands out as someone using their power and privilege in the correct way, standing up to the system and advocating fiercely for people affected by gender-based violence and by FGM especially. She knows the world we live in wasn't set up for women's benefit and works to disrupt those foundations of inequality, specifically in the legal sphere. She knows FGM must be addressed in relation to systematic oppression based on race, class, and gender, and is constantly conscious of the intersectional nature of these issues. I have great respect for her work and can't wait to see more people engage with her approach to the reasons for the continuation of FGM and the tools at our disposal to end the violence once and for all.

Something I always emphasise in my work with healthcare professionals, during interviews, and at international conferences is that a large majority of FGM cases affect the statistically most vulnerable human being on this planet: the Black, female, African child. She is most often the very last human being those who hold power and resources in this world think about. As a result of this, we must rethink and reshape the very basis of our approach to this system that rules our lives so cruelly. The system we live in accepts that abuse and control of women and children is okay, the marginalisation of Black people is okay, the oppression of those in poverty is okay – these inequalities are seen as something we can live with and move past without fully confronting. Charlotte's book does confront that reality and challenges it.

Luckily, we have entered a period of time in which more and more people are waking up to the reality. In 2020, the combination of lockdowns, political conflict, and global uncertainty did one positive thing: it forced communities to reflect, question their beliefs, and stand up to white supremacy and patriarchy. The Black Lives Matter movement re-energised age-old calls for liberation, inclusivity, and equality. Black feminist voices were amplified more than ever before, creating a moment in which the world was listening intently. However, this cannot simply be a moment. It has to be a sustained effort to foreground the voices of the marginalised and genuinely listen to the reasons for which change is urgent. Black liberation, gender equality, and ending FGM share the requirement of people from all walks of life coming together to better understand violent structures and acting in unison to dismantle them. We need to ask more questions: what and who are presenting themselves as barriers to equality? Why is the Black, female, African child so vulnerable? What do we need to do in our personal and professional lives to contribute to progress and safety? Who do we need to listen to in order to ensure change is rapid and sustainable? Which legal structures are contributing to the continuation of FGM? I know Charlotte's book is taking important steps to address these questions (among many more) and shape the future of discourse and policy surrounding FGM and equality.

I am so proud to be included in the introductory pages of this book and I hope it moves and educates readers as much as it has done so for me. I have been so fortunate to work with Charlotte over the years as we have sat on panels together, campaigned, and shared knowledge and experiences. I have learned so much from her and I know anyone who reads this book will too. From the first time we met, we were aligned in our principles and values when it comes to the status of women in the world. Our ways of thinking about equality and progress are very similar, which allowed us to have an easy and effective personal and professional relationship. Our feminism has led us to become sisters in arms, fighting together for real change in policies, laws, and attitudes. I firmly believe that people will do better and have bigger impacts when they work together in this way and support each other. Charlotte has done so much great work in this space and I admire the depth of analysis and insightful commentary she has incorporated into this book. She has done an excellent job crafting a story about the status of laws on FGM and the possibilities for future pathways to change, which I have no doubt will provoke knowledge and experience sharing around the world. The history, law, and diverse experiences of FGM are elucidated with so much care and compassion. Strong, outspoken women like Charlotte give me hope in today's world, they allow me to feel that there is a path out of the violent structures damaging the lives of so many women and girls every day. Together as barristers, activists, medical professionals, wellbeing experts, consultants, political leaders, and individuals, I am confident we can shape and improve the system to protect all people equally. FGM and all forms of violence against women and girls will end and we are all responsible for working towards that goal together.

Dr Leyla Hussein
5 April 2021

Preface

I remember when I first understood the limitations of professionals' knowledge of FGM. I was a baby barrister in the High Court, trying to soak up as much information and experience as I could. It was approximately 2012 when an FGM case was before the court. I will never forget the judge referring to FGM as 'FMG'. It was perfectly clear to me that he had never even heard of the practice. A year later and FGM was firmly put on the political agenda by my feminist ally, Dr Leyla Hussein OBE, who dared to speak her truth so that many women and girls would not suffer the same fate. I quickly became involved in changes to the law on FGM when I worked tirelessly with the Bar Human Rights Committee's Working Group on FGM, chaired by the inspirational human rights barristers, Dexter Dias QC and Kirsty Brimelow QC. We were instrumental in carving out a new legal remedy that could protect thousands of at-risk girls from FGM: Female Genital Mutilation Protection Orders. It was this very work that led me to spend several years buried in books in the University of Cambridge's library, trying to work out and understand why an ancient, patriarchal practice continued to be performed and why our society was turning a blind eye to women and girls who suffered gravely because of FGM. Reading was not enough. I needed to hear the voices of survivors and perpetrators of FGM. I wanted to understand the uncomfortable truths about FGM. I set about interviewing women who had been subjected to FGM, women at risk, and professionals working in the field of FGM. I spent hours after hours, wrestling with my feminist views alongside trying to understand a deeply entrenched cultural norm from the perspective of women who wanted to uphold FGM. I travelled to Harvard University to meet with professors who had spent decades trying to end FGM globally. I remember vividly a warm, sunny afternoon at Yale Law School, speaking with my hero, Professor Catharine MacKinnon, about my doctoral research. She inspired me to apply a feminist and critical race theory analysis to my research. After many years of highs and lows, my doctoral research was complete but my work to help end FGM was far from over. I moved from academia to legal practice as a human rights barrister. Continuing my commitment to protecting girls from FGM, I specialise in FGM law and have worked on a number of landmark cases in the UK. I have advised the United Nations on the efficacy of legal remedies to end FGM. I also taught and wrote about FGM, as a Junior Research Fellow at Queens' College, Cambridge. When I hear the stories of mothers who have been cut, mothers who desperately want to protect their children from the same trauma, I am compelled to continue my life work to end FGM. No girl or woman should suffer the irreversible harm that is FGM.

Acknowlededgments

I owe an enormous debt to all the women and stakeholders who generously gave up their time to contribute to this book. It is their voices that made this book come to life. My incredible work colleagues and friends, Dr Leyla Hussein OBE and Dexter Dias QC, the absolute dream team who have devoted their lives to ending FGM. Hoda Ali and Hibo Wardere, you are my absolute heroes.

Janet Fyle, Naana Otoo-Oyortey, Joy Clarke, Juliet Albert, Professor Hilary Burrage, Leethan Batholomew, Rohma Ullah, Millie Kerr, Natasha Rattu, Alex Adams, Stella Creasy MP, and Dr Sharon Raymond for changing women's lives and working towards ending FGM. Detector Inspective Alan Davies, Commander Ivan Balhatchet, Detective Sergeant Pal Singh, and Gill Squires for working hard to help implement the law and protect girls and women from FGM.

My PhD supervisor, Professor Manali Desai, who guided me every step of the way. My former PhD supervisor, Dr Jeff Miley, an absolute trail blazer. Catharine MacKinnon who inspired me to dedicate my life's work to feminism and the law. Helena Kennedy QC for making me believe in the sisterhood (even in law). My mentor, Michael Sternberg QC, for encouraging me to further my academic studies. I am grateful to Anthony Metzer QC for his invaluable support. Thank you to Professor Felicity Gerry QC for reaching out to me when I was a baby barrister and for inviting me to collaborate on important FGM projects. Dr Annemarie Middelburg for being a kindred spirit in every sense of the word. Kirsty Brimelow QC for championing the end FGM movement through the law. Thank you to Gunn Benjaminsen for her beady editing eye and Harriet Sheves for helping in the latter stages of this book.

A huge thank you to my Mum, Aviv, Kathryn, and Teddy for believing in me every step of the way.

Contents

Table of Cases

Table of Legislation

List of Abbreviations

ECHR	European Convention on Human Rights
FGCS	female genital cosmetic surgery
FGM	female genital mutilation
FGMPO	female genital mutilation protection order
MP	Member of Parliament
NGO	Non-government organisation
NHS	National Health Service, which exists throughout the UK
Pharaonic / pharaoni	Type III FGM
Sunna	Type I FGM
UN	United Nations
UNESCO	United Nations Economic and Social Council
UNICEF	United Nations International Children's Emergency Fund
WHO	World Health Organization

Female Genital Mutilation: An Overview

Female genital mutilation (FGM) is a violation of women's and girls' international human rights.[1] FGM was largely invisible in Britain until increased political sensitisation of the practice emerged in 2013. Survivors for the first time were given a high-profile platform to speak about FGM and the government's failure to address and work towards eliminating the practice. Survivors spoke vividly about their stories of FGM, which permeated people's consciousness and put the issue on the political agenda. FGM was rarely out of the media in 2014 and 2015. It was featured widely in newspapers and even on the television and radio. Stories about the mutilation of women's and girls' genitalia became popular news as people read articles feeling equally repulsed and moved to action. Anti-FGM campaigns sprung up in most Western countries and the UN made FGM a human rights priority. At the same time as anti-FGM discourses were gaining traction, many FGM-performing communities remained unaware of the criminal status of FGM. Alongside increasing public sensitisation about FGM were new anti-FGM policies and laws targeted at FGM. This book analyses women's and professionals' testimonies and relevant literature about FGM and relevant laws and policies. The focus is on interview participants' responses to FGM and anti-FGM laws, their experience of FGM, and the meanings attached to their lives. Much is learned about the dynamics of FGM from interview participants' descriptions of the practice and their attitudes towards the law.

In 1985, FGM was criminalised in Britain. Since criminalising the practice in the mid-1980s, it is believed that FGM continues to be performed in the UK and upon British citizens or residents abroad. The number of women and girls who have undergone FGM or are at risk of FGM in Britain is highly contested due to the challenges in obtaining reliable data. The first conviction for FGM was in 2019. The efficacy of anti-FGM laws is an unresolved topic of debate. The function of the criminal law is to prohibit behaviour and practices

---

[1] For more about the UK's international obligations to end FGM see, Bar Human Rights Committee, *Report of the Bar Human Rights Committee of England and Wales to the Parliamentary Inquiry into Female Genital Mutilation* (2014) and Theodora A Christou and Sam Fowles, 'Failure to Protect Girls from Female Genital Mutilation' (2015) 79(5) The Journal of Criminal Law 344.

Female Genital Mutilation. Charlotte Proudman, Oxford University Press. © Charlotte Proudman 2022.
DOI: 10.1093/oso/9780198864608.003.0001

in society and therefore maintain social control and to send a public message that specific behaviour and practices are unacceptable.[2] The British state has an interest in FGM because criminalising the practice ensures the protection of British values and the enforcement of norms upon 'other' communities.

The role of the British state in attempting to eliminate FGM must be carefully considered alongside the Black Lives Matter movement, a global movement that re-emerged following the murder of George Floyd by four police officers in the US in the summer of 2020. In this book, FGM is examined and understood in a context of social and legal structures that reproduce systematic race, gender, and class inequalities. Black, Asian, and Minority Ethnic women experience higher levels of social exclusion and gender-based violence than white women, thus accessing support from service providers can often be limited and seeking redress through the law can compound racial and gender inequalities. For example, women who do not have secure immigration status may fear that reporting FGM could result in them being removed from the country or they may lack recourse to public funds to seek additional support from the public sector. As such, this book applies an intersectional, feminist, and human rights framework to ensure that the multiple axes of women's inequality are situated within women's experiences of FGM.

When the law is not, or rarely, implemented, one must question whether the law has a deterrent effect or has any real impact on eliminating the prohibited behaviour. However, FGM is a unique practice deeply rooted in cultural norms and values over generations, causing clashes between culture and law.[3] Research studies ordinarily proceed without scrutiny of the impact of the law and its apparent impenetrable nature. The law has been subject to criticism for failing to recognise the diversity of individuals within particular groups, instead regarding them as a homogeneous category.[4] At present, the law targets migrant communities, which creates a perception that anti-FGM laws reproduce the discrimination that FGM-performing communities' experience in

---

[2] Andrew Ashworth and Lucia Zedner, 'Defending the Criminal Law: Reflections on the Changing Character of Crime, Procedure, and Sanctions' (2015) 2(1) Criminal Law and Philosophy 21.

[3] Literature often focuses on a clash between the societal understandings of violence and so-called cultural practices such as forced marriage, honour-based violence, and the wearing of the veil. See, Lynn Welchman and Sara Hossain (eds), 'Honour': Crimes, Paradigms and Violence against Women (Zed Books 2005); Susan Moller Okin, Is Multiculturalism Bad for Women? (Princeton University Press 1999); Tamsin Bradley, Women, Violence and Tradition: Taking FGM and Other Practices to a Secular State (Zed Books Ltd 2013) (hereafter Bradley, Women, Violence and Tradition); Chia Longman and Tamsin Bradley, Interrogating Harmful Cultural Practices: Gender, Culture and Coercion (Routledge 2016); Jocelynne A Scutt (ed), Women, Law and Culture: Conformity, Contradiction and Conflict (Springer 2016).

[4] Paola Uccellari, 'Multiple Discrimination: How Law Can Reflect Reality' (2008) 1 The Equal Rights Review 24.

wider society and through the law. This could account in part for FGM-per-forming communities' resisting anti-FGM laws and initiatives.

The government was compelled to move to action in 2013 following increasing pressures to eliminate FGM and no prosecutions for the practice.[5] Addressing the lacunas in the criminal law, the law was amended in 2003 and 2015. In 2015, the Conservative-led coalition government introduced Female Genital Mutilation Protection Orders (FGMPO), a novel legal remedy in family courts that aim to prevent FGM from taking place without puni-tive remedies being imposed upon potential perpetrators unless the order is breached. The failure of the criminal law to secure convictions for FGM has been the subject of sustained academic, political, and legal debate. Sociologists, anthropologists, and legal scholars have produced a volume of literature at-tempting to explain the persistence of the practice in a context of criminal-isation.[6] Academics continue to question whether the law is a suitable tool for deterring and eliminating FGM or whether other initiatives could have a more significant impact on ending FGM.[7] More recently, the conviction for FGM in 2019 has sparked renewed interested in the criminalisation of FGM.

The aim of this book is to examine the impact of anti-FGM laws on deterring FGM and changing the attitudes and beliefs of FGM-performing communities' members towards the practice. A core theme in the book is the potential and limitations of social and cultural change through the law. The perspective of individuals involved is at the heart of this book. Interviews with women from FGM-performing communities and professionals[8] highlight the complex and varying attitudes towards the practice and legal remedies designed to prevent FGM. There is limited qualitative material about women's attitudes towards FGM and the criminal law as well as their own experiences of the practice. It is imperative that one listens to the voices of women who have undergone FGM and advocate for and against the practice. Information about profes-sionals who are law enforcement agents or work closely with FGM-performing communities is inadequate, yet they play key roles in enforcing the law and

---

[5] For a discussions about the limits of the law in ending FGM see, Jenaye M Lewis and Dexter Dias, 'Feminism, Morality, and Human Rights: Assessing the Effectiveness of the United Kingdom's FGM Act' in Irehobhunde O Iyioha (ed), *Women's Health and the Limits of Law* (Routledge 2019) 65.

[6] In a UK context, see for example, Hilary Burrage, *Eradicating Female Genital Mutilation: A UK Perspective* (Routledge 2016).

[7] For arguments that the UK response to FGM is disproportionate see, Sarah M Creighton and others, 'Tackling Female Genital Mutilation in the UK' (2019) 15 British Medical Journal 364; Marge Berer, 'Prosecution of Female Genital Mutilation in the United Kingdom: Injustice at the Intersection of Good Public Health Intentions and the Criminal Law' (2020) 19(4) Medical Law International 258.

[8] Professionals responsible for designing and enforcing the law and who work with communities were interviewed.

encouraging communities to abandon FGM. This book provides a thorough analysis of the impact of the law on the dynamics of FGM and it aims to analyse the core barriers and obstacles to the elimination of FGM, including whether criminal laws designed to prohibit FGM have resulted in unintended consequences of communities resisting the law and continuing the practice. It is important to analyse the ways in which FGM-performing communities negotiated and maintained the practice of FGM in a context where it is a criminal offence and thus is performed underground to prevent detection and evade the law. It is in this context that this book seeks to explore the continuation of FGM and the impact of laws on the practice. There are five main areas of enquiry: women's experiences of FGM and the motivations for the practice; the evolution of the criminalisation of FGM since the mid-1980s to present day; women's attitudes towards anti-FGM laws and FGM narratives; the barriers to criminal laws working effectively; and the impact of FGMPOs in protecting girls and women from FGM.

Dealing with issues of reflexivity, my background is relevant in reflecting on how my position has impacted upon the theoretical and practical design of this thesis.[9] I practice as a family and immigration law barrister specialising in violence against women and girls. I have advised NGOs in relation to cases of FGM and I have represented women and girls who have undergone FGM or are at risk of the practice.[10] My experience has driven me towards wanting to understand the practice from the perspective of communities including those that defend FGM. I chose a qualitative methodological approach and applied a feminist framework to allow the participants' voices to be heard through the research. My personal and professional position is to further the elimination of FGM; however, I recognise that there are a multitude of perspectives towards the practice including defending FGM or sympathising with the practice. Furthermore, I recognise that anti-FGM laws appear to have had limited effect in furthering the end-FGM movement. I am curious to explore all sides of the debates about FGM, to examine why there is limited dialogue between the different positions, and to analyse the nexus between attitudes towards FGM and the efficacy of the law. My approach is to attempt to remain neutral and objective in exploring FGM whilst recognising my own position and biases that might influence the research. In the conclusion I draw on the competing

---

[9] Reflexivity and ethics are explored further throughout the book.
[10] While I am an anti-FGM advocate, I attempted, in so far as I could, to suspend my own activism and assumed as neutral a position as possible. This allowed me to document and give space to the views of women of colour from a range of backgrounds.

narratives about FGM and pull together a coherent overview of the impact of anti-FGM laws.

This book will use interviews in conjunction with a literature review[11] and a socio-legal analysis of case law in criminal and family law to explore emerging FGM jurisprudence. Information about FGM is usually confined to recorded statistics about women and girls who have undergone FGM from health providers and limited research studies about FGM.[12] Given the paucity of empirical research, interviews with women and professionals have greatly enriched understandings about FGM and the potential and challenges of anti-FGM legal remedies. The empirical research for this book represents, for the first-time in

---

[11] This book explores the conflict and tensions between the often polarised theoretical positions of feminism, international human rights, cultural relativism, and critical race theory, which take different positions on the practice. In simple terms, feminism regards FGM as control over women's and girls' sexuality: see, Fran P Hosken, *The Hosken Report: Genital and Sexual Mutilation of Females* (Women's International Network News 1979); Mary Daly, *Gyn/Ecology: The Metaethics of Radical Feminism* (Beacon Press 1990); Alice Walker and Pratibha Parmar, *Warrior Marks: Female Genital Mutilation and the Sexual Blinding of Women* (Harcourt Brace 1993). International human rights defines the practice as a violation of the child's right to bodily integrity: see, Charlotte Bunch, 'Women's Rights as Human Rights: Toward a Re-vision of Human Rights' (1990) 12(4) Human Rights Quarterly 486; Radhika Coomaraswamy, 'Integration of the Human Rights of Women and the Gender Perspective: Violence against Women' (Report of the Special Rapporteur on Violence Against Women, its Causes and Consequences, Ms Radhika Coomaraswamy, submitted in accordance with Commission on Human Rights resolution 2001/49: cultural practices in the family that are violent towards women, United Nations Economic and Social Council 2002). Colliding with these two positions, cultural relativism often regards FGM as a legitimate cultural practice while Western opposition is perceived as neo-colonial imposition: Fuambai Ahmadu, 'Rites and Wrongs: An Insider/Outsider Reflects on Power and Excision' in Bettina Shell-Duncan and YIva Hernlund (eds) *Female 'Circumcision' in Africa: Dimensions of the Practice and Debates* (Lynne Rienner Publishers 2000) (hereafter Ahmadu, 'Rites and Wrongs'); Richard A Shweder, 'What About "Female Genital Mutilation"? And Why Understanding Culture Matters in the First Place' (2000) 129(4) Daedalus 209 (hereafter Shweder, 'What About "Female Genital Mutilation"'). Finally, critical race theory identifies the distinctive legal control exercised over ethnic minority women from a racial perspective: Kimberle Crenshaw, 'Mapping the Margins: Intersectionality, Identity Politics, and Violence against Women of Color' (1991) 43(6) Stanford Law Review 1241 (hereafter, Crenshaw, 'Mapping the Margins').

[12] For small empirical research studies on FGM see, Kate Norman and others, 'FGM is Always with Us: Experiences, Perceptions, Beliefs of Women Affected by Female Genital Mutilation in London: Results from a PEER Study' (2009) Options Consultancy Services Ltd <https://options.co.uk/sites/default/files/uk_2009_female_genital_mutilation.pdf> accessed 9 September 2021; Eiman Hussein, 'Women's Experiences, Perceptions and Attitudes of Female Genital Mutilation: The Bristol PEER Study' (2010) FORWARD <https://www.forwarduk.org.uk/wp-content/uploads/2019/06/Forward-Womens-Experiences-Perceptions-and-Attitudes-of-FGM-The-Bristol-PEER-Study.pdf> accessed 9 September 2021; Kate Norman, Seblework Belay Gegzabher, and Naana Otoo-Oyortey '"Between Two Cultures": A Rapid PEER Study Exploring Migrant Communities' Views on Female Genital Mutilation in Essex and Norfolk, UK' (2016) FORWARD & National FGM Centre Report <http://nationalfgmcentre.org.uk/wp-content/uploads/2015/12/Peer-Research-National-FGM-Centre.pdf> accessed 9 September 2021; Eleanor Brown and Chelsey Porter 'The Tackling FGM Initiative: Evaluation of the Second Phase (2013–2016)' (2016) Options Consultancy Services Ltd (hereafter Brown and Porter, 'Tackling FGM Initiative'); Bradley, *Women, Violence and Tradition* (n 3); Efua Dorkenoo, *Cutting the Rose: Female Genital Mutilation: the Practice and its Prevention* (Minority Rights Group 1994) (hereafter Dorkenoo, *Cutting the Rose*); Comfort Momoh, *Female Genital Mutilation* (Radcliffe Publishing 2005) (hereafter Momoh, *Female Genital Mutilation*); Linda A Morison and others, 'How Experiences and Attitudes Relating to Female Circumcision Vary According to Age on Arrival In Britain: A Study Among Young Somalis in London' (2004) 9(1) Ethnicity & Health 75.

Britain, substantial and in-depth interviews with women[13] and professionals[14] about the dynamics of FGM and the accompanying laws. Detailed interviews were conducted with seventy-nine individuals and two focus groups involving eleven women in each focus group.[15] The women from FGM-performing communities came from a range of demographic backgrounds and were of different ages, the vast majority had undergone FGM. The survivors of FGM whom were interviewed are women of colour mainly of Sub-Saharan African origin. Race is a critical issue that is explored throughout this book. The professionals came from a wide variety of professions including front-line professionals such as police, teachers, social workers and medical practitioners, and professionals responsible for designing the law including politicians and lawyers. Interviews with influential professionals provided a historical analysis of the trajectory of the evolution of law from the 1980s to present day. Women's and professionals' narratives provide colourful and complex material about FGM and the law rarely explored in the available literature. In-depth interviews with women from FGM-performing communities have provided evidence about their unique experiences of FGM, the meaning and purpose ascribed to FGM, what information about anti-FGM laws is known, and their attitudes towards criminal laws. Women's experiences of FGM and the criminal justice system are bound up with their lived experiences as ethnic minority women subject to sexism, racism, and classism. The defence of FGM is not merely about protecting a group right to perform a cultural practice, FGM is representative of other issues of migrant culture, group rights, cultural norms,

---

[13] Eleven women from a Somalian background in two focus groups (twenty-two women in total) and thirteen individual interviews with women and two interviews with men.

[14] Professionals included law enforcement agents, civil servants, Members of Parliament, Members of the House of Lords, NGO workers, medical professionals, social workers, teachers, and religious leaders. Sixty-four of seventy-nine interviews were with professionals from non-FGM-performing communities. Further updating interviews were undertaken where possible.

[15] The interviews were undertaken as part of a PhD thesis on the impact of the criminalisation of FGM on the prevalence of the practice in England and Wales; the research and thesis concluded in 2017. Appendix I provides information pertaining to the interviewees and interview process. The participants included thirteen women from FGM-performing backgrounds, two men from performing communities, and sixty-four professionals working in FGM-related areas. I also conducted two focus groups, each comprised of eleven women of Somali heritage, the majority of whom disclosed that they had undergone FGM. Some of the women interviewed from FGM-performing communities were also professionals as they held jobs such as teachers, social workers, or midwives. Where women held jobs that are relevant to this research study their occupation is identified in the description of the interview participant (see Appendix I). However, women's attitudes and beliefs as women from FGM-performing communities were considered the most important factor when interviewed because they could share insights into a closed community. Women who were also professionals often held a nuanced view, as they were insiders in their community and had knowledge of how FGM is perceived by outsiders. Where relevant, women were questioned about their professional experience. All participants were habitually resident in England, which means their primary residence at the time of the interviews was England.

and race. Highlighting the intersectionality[16] of the common modes of oppression and FGM shows the impact of different structural inequalities upon women's lives, their attitudes and beliefs towards FGM, their experiences of working with professionals, and the barriers to seeking support. In addition, professionals' testimony highlights both their knowledge and lack of insight into the dynamics of FGM and the contested role of anti-FGM laws in ending FGM. Interviews reveal that the law could constitute a barrier to FGM being eliminated, as women used the law as an advocacy tool to argue that it discriminates specifically against ethnic minority women, particularly when the law prohibits FGM for adult women while permitting female genital cosmetic surgery (FGCS) for so-called white, Western women who exercise their agency and choose FGCS. It is rare for professionals, particularly in the field of law, to have a thirst for learning about the nuances of prohibited practices within migrant communities. This is one of the reasons that professionals struggle with applying an intersectional lens to understand the motivations for performing prohibited practices and the impact of the law upon women's lives.

The evidence from interviews provides a more robust account of the deliberate choices to undergo FGM, which is negotiated in a context of criminalisation. Many women stressed the continuities of performing FGM, for example, continuing a cultural norm, maintaining ties to kinship groups, and preventing social ostracisation of girls who are not cut. There was little shift in the consciousness between themselves, their parents, and grandparents. In contrast to widespread assumptions that women are victims of FGM or cultural dupes, women asserted that they valued the practice even if it was a means of controlling their sexuality because it gave them power within a patriarchal community as a wife, mother, and grandmother. The reasons for FGM are rich, complex, and woven into the beliefs and values that various communities uphold.[17] There is no single reason for the continuation of FGM and instead, the factors are multiple and layered. Motivations are rarely specific to each community and instead can be deeply individual and community related, as such the rationale for the continuation of FGM varies within each community that performs FGM. This book provides a unique insight into the motivations for FGM.[18] The most common motivations for the practice include control of

---

[16] Critical race theorist, Kimberley Crenshaw, coined the term 'intersectionality' in 1989, which involves the analysis of 'intrinsically negative frameworks in which social power works to exclude or marginalise those who are different', Crenshaw, 'Mapping the Margins' (n 11).

[17] See, Anika Rahman and Nahid Toubia, *Female Genital Mutilation: A Practical Guide to Worldwide Laws & Policies* (Zed Books 2000) (hereafter Rahman and Toubia, *Female Genital Mutilation*).

[18] See Chapter 1, which outlines women's stories of FGM.

women's sexuality, custom and tradition, social pressure, and religion. Scholars rarely explore the intersection of the motivations for FGM with the multiple forms of oppression women experience, such as gender, race, and class, which have an impact on their attitudes about the rationale for performing FGM.[19] An intersectional analysis allows for an exploration of women's experiences of FGM and the law, which are situated within systems of discrimination.

It is through investigation of the ways in which FGM-performing communities negotiate continuing or abandoning the practice that the impact of anti-FGM laws can be understood. The first chapter gives voice to women's rich and diverse stories about FGM, which are rarely featured in anti-FGM narratives. Instead, women's stories of FGM that feature in the media are often one-dimensional, depicting FGM as cruel and horrific. Women's divergent experiences are frequently silenced by dominant anti-FGM discourses which depict FGM as a barbaric practice. Indeed, some survivors described FGM as torture. However, the use of vocabulary in story-telling makes explicit the complexities of defining FGM as child abuse and violence against women. Women's competing narratives of FGM are often silenced at the expense of making women's lived experiences a known reality. Whilst some women described FGM as a traumatic event that has an impact on their life and identity, other women either had no recollection of FGM or defined the practice as important to their sense of identity. The distinctions in women's experiences and attitudes towards FGM reflect their differences in beliefs about the drivers of the practice. There was no single factor or group of factors that explained the rationale for FGM. Many women did not speak openly about FGM with their family or kinship group. Issues relating to women's bodies and sexuality are sensitive areas that remain shrouded in secrecy.

There is a consensus amongst the anti-FGM movement that the most commonly cited reason for FGM is to control a girl and woman's sexuality, to maintain her role as a faithful wife and child bearer. Scholars argue that FGM impacts on women's sexual responses,[20] which was highly contested amongst women interview participants. Some women claimed that representations of FGM purport to show that all women lack agency and autonomy to consent to FGM, which is essentialist and ethnocentric.[21] Regardless of women's attitudes

---

[19] For a discussion about the criminalisation of FGM and intersectionality, see, Arianne Shahvisi, 'Female Genital Alteration in the UK' in Katja Kuehlmeyer, Corinna Klingler, and Richard Huxtable (eds), *Ethical, Legal and Social Aspects of Healthcare for Migrants: Perspectives from the UK and Germany* (Routledge 2018) 156 (hereafter Shahvisi, 'Female Genital Alteration').

[20] See, Rahman and Toubia, *Female Genital Mutilation* (n 17).

[21] See, Chima Korieh, '"Other" Bodies: Western Feminism, Race, and Representation in Female Circumcision Discourse' in Obioma Nnaemeka, *Female Circumcision and the Politics of Knowledge: African Women in Imperialist Discourses* (Praeger 2005) 111; L Amede Obiora, 'A Refuge

towards FGM, the practice remains deeply embedded within families and communities and represents the inter-generational perpetuation of the practice. The second core motivation for FGM was the preservation of cultural traditions in migrant communities. The performance of FGM affirms families and communities' relationship with kinship groups over generations. FGM can also reaffirm boundaries between migrant cultural norms and mainstream cultural values. Cultural relativists[22] criticise attempts to criminalise cultural practices which are viewed as integral to migrant communities and the law is perceived as representing neo-colonial interests. The third rationale for continuing FGM is a religious belief that FGM ought to be performed. Whilst it is generally accepted that FGM has no religious basis, some women defined FGM as a religious practice, which is advised in Islam. Women's understanding of contested religious scriptures was eloquently explained in the interviews, highlighting their religious and cultural consciousness. Changing religious beliefs is likely to be a further challenge for the anti-FGM movement but a necessary advocacy tool. A third explanation for FGM is the fear of transgressing social norms by abandoning the practice, which could result in social ostracisation and condemnation. Women described the social costs of abandoning the practice as life-changing, for example, not being able to marry within their community or fearing social isolation, which reinforces the duress girls and women are under when considering whether to perform FGM. For considerable numbers of women, FGM was perceived and experienced as debilitating and oppressive. Women's stories of abuse legitimise the implementation of anti-FGM laws, to deter FGM and to prosecute perpetrators.

The second chapter explores the evolution of anti-FGM legislation in Britain from the 1980s, the amendments to legislation in 2003 and 2015. Explicit, detailed interviews from House of Lords Peers are key to understanding the intention of legislation. For many, anti-FGM laws were used to reinforce British values and norms and to criminalise migrant communities for performing a perceived barbaric custom. Lord Glenarthur described the practice in the 1980s as 'not compatible with the culture of the country' and 'thoroughly repugnant to our way of life'.[23] The stereotypical view of women as abusers of children led

---

from Tradition and the Refuge of Tradition: On Anticircumcision Paradigms' in Ylva Hernlund and Bettina Shell-Duncan (eds), *Transcultural Bodies: Female Genital Cutting in Global Context* (Rutgers University Press 2007) 67.

[22] See, Shweder, 'What About "Female Genital Mutilation"' (n 11).
[23] Prohibition of Female Circumcision Bill, HL Deb 18 June 1985, vol 465, cols 207–24 <https://api.parliament.uk/historic-hansard/lords/1985/jun/18/prohibition-of-female-circumcision-bill> accessed 4 March 2021.

to racist narratives that engendered an urgency to criminalise FGM. The anti-FGM narrative emerged from the echelons of power in a top-down approach, which led to accusations of racial and cultural superiority. House of Lords Peers commented that they did not consider how the law would be implemented nor did they engage FGM-performing communities in the consultation process for new legislation. Unsurprisingly there were no prosecutions and convictions following the enactment of the Prohibition of Female Circumcision Act 1985, which led to further amendments through the Female Genital Mutilation Act 2003. Despite legal changes to close the gaps in legislation through the FGM Act 2003, there were still no criminal cases. From 2012 there was increasing media and political awareness about FGM following the bravery of survivors mobilising and speaking about FGM. Further political intervention came through the House of Commons Home Affairs Committee inquiry into FGM which published a report in 2014 and recommended a number of legal changes. The government was shamed into acknowledging that the law appeared ineffective as there had not yet been one prosecution or conviction for FGM resulting in yet more amendments to anti-FGM laws in 2015. The government responded to public calls to prosecute a case of FGM and show that the law is effective in deterring and criminalising unwanted behaviours.

Despite the constant change to legislation, the first conviction for FGM did not take place until 2019. The first FGM conviction and three failed prosecutions are explored in further detail. The barriers to prosecuting cases are actively explored to understand and resolve the tensions towards the efficacy of anti-FGM laws. There is a fundamental clash between the practice of FGM and the laws that seek to regulate the practice. A significant challenge to implementing anti-FGM laws is that the law criminalises a cultural practice, which stirs tensions amongst FGM-performing communities who are disproportionately affected by the laws. Links between cultural practices and the criminal law lead to heated debates about whether individuals should be permitted to perform cultural practices that are sacred to their identity and belonging. The criminalisation of girls' parents and family members highlights the unique nature of the practice. FGM is often perceived as controlled by women and performed by women on girls who are often too young to speak about their experiences and socialised to normalise FGM. The criminal cases that are analysed in the chapter range from prosecuting a doctor charged with performing FGM on a patient after giving birth, to a Bristol taxi driver accused and acquitted for organising FGM for his daughter, to a solicitor who was accused and acquitted of organising and watching his daughter being cut at home on two occasions, to the first conviction of a mother who performed witchcraft in the family home and then cut her daughter's genitalia. An exploration of the four FGM trials, one resulting in a conviction and three cases not resulting in a conviction, highlights the complexity of prosecuting cases of FGM. The cases outlined do not represent so-called conventional FGM cases where FGM is performed within the family for generations. These cases could be regarded as 'outliers' which suggests that the criminal law is still struggling to permeate FGM-performing communities. The barriers to potentially convicting alleged perpetrators of FGM in three of the FGM cases ranged from public perceptions that FGM is a woman's issue and thus men have no control or involvement in FGM; the difficulty in detecting FGM on a girl's genitalia; and the need to iden-tify a traditional motivation for FGM, for example, that it was performed to control a girl or woman's sexuality, in order for the case to have credibility.

Chapter Three explores the barriers and obstacles to criminalising FGM. Interviews with women from FGM-performing communities allowed an ex-ploration of their attitudes towards the criminal law and ways in which they have changed the dynamics of FGM to continue the practice underground. Education about anti-FGM laws was lacking at a grassroots level leaving many community members unaware about the criminal status of FGM. A further barrier to the criminalisation of FGM was women's sympathetic attitudes to-wards FGM and opposition towards anti-FGM laws. At present, the criminal law prohibits FGM regardless of age or consent. Women opposed a blanket ban on the prohibition of FGM, which they say amounts to adult women being in-fantilised by the law. Whilst it is largely accepted that FGM is child abuse, the rhetoric and discourse framing FGM as an inhumane practice performed on innocent children by abusive parents resulted in resistance to anti-FGM initia-tives. Many women described FGM as performed to safeguard children from living a life uncut and ostracised from wider society. Labelling FGM as child abuse appears to have the unintended consequence in women disengaging from the anti-FGM movement because they disassociate with descriptions of parents as mutilators. The hyperbole discourse and visceral images of child abuse could ignite racist and imperialist stereotypes of a victim and a rescuer.

A further obstacle to anti-FGM legislation eliminating FGM is the top-down approach, as politicians and law enforcement agents impose legislation that targets migrant communities leaving FGM-performing communities feeling stigmatised and alienated. Increasing police surveillance of already marginalised communities compounds the structural inequalities that many women experience through the law, such as institutional racism and sexism, which could deter them from relying on the criminal justice system. There are limited studies exploring links between race, racism, and FGM, frequently such studies lack an intersectional lens to examine the wider impact of anti-FGM laws on women of colour's lives. Service providers assisting women who are victims of abuse could be described as reluctant to intervene in so-called cultural violence due to fears that they could be branded racist, which renders the violence invisible and leaves women and girls unprotected. There is now a mandatory duty for frontline professionals to report cases of FGM to the police when they have discovered FGM in the course of their work.[24] The law was clarified in 2015 due to concerns that professionals were not reporting cases of FGM to the police. With increasing pressure on the police to detect a case of FGM and ensure that perpetrators are brought to justice, FGM-performing communities have pushed the practice further underground. The dynamics of FGM are believed to have changed to allow the practice to continue without detection, thereby evading the law. For example, girls are cut younger before they are able to explain the event, girls are cut abroad where FGM is medicalised or by medical practitioners in Britain on the black market, the type of FGM has changed to the least physically invasive which is increasingly difficult to detect. The assumption that FGM persists but has changed in practice is supported in the interviews with FGM-performing communities and professionals that work closely with communities at a grassroots level. Studies remain largely silent about whether the dynamics of FGM have changed perhaps due to the difficulties in obtaining empirical evidence.

Chapter Four continues the theme of barriers to the criminalisation of FGM by focusing on the legal double standard of prohibiting FGM while permitting FGCS. Questions about whether FGM continues under the guise of FGCS are explored in detail. The two practices are compared and contrasted to ascertain if there is a marked difference between FGM and FGCS. Women's attitudes towards the two practices varied; however, the majority of women argued that permitting FGCS on so-called white Western women whilst banning a form of body modification for women of colour is discriminatory and quasi-racist. The legal double standard roused anger and hostility towards anti-FGM laws. Similarly, the two practices are described in the literature as emanating from patriarchal cultural norms about how a woman's body should look and function, which legitimises both practices continuing.[25] Fundamentally, women

---

[24] Female Genital Mutilation Act 2003, s 5B (hereafter FGM Act 2003).

[25] See, Sheila Jeffreys, *Beauty and Misogyny* (Routledge 2005); Simone Weil Davis, 'Loose Lips Sink Ships' (2002) 28(1) Feminist Studies 7; Linda Duits and Liesbset Van Zoonen, 'Headscarves and Porno-Chic: Disciplining Girls' Bodies in the European Multicultural Society' (2006) 13(2) European Journal of Women's Studies 103; Carolyn Pedwell, 'Theorizing "African" Female Genital Cutting and "Western" Body Modifications: A Critique of the Continuum and Analogue Approaches' (2007) 86(1) Feminist Review 45.

chose to compare the practices for different political ends, some women argued that both practices should be permitted on adult women whilst others argued that both practices should be prohibited as they emanate from the control of women's bodies. In contrast, professionals contrasted the two practices, believing that they are fundamentally different with FGM stemming from a belief that a woman's and girl's sexuality needs to be controlled whilst FGCS is intended to liberate women's sexuality. The permissibility of FGCS is likely to result in unhelpful consequences for the end-FGM movement. First, FGM could be performed under the guise of FGCS and second, women use the legal status of FGCS as an effective advocacy tool to resist anti-FGM laws and oppose anti-FGM initiatives. The revealing testimonies of women and professionals challenge traditional understandings about FGM as a cultural practice. A closer analysis of the practice shows the complexities and contradictions inherent in criminalising body modification practices on adult women.

The final chapter takes a step back from the criminalisation of FGM, which is riddled with questions and critiques and instead focuses on exploring an alternative legal remedy that could prevent FGM and protect girls and women. FGM is explored in a family law context where punitive sanctions are rare and instead the child and the family are the focus of court litigation. Care proceedings are explored, as a means of the state taking robust legal steps to ensure the protection of children who have undergone FGM or are at risk of undergoing FGM. Whilst care proceedings are considered a draconian step, removing children from their families and interfering with family life,[26] such litigation can be necessary to protect the safety and welfare of children. This chapter reviews two reported cases involving FGM in care proceedings, as a means of highlighting the challenges in proving on the balance of probabilities that a child has been cut or is at risk of being cut. In 2015, a novel legal remedy was introduced, FGMPOs,[27] which is an injunctive legal remedy to prevent FGM. Such court orders might involve removing a child's passport and prohibiting international travel. There is limited literature and empirical research about the efficacy and impact of FGMPOs on ending FGM.

A review of FGMPO case law shows broader themes in FGM cases, for example that many cases are likely to involve travel restrictions which highlights the nexus between families in Britain and kinship groups in their country of heritage. There were implicit challenges in FGM cases. When families claimed that FGM had been abandoned, women in the family were required to undergo

---

[26] European Convention of Human Rights, art 8.
[27] FGM Act 2003 (n 24) sch 2.

a medical examination to prove that they had not been cut. The suggestion in such cases is that families from high prevalence FGM countries are viewed with suspicion and hostility. The glaring loophole is the inability of family courts to use FGMPOs to protect girls with insecure immigration status from being deported to their home countries where they are at risk of FGM. The inconsistent protection afforded to girls at risk of FGM who have British status compared to those who have insecure immigration status is stark. This reinforces perceptions that the law discriminates against women and girls of colour who are not British nationals. The focus on prosecuting and convicting cases of FGM whilst refusing to provide families at risk of FGM abroad with immigration status highlights the government's focus in targeting and punishing ethnic minority families for a so-called cultural practice rather than supporting them and providing vital protection.

Overview of the Practice FGM

Before embarking on a detailed exploration of FGM and anti-FGM laws, it is first important to explore the fundamental dynamics of the practice. It is important to acknowledge that there are limited in-depth, large-scale studies of FGM and much of the literature cities previous academic work without applying new empirical research, thus some of the material is limited in the weight that can be attached to it. Furthermore, many academic studies are dated but there are relevant principles that can be applied. By way of an introduction to FGM, the four types of FGM are described below. The four types of FGM are important to understand, as there are different meanings associated with each type of FGM. The different types of FGM show the variations in types of FGM over generations. Furthermore, there are challenges to medical practitioners identifying Types I, II, and IV FGM. The language and terminology used to define the practice is a contentious issue subject to fierce debate. FGM is a value-laden term that is rejected by many FGM-performing communities. The variety of terms used to define the practice, the heritage of these terms, and the meanings associated with them are further explored. The prevalence of FGM remains subject to debate because there are few empirical studies exploring the prevalence of the practice in Britain and thus it is unknown with any degree of accuracy the numbers of women and girls living with FGM in Britain.[28] The

---

[28] See clinical findings of FGM or suspected FGM on children in the UK alongside the referral mechanisms, Sarah M Creighton and others, 'Multidisciplinary Approach to the Management of Children

final section is an overview of the key motivations for performing FGM and the consequences of performing FGM on women's health is briefly. These issues are grappled with in further detail throughout the book.

Four Types of FGM

Eliminating Female genital mutilation, an interagency statement developed by the World Health Organization (WHO)[29] provides the international anatomical typology of FGM. The four types of FGM identified by the WHO are applied throughout this book.

Type I: Partial or total removal of the clitoris and/or the prepuce (*clitoridectomy*). When it is important distinguish to between the major variations of **Type I** mutilation, the following subdivisions are proposed: **Type Ia**, removal of the clitoral hood or prepuce only; **Type Ib**, removal of the clitoris with the prepuce. FGM-performing communities usually refer to Type I as *sunna*, which is Arabic for 'tradition' or 'duty'.[30]

Type II: Partial or total removal of the clitoris and the labia minora, with or without excision of the labia majora (*excision*). When it is important to distinguish between the major variations that have been documented, the following subdivisions are proposed: **Type IIa**, removal of the labia minora only; **Type IIb**, partial or total removal of the clitoris and the labia minora; **Type IIc**, partial or total removal of the clitoris, the labia minora, and the labia majora.

Type III: Narrowing of the vaginal orifice with creation of a covering seal by cutting and appositioning the labia minora and/or the labia majora, with or without excision of the clitoris (*infibulation*). When it is important to distinguish between variations in infibulations, the following subdivisions are proposed: **Type IIIa**: removal and

---

with Female Genital Mutilation (FGM) or Suspected FGM: Service Description and Case Series' (2016) 6(2) British Medical Journal 1.

[29] It was developed in 1995 and updated in 2008. The WHO identified four types of FGM, which originate from a study conducted by Felix Bryk in 1910 that identified eight types of FGM based partially on his fieldwork in Kenya: Chantal J Zabus, *Between Rites and Rights: Excision in Women's Experiential Texts and Human Contexts* (Stanford University Press 2007).

[30] See, UNICEF, 'Female Genital Mutilation/Cutting: A Statistical Overview and Exploration of the Dynamics of Change' (2013) UNICEF (hereafter UNICEF, 'Dynamics of Change').

apposition of the labia minora; **Type IIIb**: removal and apposition of the labia majora. The seal of the labia results in near complete covering of the urethra and the vaginal orifice, which must be re-opened for sexual intercourse and childbirth, a procedure known as deinfibulation.[31] In some cases, the seal of the labia is closed again with reinfibulation. Community members usually refer to Type III FGM as pharaonic circumcision or pharaonic infibula-tion.[32] It is thought pharaonic refers to the heritages of the prac-tice in ancient Egypt.[33]

Type IV: Unclassified: All other harmful procedures to the female genitalia for non-medical purposes, for example, pricking, piercing, incising, scraping, and cauterization. Pricking or nicking involves cutting to draw blood, but no removal of tissue and no permanent alteration of the external genitalia.[34] Some communities call this 'symbolic cir-cumcision'.[35] Although symbolic circumcision is still highly contro-versial, it has been proposed as an alternative to more severe forms of cutting in countries where there is a high prevalence of FGM.[36]

Terminology

The language and terminology adopted to describe FGM is political and epis-temologically important and is the subject of heated debate amongst aca-demics. Choosing terminology to describe these practices is 'fraught with political land mines' and one of the most controversial issues.[37] Attention to language is essential to understanding the political and ideological debates in which FGM is situated.[38] Until the 1980s, 'female circumcision' was historically

---

[31] See, ibid.

[32] See, Momoh, *Female Genital Mutilation* (n 12).

[33] See, Dorkenoo, *Cutting the Rose* (n 12).

[34] See, UNICEF, 'Dynamics of Change' (n 30).

[35] See, ibid.

[36] See, L Amede Obiora, 'Bridges and Barricades: Rethinking Polemics and Intransigence in the Campaign against Female Circumcision' (1997) 47 Case Western Reserve Law Review 275 (here-after Obiora, 'Bridges and Barricades'); Doriane L Coleman, 'The Seattle Compromise: Multicultural Sensitivity and Americanization' (1998) 47 Duke Law Journal 717; American Association of Pediatrics, 'Policy Statement: Ritual Genital Cutting of Female Minors, American Academy of Pediatrics' (2010) 125(5) Pediatrics 1088, 1088–93; UNICEF, 'Dynamics of Change' (n 30).

[37] See, Bettina Shell-Duncan and Ylva Hernlund, *Female 'Circumcision' in Africa: Dimensions of the Practice and Debates* (Lynne Rienner Publishers, Inc 2000) 1 (hereafter Shell-Duncan and Hernlund, *Female 'Circumcision' in Africa*).

[38] See, Rogaia M Abusharaf, *Female Circumcision: Multicultural Perspectives* (University of Pennsylvania Press 2013) (hereafter Abusharaf, *Female Circumcision*).

used to describe these practices in the international literature.[39] However, the growth of the feminist movement and public concern from international health organisations resulted in objection to the term, as it de-emphasises the severity of the practice.[40] The use of 'female circumcision' to describe FGM suggests that a parallel can be drawn with male circumcision, which creates confusion about the significance of the practice.

In 1990, the term 'female genital mutilation' was adopted at the third conference of the Inter-African Committee on Traditional Practices Affecting the Health of Women and Children in Addis Ababa, Ethiopia.[41] In 1991, the WHO recommended the UN adopt the term. From the late 1990s, the term has been increasingly used by international and national agencies.[42] A joint statement issued in 1997 by the WHO, UNICEF, and UNFPA defined the practices as 'female genital mutilation'.[43] The joint statement concluded that adopting FGM as the standard term for the practices reinforced the gravity of the act and promoted the abandonment of the practices. The term was used as an advocacy tool to encourage the abandonment of a practice widely condemned.[44] There was some evidence that the term 'mutilation' has estranged communities, hindering the process of social change for the elimination of FGM.[45] Indeed, FGM could be considered an offensive term to women who do not regard themselves as mutilated or their families as mutilators.[46] FGM could be considered moral condemnatory language that prejudices women's autonomy to choose the practice; instead they are automatically viewed as victims incapable of choosing FGM.[47]

Female circumcision continues to be used by fieldworkers and researchers to show respect for women's understandings of the practice[48] and the term was used when undertaking interviews with women from FGM-performing communities who expressed a preference to use the term. Scholars argue that to adopt mutilation shows disrespect for women and their cultures and could be

---

[39] See, Rahman and Toubia, *Female Genital Mutilation* (n 17).

[40] See, Shell-Duncan and Hernlund, *Female 'Circumcision' in Africa* (n 37).

[41] See, UNICEF, World Health Organisation, and UNFPA, 'Female Genital Mutilation: A Joint Statement' (1997) (hereafter UNICEF, WHO, and UNFPA, 'Joint Statement').

[42] ibid.

[43] ibid.

[44] See, Suzan Izett and Nahid Toubia, *Learning About Social Change. A Research and Evaluation Guidebook Using Female Circumcision as a Case Study* (RAINBO 1999).

[45] UNICEF, WHO, and UNFPA, 'Joint Statement' (n 41).

[46] See, Rahman and Toubia, *Female Genital Mutilation* (n 17).

[47] See, Diana Tietjens Meyers, 'Feminism and Women's Autonomy: The Challenge of Female Genital Cutting' (2000) 31(5) Metaphilosophy 281 (hereafter Meyers, 'Feminism and Women's Autonomy').

[48] See, Els Leye and others, 'An Analysis of the Implementation of Laws with Regard to Female Genital Mutilation In Europe' (2007) 47(1) Crime, Law and Social Change 1 (hereafter Leye and others, 'An Analysis').

an example of cultural imperialism; however, opposing scholars contend that any other language than 'mutilation' condones the practice and sustains male dominance.[49] African-American legal scholar, Isabelle Gunning, proposed the term 'genital surgeries' as a value-neutral term, but the term could suggest medical necessity.[50] Legal scholar, Maria Caterina La Barbera, attempted to avoid a colonialist approach and adopted the term 'ritual female genital interventions'.[51] The term 'ritual' was supposed to highlight the cultural and ethnic dimensions of surgeries on the genitalia. In yet another attempt to change the language used, Arianne Shahvisi adopts the term 'Female genital Alteration' as she argues that no community practising FGM describes the act as mutilation—but equally no FGM-performing community describes the act as 'alteration'.[52]

Some non-government organisations (NGOs) have adopted the term female genital cutting (FGC), which appears more neutral and sensitive to FGM-performing communities' beliefs.[53] This book adopts the widely used term, female genital mutilation because it situates FGM within current political and public discourse. Furthermore, the aim of this book is to better understand the practice and the law but ultimately the objective is to eliminate the practice, which is a human rights violation.

A further contentious debate persists in the feminist literature as to whether 'victim' or 'survivor' should be used to describe women who have experienced FGM. Victim suggests a lack of agency and autonomy, which could alienate women further from end-FGM initiatives. Survivor could be viewed as suggesting women have survived mutilation. Some women reject the label survivor as they view FGM as a legitimate cultural practice. Survivor is not a term widely used in political or public discourse to describe women who have undergone FGM. The term survivors is used when women attributed the identity of survivors to themselves. Steering away from using specific labels, this book instead referred to women as 'women', a value neutral term that reinforces their gender identity, which no interview participant took issue with. Out of respect and accuracy, I intend to disaggregate descriptors such as BAME which are increasingly contested by the communities they purport to describe. I will

---

[49] See, Meyers, 'Feminism and Women's Autonomy' (n 47).

[50] Isabelle R Gunning, 'Arrogant Perception, World-Travelling and Multicultural Feminism: The Case of Female Genital Surgeries' (1991) 23 Columbia Human Rights Law Review 189 (hereafter Gunning, 'Arrogant Perception'). Also see criticism of the term genital surgeries by anthropologists, Shell-Duncan and Hernlund, Female 'Circumcision' in Africa (n 37).

[51] Maria Caterina La Barbera, 'Multicentred Feminism: Revisiting the "Female Genital Mutilation"' (2009) Discourse.

[52] Shahvisi, 'Female Genital Alteration' (n 19).

[53] See, Abusharaf, Female Circumcision (n 38).

generally use the terms 'women of colour', 'ethnic minority women', and 'ethnic minority communities' and wherever possible seek to identify the particular region, country or ethnic heritage of the people referred to. I appreciate this solution is not perfect and in itself may be contested by some, understandably. I would welcome suggestions for future editions of my book. The term 'FGM–performing community' is used to refer to a broad category of people whose family originate from countries where FGM is performed.[54] This fluid category includes women from FGM-performing communities who have undergone FGM, women who have not undergone FGM,[55] and women who did not disclose whether they had been cut. There is no intention to stigmatise or label communities but instead to clarify for the reader the group of individuals referred to.

Complex Dynamics of FGM

Historically, FGM is thought to have originated in southern Egypt or northern Sudan and was practised by many cultures including the Phoenicians, Hittities, and the ancient Egyptians.[56] Due to a lack of data collection about FGM worldwide, the exact number of women and girls who have undergone FGM is not known. The prevalence rates and the types of FGM performed vary according to each ethnic group within every country.[57] It is possible to detect trends in dynamics of FGM that are performed in high prevalence FGM countries including the types of FGM, the age at which girls are cut, and the organiser of FGM. A report by UNICEF in 2016, *Female Genital Mutilation/Cutting: A Global Concern*, estimates that more than 200 million girls and women alive today have undergone FGM in the 31 countries where FGM is concentrated. The practice is almost universal in Somali, Guinea, and Djibouti with levels around 90 per cent, while it affects no more than 1 per cent of adolescent girls in Cameron, the Maldives, and Uganda. The report states that FGM can also be traced to Colombia, India, Malaysia, Oman, Saudi Arabia, and the United Arab Emirates. However, there are no reliable estimates about FGM prevalence rates in these countries. In Somalia, Eritrea, Niger, Djibouti, and Senegal, more

---

[54] See report by UNICEF which identifies the countries where FGM is performed: UNICEF, 'Dynamics of Change' (n 30).

[55] While some women had not undergone FGM, they were able to speak about the practice from their position within an FGM-performing community, which supports the practice.

[56] See, Rahman and Toubia, *Female Genital Mutilation* (n 17).

[57] See, Momoh, *Female Genital Mutilation* (n 12).

than one in five girls have undergone Type III, the most physically invasive type of FGM.[58]

In Britain and other Western countries, FGM tends to occur amongst immigrants, refugees, and asylum seekers when their families originate from high FGM prevalence countries.[59] It is challenging to gain empirical evidence about the dynamics of a practice that is increasingly scrutinised and subject to criminal laws and amongst communities that live on the margins of mainstream society. There are limited reports about the prevalence rates of FGM in Britain.[60] However, it is reported in the literature that FGM is usually prevalent amongst FGM-performing communities in Britain from Somalia, Sudan, Djibouti, Nigeria, Eritrea, Ethiopia, and Sierra Leone.[61] The largest populations of people whose families can be traced to high prevalence FGM countries tend to reside in London, Bristol, Cardiff, Coventry, Reading, Thurrock, Manchester, Sheffield, Northampton, Birmingham, Oxford, Slough, and Milton Keynes.[62] In 2014, a study estimated that approximately 60,000 girls aged 0–14 were born in England and Wales to mothers who had undergone FGM and 137,000 women and girls born in countries where FGM is performed were permanently resident in England and Wales.[63] However, one of the authors of this study, Macfarlane, argues that the data available from the Department of Education and the Department of Health and Social Care cannot support the claims that FGM is widespread among girls born in England and Wales to mothers from FGM prevalent countries.[64] Indeed, Macfarlane suggests that following migration to the UK, large numbers of families have abandoned the practice, thus projected numbers of victims may not be accurate.[65] Women's rights campaigner, Julie Bindel, estimated that 65,000 girls in the UK are at risk of FGM.[66]

---

[58] See, UNICEF, 'Dynamics of Change' (n 30).

[59] See, Harry Gordon, 'Female Genital Mutilation: A Clinician's Experience' in Comfort Momoh (ed), *Female Genital Mutilation* (Radcliffe Publishing 2005).

[60] N Ayadi O'Donnell and others, 'G142 Female Genital Mutilation (FGM) Surveillance in Under 16 Years Olds in the UK and Ireland' (2018) 103(1) British Medical Journal . In a study on prevalence of FGM during a data set from the national British Paediatric Surveillance Unit reporting system from November 2015 to November 2017 with a 12-month follow up, the authors found 120 reported cases, of which 51% had confirmed FGM; 80% of children were four years or older; 93% of cases were performed before arrival to the UK. The authors conclude that the numbers reported were lower than expected for UK-estimated prevalence with fewer physical and mental symptoms than anticipated.

[61] See, Sadiya Mohammad, 'Legislative Action to Eradicate FGM in the UK' in Comfort Momoh (ed), *Female Genital Mutilation* (Radcliffe Publishing 2005) (hereafter Mohammad, 'Legislative Action').

[62] See, AJ Macfarlane and E Dorkenoo 'Female Genital Mutilation in England and Wales: Updated Statistical Estimates of the Numbers of Affected Women Living in England and Wales and Girls at Risk: Interim Report on Provisional Estimates' (2014) City University London.

[63] See, ibid.

[64] ibid.

[65] ibid.

[66] Julie Bindel, 'An Unpunished Crime: The Lack of Prosecutions for Female Genital Mutilation in the UK' (2014) New Culture Forum (hereafter, Bindel, 'Unpunished Crime').

To gain a more accurate reflection of FGM prevalence rates, the Health and Social Care Information Centre began collecting data on FGM within England in September 2014, on behalf of the Department of Health and National Health Service (NHS) England to improve the NHS response to FGM and help commission services to support women and girls. However, the statistics are only based on the number of women and girls treated by NHS medical practices rather than an accurate reflection of the prevalence rates in Britain more generally. Between April 2015 and September 2019, a total of 45,950 attendances to health services occurred in England by individuals who have been identified to have suffered FGM, or where the attendance to services was due to a consequence of suffering FGM.[67] Any individuals who have presented to health services on more than one occasion due to complications associated with FGM have only been recorded in this figure once.

Medical professionals undertook a study to describe the 'presentation and management' of victims of FGM who were referred to a specialist paediatric clinic.[68] They found that between 2014 and January 2019: 148 children attended the clinic of whom 55 (37.2%) had confirmed FGM; police or social care referred 112 (76% of the children); the proportion of looked-after children was significantly higher in the group with confirmed FGM (17/55—31%) compared with children where FGM was not confirmed (5/93—5%); Of these, 48/55 (87%) underwent FGM prior to UK entry; the remaining seven cases were British children, potentially meeting legal criteria under the FGM Act 2003, and one resulted in successful prosecution. This study illustrates that children continue to experience FGM and there appears to be a lack of recourse to the criminal justice system.

The dynamics of FGM can be contextualised according to the subject individuals and community; it is dangerous to extrapolate and normalise the practice on groups of people that are not homogenous. However, there are useful norms about the performance of FGM identified in the literature, which assist understandings about the practice. FGM is commonly performed on girls between the ages of four and twelve as a rite of passage to womanhood.[69] However, the age that FGM is performed varies according to the country, tribe, and circumstances and ranges from a few days old to adolescence, adulthood, just

---

[67] NHS Digital, 'Female Genital Mutilation Datasets: The Female Genital Mutilation (FGM) Enhanced Dataset' (28 November 2019) <https://digital.nhs.uk/data-and-information/clinical-audits-and-registries/female-genital-mutilation-datasets> accessed 7 March 2021.

[68] Sakaria Ali and others, 'Female Genital Mutilation (FGM) in UK Children: A Review of a Dedicated Paediatric Service for FGM' (2020) 105(11) Archives of Disease in Childhood 1075.

[69] See, Nahid Toubia, *Female Genital Mutilation: A Call for Global Action* (RAINBO 1995) (hereafter Toubia, *A Call for Global Action*).

before marriage, or after the first pregnancy.[70] Indeed, FGM may be performed at various stages of an individual's life, at infancy, before puberty, at puberty, with or without initiation rites, upon contracting marriage, during pregnancy, and after the birth of the first child.[71] Late anti-FGM campaigner, Dorkenoo, states that girls in Britain are most likely to be subjected to FGM between five and ten years of age. However, as the campaign against FGM deepens parents are believed to be cutting children younger to avoid detection.[72] Girls may be cut alone or with a group of family members or peers from their community.[73] Infibulated[74] women are often deinfibulated[75] to enable them to have sexual intercourse after marriage and to give birth to a child. In some cases, women are reinfibulated[76] after birth to leave a small hole.[77]

FGM is usually performed by a traditional practitioner, often an older woman, who comes from a family in which generations of women were traditional practitioners.[78] In some countries, trained medical practitioners such as midwives, nurses, and physicians have in recent years performed FGM on the 'black market'.[79] In Britain, it is believed that medical practitioners or traditional excisors perform FGM or British girls are taken to countries of heritage or to countries where FGM is medicalised.[80] Girls who are subjected to FGM overseas are usually taken abroad at the start of the school holidays, typically in the summer, in order for them to recover before returning to school. This is commonly known as the 'cutting season'.

Highlighting the impact of FGM upon girls' and women's health is often suggested as an advocacy strategy to encourage communities to abandon FGM. The health consequences of FGM vary depending on multiple factors such as the type of FGM, the medical experience of the excisor, and the medicalised or non-medicalised context in which FGM is performed. The use of

---

[70] See, Momoh, *Female Genital Mutilation* (n 12) 2.

[71] See, Gerry Mackie, 'Female Genital Cutting: The Beginning of the End' in Lynne Rienner (ed), *Female "Circumcision" in Africa: Culture, Controversy, and Change* (Lynne Rienner Publishers 2000) 253.

[72] See, Dorkenoo, *Cutting the Rose* (n 12) 131.

[73] See, Rahman and Toubia, *Female Genital Mutilation* (n 17).

[74] Infibulated refers to Type III FGM.

[75] Deinfibulation refers to the practice of cutting open the sealed vaginal opening in a woman who has been infibulated: World Health Organization 'Eliminating Female Genital Mutilation: An Interagency Statement OHCR, UNAIDS, UNDO, UNECA, UNESCO, UNFPA, UNHCR, UNICEF, UNIFEM, WHO' (2008)

[76] Reinfibulation refers to re-sealing the vaginal opening after an infibulated woman has undergone deinfibulation: ibid.

[77] See, Hanny Lightfoot-Klein and Evelyn Shaw, 'Special Needs of Ritually Circumcised Women Patients' (1991) 20(2) Journal of Obstetric, Gynecologic, & Neonatal Nursing 102 (hereafter Lightfoot-Klein and Shaw, 'Special Needs').

[78] See, Rahman and Toubia, *Female Genital Mutilation* (n 17).

[79] See, Toubia, *A Call for Global Action* (n 69).

[80] See, Dorkenoo, *Cutting the Rose* (n 12).

unsterile instruments can cause infections after the procedure, particularly if the wounded area is contaminated with urine or faeces. While long-term health complications can arise from any type of FGM, Types II and III usually result in the severest complications due to the grave nature of the injury. The possible immediate physical complications of all types of FGM include severe pain, bleeding, and haemorrhage, which if not controlled can result in death.[81] The most common long-term complications are dermoid cysts in the line of the scar, chronic urinary tract infections, which can evolve and lead to urinary stones and kidney damage and fistulae.[82] Women may suffer pain during menstruation, pain from sexual intercourse, and complications during childbirth. Infibulated women usually have to undergo deinfibulation prior to the delivery of the child. If deinfibulation is not performed, the mother and child's life could be threatened.

While there are few studies on the psychological effects of FGM available,[83] it is understood that shortly after undergoing FGM women and girls can experience disturbances in appetite, sleep, mood, and cognition as well as emotional responses such as fear, submission, and suppressed feelings of anger, bitterness, or betrayal.[84] A tragic irony is that symptoms of depression are labelled as hysteria rather than attributable to FGM.[85] A systematic review of the evidence about the association between FGM and adverse mental health consequences was carried out by epidemiologists, which found that there was a correlation between the severity of FGM and the severity of adverse mental health outcomes but they cautioned that more rigorous research on the topic is required before conclusions can be confidently made.[86]

The issue of how women experience their own sexuality is an area of limited research and highly contested, with some studies suggesting that FGM interferes with women's sexual responses and other studies stating that the practice does not necessarily eliminate sexual pleasure and climax[87] and that FGM can

---

[81] See, Rahman and Toubia, *Female Genital Mutilation* (n 17).

[82] See, Nahid Toubia, 'Female Circumcision as a Public Health Issue' (1994) 331(11) New England Journal of Medicine 712.

[83] A study of a community in Sudan that performs FGM shows that FGM had negative effects on self-identity and self-esteem: Janice Boddy, *Wombs and Alien Spirits. Women, Men, and the Zar Cult in Northern Sudan* (The University of Wisconsin Press 1989).

[84] See, Rahman and Toubia, *Female Genital Mutilation* (n 17).

[85] See, Toubia, *A Call for Global Action* (n 69) 230.

[86] Salma M Abdalla, and Sandro Galea. 'Is Female Genital Mutilation/Cutting Associated with Adverse Mental Health Consequences? A Systematic Review of the Evidence' (2019) 4(4) BMJ Global Health e001553.

[87] See, AA Shandall, 'Circumcision and Infibulation of Females: A General Consideration of the Problem and a Clinical Study of the Complications in Sudanese Women' (1967) 5(4) Sudan Medical Journal 178; Asma El Dareer, *Woman, Why Do You Weep? Circumcision and its Consequences* (Zed Press 1982); U Megafu, 'Female Ritual Circumcision in Africa: An Investigation of the Presumed Benefits

in fact increase women's sexual pleasure.[88] Adverse health risks form the main opposition to FGM yet they do not always reflect *all* women's and girls' experiences of FGM. Scholars contend that little attention is given to the original source of medical information, which usually emanates from British colonial surgeons and gynaecologists in the 1930s and 1940s.[89] Instead, the health consequences of some cases of infibulation are generalised to describe the health risks of *all* types of FGM to support the dominant narrative that FGM should be treated as a public health problem.[90] Some scholars argued that FGM research is often based on a singular anecdote and published reports have become repeated and subject to uncritical citations.[91]

Spoken Testimony about FGM

This book relies on interviews with women from FGM-performing communities and professionals. The professionals interviewed have a unique insight into FGM as they work closely with communities and are responsible for designing and enforcing the law.[92] Alongside testimony, this book explores relevant literature from a variety of disciplines. This method allowed an investigation into a sensitive subject, FGM, where there is limited empirical research about attitudes towards FGM, how the practice is performed in Britain, and beliefs in anti-FGM laws in the academic literature. Where research includes women's voices about FGM, it usually takes a specific view about women's attitudes about FGM and the horrors of the practice, which reinforce the need for anti-FGM campaigns and anti-FGM legislation, rather than grounding interviews in the context of the criminalisation of FGM. However, this body of work has

---

Among Ibos of Nigeria' (1983) 60(11) East African Medical Journal 793; Olayinka Koso-Thomas, *The Circumcision of Women: A Strategy for Eradication* (Zed Books 1987).

[88] Lightfoot-Klein and Shaw, 'Special Needs' (n 77); Maria Frederika Malmström, 'The Production of Sexual Mutilation Among Muslim Women in Cairo' (2013) 3(2) Global Discourse 306; Ahmadu, 'Rites and Wrongs' (n 11).

[89] See, Obiora, 'Bridges and Barricades' (n 36).

[90] See, Shell-Duncan and Hernlund, *Female 'Circumcision' in Africa* (n 37).

[91] See, Carla M Obermeyer, 'Female Genital Surgeries: The Known, the Unknown, and the Unknowable' (1999) 13(1) Medical Anthropology Quarterly 79 (hereafter Obermeyer, 'Female Genital Surgeries').

[92] As a barrister, I spend considerable time listening to the stories of women and conveying them to judges in a court arena. I was keen to interview women and professionals and share their intimate views which are often marginalised from popular media coverage.

concentrated almost exclusively on women affected by FGM and the majority of studies are small in sample size.[93]

Interviews were the preferred methodology because they allow the researcher to frame the research with a specific focus whilst understanding women's lived realities. A broad cross-section of interview participants allowed an exploration of the potential and limitations of social change through the law. Semi-structured and open-ended questions gave participants the power to define the research agenda and the issues they want to talk about.[94] Applying a feminist framework[95] to this book, qualitative interviews allowed women's and girls' experiences to be fully explored and put at the forefront of this research.[96] Interviews were critical in ensuring the following core tenets of feminist research were met: experiences of women's lives are heard;[97] an ethic of commitment and egalitarianism through openness and engagement;[98] the need to alter and critique the power dynamics in the formulation of knowledge and the need to critically reflect on research processes because most of the knowledge and the research processes in our society have been produced by men;[99] and woman-to-woman interviewing using categories that represent women's lives rather than categories that reflect men's activities or social science terminology.[100]

While there have been anthropological studies about FGM internationally— partly because FGM is considered a cultural and traditional practice prevalent

---

[93] For recent empirical work about FGM in the UK see, for example, Kate Norman and others, 'FGM is Always with Us: Experiences, Perceptions, Beliefs of Women Affected by Female Genital Mutilation in London: Results from a PEER Study' (2009) FORWARD, Options Consultancy Services Ltd; Bradley, *Women, Violence and Tradition* (n 3), which includes the stories of a small sample of women interview participants; Brown and Porter, 'Tackling FGM Initiative' (n 12).

[94] In contrast, structured interview questions or surveys often create a perception that participants are expected to disclose personal information that could leave participants feeling exposed: Ann Oakley and Helen Roberts, 'Interviewing Women: A Contradiction in Terms' in Helen Roberts (ed), *Doing Feminist Research* (Routledge & Kegan Paul Plc 1997) 30 (hereafter Oakley and Roberts, *Doing Feminist Research*). Moreover, quantitative methods do not always allow for the free interaction between researcher and participant and social researchers that is required for an exploratory study.

[95] While feminist research shares some common goals and visions, there is no single feminist epistemology or methodology: Sharlene Hesse-Biber, 'Feminist Research: Exploring, Interrogating, and Transforming the Interconnections of Epistemology, Methodology, and Method' in Sharlene Hesse-Biber (ed), *Handbook of Feminist Research* (Sage Publications 2012) 2.

[96] Feminist social research studies have 'powerful liberating effects' by bringing forth 'a wealth of previously untold stories': Marjorie L DeVault and Glenda Gross, 'Feminist Interviewing: Experience, Talk, and Knowledge' in Sharlene Hesse-Biber (ed), *Handbook of Feminist Research* (Sage Publications 2007) 173 (hereafter DeVault and Gross, 'Feminist Interviewing').

[97] Janet Finch, '"It's Great to Have Someone to Talk to": Ethics and Politics of Interviewing Women' in Martyn Hammersley (ed), *Social Research, Philosophy, Politics and Practice* (Sage 1993) 166.

[98] Oakley and Roberts, *Doing Feminist Research* (n 94).

[99] Dale Spender, *Men's Studies Modified: The Impact of Feminism on the Academic Disciplines* (Pergamon Press 1981).

[100] Shulamit Reinharz, *Feminist Methods in Social Research* (Oxford University Press 1992).

abroad—scant attention has been paid to responding to FGM in Britain. The increase of the practice in Britain following the arrival of women and girls from FGM-performing countries has received relatively little critical academic attention.[101] While there has been public critique of the lack of prosecutions for FGM,[102] as well as scholarly attention directed at the design of FGM legislation and enforcement mechanisms, notably through a cross-European legislative lens,[103] much less effort has been invested in listening to the voices of women from FGM-performing communities whose lives are affected by FGM and anti-FGM laws as well as the views of those responsible for designing and enforcing FGM legislation.

I questioned whether consideration of FGM could be done fairly by a white woman, or whether women of colour who have experience of FGM are in a better position to address the topic. A white woman would again be given yet more public space to address FGM. I am only able to undertake this research because women of colour agreed to speak with me about FGM and because Black and Ethnic Minority women have, for many years, developed critiques of mainstream feminist scholarship.[104] It is important that white women take responsibility and identify our racism and work to eliminate it, rather than leaving the work to Ethnic Minority women.[105] The purpose of this book is to continue the development of feminist approaches to law by applying it to issues that affect Ethnic Minority women, particularly women of colour's bodies, which have previously been marginalised.

Scholars, including myself, have been warned against essentialising women and treating gender as a homogenous variable and thereby neglecting women's diverse experience situated in race, class, age, and socio-economic position. Reflexivity was imperative in this research; it was deeply important to maintain reflexive awareness throughout of the impact of my cultural, political, and

---

[101] Mohammad, 'Legislative Action' (n 61).

[102] Bindel, 'Unpunished Crime' (n 66).

[103] Els Leye and Jessica Deblonde, 'Legislation in Europe Regarding Female Genital Mutilation and the Implementation of the Law in Belgium, France, Spain, Sweden and the UK' (2004) International Centre for Reproductive Health (ICRH); Els Leye, 'Strategies for FGM Prevention in Europe' in Comfort Momoh (ed., *Female Genital Mutilation* (Radcliffe Publishing 2005); Leye and others 'An Analysis' (n 48); Els Leye and Alexia Sabbe, 'Responding to Female Genital Mutilation in Europe. Striking the Right Balance between Prosecution and Prevention. A Review of Legislation' (2009) International Centre for Reproductive Health.

[104] See, Obiora, 'Bridges and Barricades' (n 36); Carla M Obermeyer, 'The Consequences of Female Circumcision for Health and Sexuality: An Update on the Evidence' (2005) 7(5) Culture, Health & Sexuality 443; Obermeyer, 'Female Genital Surgeries' (n 91); Ahmadu, 'Rites and Wrongs' (n 11); Gunning, 'Arrogant Perception' (n 50).

[105] This critique is developed further by Marlee Kline, 'Race, Racism, and Feminist Legal Theory' (1989) 12 Harvard Women's Law Journal 115; Bell Hooks, *Ain't I a Woman* (South End Press 1981).

social context on the construction of this project[106] and the development of knowledge.[107] My background differed[108] with the backgrounds of the participants who were women of colour mainly from a socio-economically disadvantaged background. Discussions of class were evident in the interviews, as they described how their life conditions were manifested in their educational and socio-economic background and one's position in the community, presenting a complex picture.[109] All participants knew and had experienced, either personally or through their communities, that poverty was a reality in the lives of many Black people. Interview participants described their experiences of war having fled Somalia as asylum seekers and then living in the UK as refugees. Race, gender, class, age, education, and profession are all key differences between the participants and myself. Race was a significant theme of difference during the interviews. Race is an important aspect of women of colour's identities in their experience of the world and their interactions between themselves and law enforcement agents. Following Rosalind Edwards' suggestion, I addressed racial identities explicitly by highlighting the difference in social location between me and the interview participant.[110] For example, I would start the interview by openly stating my limitations in researching FGM but I am interviewing women because I want to learn, understand, and listen to their voices. My status as an outsider, unfamiliar with the cultural practices, religion, family, and community traditions gave participants the status of experts of their social worlds, as they explained aspects of their lives,[111] sometimes in intricate detail.[112] Furthermore, the 'stranger value' allowed interview participants to vent a sense of injustice and anger, which they said they felt unable to express to women and men from their community for fear of discussing a

---

[106] Differences and similarities impact on every aspect of the interview process from designing questions, deciding not to ask certain questions, the ease of difficulties of recruiting participants, the relationship with the participant, and the lenses through which researchers produce and analyse data: see, Susan E Chase, *Ambiguous Empowerment: The Work Narratives of Women School Superintendents* (University of Massachusetts Press 1995).

[107] See, Alan Bryman, *Social Research Methods* (Oxford University Press 2012); DeVault and Gross, 'Feminist Interviewing' (n 96).

[108] As a white, privileged woman in her twenties at the time the research was undertaken.

[109] See Juanita Johnson-Bailey, 'The Ties that Bind and the Shackles that Separate: Race, Gender, Class, and Color in a Research Process' (1999) 12(6) International Journal of Qualitative Studies in Education 659.

[110] Rosalind Edwards, 'Connecting Method and Epistemology: A White Woman Interviewing Black Women' (1990) 13(5) Women's Studies International Forum 477.

[111] I was concerned about exposing women to trauma as they divulged their personal narratives. As a result, I avoided asking women directly about *their own* story of FGM, instead I asked them about FGM more broadly. Interviewees appeared comfortable in discussing their personal experiences, often in detail.

[112] Jody Miller and Barry Glassner, 'The "Inside" and the "Outside": Finding Realities in Interviews in David Silverman (ed), *Qualitative Research* (Sage Publications 2004) 125.

taboo, expressing opinions they assumed would be different, therefore risking social ostracisation.[113] My outsider status meant that some women treated the research as a mode of conveying their views about FGM to a wider audience.[114] African-American legal scholar, Isabelle Gunning, recommended a method for feminist 'outsiders' requiring them to criticise their own, often invisible culture-based practices from the perspective of the 'other'.[115] Taking on board this approach, one of the double standards in law is explored, the toleration of FGCS on 'white' women whilst FGM is prohibited.

Feminists of colour[116] have suggested that analyses of women of colour are often problematic because they reinforce stereotypes and assumptions about women of colour, for example women of colour are victims of oppressive cultural norms.[117] These stances can erase the work and agency of women in transforming their social worlds.[118] This book does not intend to highlight a monolithic view of FGM but rather to locate women's agency in acts of resistance and accommodators of FGM, however uncomfortable this might be for anti-FGM campaigners (including myself), rather than portraying them as victims, which some women do not identify with.[119]

Procedures were adopted to ensure that as wide a range of interview participants as possible were chosen and that interviews were conducted to the highest ethical standard. There are serious limitations to interviewing women from FGM-performing communities, such as gaining access to interview participants. Discussion about FGM is subjective which is a strength of understanding women's unique experiences. Given my outsider status, I was initially reliant on meeting members of the community through NGOs. Once in contact with women from FGM-performing communities, snowball sampling took effect with women providing the contact details of other women to interview. Two focus groups were conducted with eleven women from a Somalia background, which were organised by two small NGOs that might better be referred to as community organisations, in different parts of the country. The NGOs agreed to organise the focus groups because it formed part of their required advocacy work, which comprised part of their projects on women's rights and helped raise awareness about FGM through sharing experiences and stories.

---

[113] PJ Rhodes, 'Race-of-Interviewer Effects: A Brief Comment' (1994) 28(2) Sociology 547.

[114] ibid.

[115] Gunning, 'Arrogant Perception' (n 50).

[116] See, Uma Narayan, *Dislocating Cultures: Identities, Traditions, and Third-World Feminisms* (Routledge 1997) (hereafter Narayan, *Dislocating Cultures*).

[117] S Wise, 'A Framework for Discussing Ethical Issues in Feminist Research: A Review of the Literature' (1987) 19 Studies in Sexual Politics 47; DeVault and Gross, 'Feminist Interviewing' (n 96).

[118] According to Narayan, *Dislocating Cultures* (n 116).

[119] Meyers, 'Feminism and Women's Autonomy' (n 47).

Interestingly, many of the NGO workers sympathised or defended the practice. The women they invited to the focus groups came from a broad cross-section of the community, from three different generations,[120] with varied educational backgrounds and diverse views on the elimination of FGM; they were all from lower socio-economic backgrounds. There is the possibility of selection bias, as the interview participants are likely to know the NGO and thus likely to support anti-FGM work. However, the findings show that many women in the focus group were vocal proponents of FGM and spoke openly about their attitudes. In the focus groups, NGO workers organised a Somali interpreter who was also from the same community to assist with translation.[121] The balance of power shifted[122] to the participants in both focus groups when they took control of the topic of conversation and determined their own agenda. They allowed women of a similar socio-economic class and race background to share their experiences of vulnerability through dialogue and debate. It was particularly interesting to observe the extent to which personal experiences of FGM were revealed, how participants challenged and supported other participants, and the meanings ascribed to FGM among different generations. Women's approach to discussing the intimate detail of FGM varied, some discussed FGM with little prompting, others appeared concerned and kept their stories short. In some cases, the subject was changed from discussing the practice to the laws or wider policies.

Meanwhile, one-to-one interviews were conducted in English, which is an additional selection bias. Such exploratory research often has selection biases. Men are an important group of participants because they are one of the main reasons that FGM is performed. NGOs and women participants were unable to put me in contact with men who might be amenable to being interviewed due to the embarrassment about speaking about FGM.[123] Further research has been conducted by a partnership of anti-FGM NGOs in respect of men's attitudes

---

[120] At the first focus group women varied in age from eighteen to sixty and at the second focus group women varied from the age of eighteen to sixty.

[121] Stephen C King, 'The Sociologist and the Community Developer: Autonomy and Role Conflict in Qualitative Research' (1981) 1(2) Sociological Spectrum 185 argues for the need to extend critical reflexivity to the role of interpreters who are active in producing research accounts. The primary consideration when recruiting an interpreter is the interpreter–participant match, in terms of the same sex, culture, religion, and age—this is according to Bogusia Temple and Rosalind Edwards, 'Interpreters/ Translators and Cross-Language Research: Reflexivity and Border Crossings' (2002) 1(2) International Journal of Qualitative Methods 12; Monique Hennink, 'Language and Communication in Cross-Cultural Qualitative Research' (2008) 34 Doing Cross-Cultural Research 21. Both interpreters matched the background of participants: women, Somali heritage, and Muslim.

[122] It is generally understood that in focus groups the researcher's power and influence is reduced because she has much less power over a group than over an individual.

[123] Two men were interviewed; I met one man at an African cultural community event and another man at an FGM conference.

towards FGM.[124] The professionals interviewed were identified through mapping their status and involvement working in the FGM arena or as law enforcement agents in the FGM area, which was often a matter of public or community knowledge; as such the key individuals to interview were identified and contacted. The consent form addressed concerns about disclosure, stating that if the participant identified that a person or child is at risk of FGM or another criminal offence, I would report this information to the police. All of the interviews were recorded using a tape recorder and transcribed into English. The interviews lasted between twenty minutes and ninety minutes and the focus groups lasted over two hours.[125]

---

[124] See, Sarah O' Neill and others, 'Men Have a Role to Play but They Don't Play It": A Mixed Methods Study Exploring Men's Involvement in Female Genital Mutilation in Belgium, the Netherlands and the United Kingdom' (2016) Full Report, Men Speak Out Project. The research found that encouraging men to speak about FGM continues to be difficult due to taboos around the practice linked to codes of social decency and shame. The belief that FGM is a religious requirement is an important factor in influencing attitudes about the continuation of FGM. Men who think that FGM is required by religion are fifteen times more likely to seek to continue FGM.

[125] I conducted follow-up interviews to ascertain whether legal changes such as the introduction of FGMPOs and the first conviction for FGM has changed attitudes and beliefs to the law.

1

Women's Stories of Female Genital Mutilation

Introduction

Women's voices must be put at the centre of the anti-FGM movement. This chapter outlines women's diverse experiences of a practice that is universally condemned as child abuse as well as their experiences of the long-term consequences for their bodies and their lives. Often a few hand-picked stories dominate media headlines with FGM depicted as a cruel and traumatic ordeal that girls are subjected to by their family members. Whilst FGM is an inhumane practice, women's voices are lost in dominant anti-FGM discourse. The description of FGM is one-dimensional rarely featuring alternative narratives. Women's divergent experiences of FGM have been shielded from public view, particularly women that support rather than oppose the practice.[1] The purpose of this chapter is to highlight women's competing and nuanced narratives about FGM rather than merely condemning FGM, which silences and marginalises many other women's lived experiences. Interviews with women who have undergone FGM show that women's experiences of FGM vary enormously. Some women describe FGM as a traumatic event that has had lifelong consequences for their mental and physical health whilst other women do not have any recollection of undergoing the practice and some women describe the practice as giving them an important sense of identity.[2] Women's divergent experiences and views about FGM indicate the challenges in eliminating and criminalising FGM.

---

[1] As highlighted in qualitative research published by Eleanor Brown and Chelsey Porter 'The Tackling FGM Initiative: Evaluation of the Second Phase (2013–2016)' (2016) Options Consultancy Services Ltd. There was a wide variation in attitudes to FGM by age, location, ethnicity, education, and place of birth.

[2] This book is underpinned by a fundamental premise that FGM is a human rights violation and should be a criminal offence. The research applies a human rights and feminist framework. Despite this stance towards the practice, it is imperative that women's and girl's nuanced attitudes towards FGM are highlighted. FGM can only be eliminated if *all* women are part of the movement whilst women who support FGM must be understood and recognised rather than silenced.

Female Genital Mutilation. Charlotte Proudman, Oxford University Press. © Charlotte Proudman 2022.
DOI: 10.1093/oso/9780198864608.003.0002

The motivations for continuing the practice of FGM also vary depending on the family or kinship group that the individual who has undergone FGM belongs to. There is no single reason for the continuation of FGM because the practice is based on a belief system rather than a single factor.[3] The reasons for performing FGM usually depend upon the meanings ascribed to FGM by different tribes and communities. The reasons for FGM are complex, interrelated, and woven into the beliefs and values that various communities uphold.[4] The most common motivations that are identified in the literature on FGM and in the interviews with women are as follows: control of a girl's and woman's sexuality, preservation of a cultural practice, a religious requirement to undergo FGM, and fear of transgressing a social norm. Whilst some women regard FGM as a choice which girls and women choose to undergo, others argue that when faced with the possibility of social ostracisation from one's family and community, girls and women do not have any reasonable means of rejecting FGM. The complex motivations for FGM show the difficulties in eliminating a deeply entrenched practice over generations.

Control of a Girl's and Woman's Sexuality

The most prevalent reason for FGM, as stated in the literature and in interviews with FGM-performing communities, is the need to control a girl's and woman's sexuality. Anti-FGM activists, Dorkenoo and Toubia, have both written extensively on the purpose of FGM as a means of controlling who, when, and how a woman has sex and reproduces.[5] Toubia rather controversially referred to FGM as a physical chastity belt.[6] However, the meanings attached to a girl's and woman's sexuality depend on the community performing the practice. Anti-FGM campaigners, Rahman and Toubia, state that in some patriarchal communities, a family or kinship group's honour is tied to a girl's and woman's virginity and chastity.[7] FGM is often performed to prevent premarital

---

[3] For a review of FGM initiatives across the world and women's stories of FGM in different countries, see, Hilary Burrage, *Female Mutilation: A Global Journey Behind the Curtains of the Horrifying Worldwide Practice of Female Genital Mutilation* (New Holland Publishers 2016).

[4] See background to FGM in Anika Rahman and Nahid Toubia, *Female Genital Mutilation: A Guide to Laws and Policies Worldwide* (Zed Books 2000).

[5] Efua Dorkenoo, *Cutting the Rose: Female Genital Mutilation: The Practice and its Prevention* (Minority Right Publications 1994) (hereafter Dorkenoo, *Cutting the Rose*); Nahid Toubia, 'Female Circumcision as a Public Health Issue' (1994) 331(11) New England Journal of Medicine 712; Nahid Toubia, *Female Genital Mutilation: A Call for Global Action* (RAINBO 1995) (hereafter Toubia, *Call for Global Action*).

[6] Toubia, *Call for Global Action* (n 5) 299.

[7] Anika Rahman and Nahid Toubia, *Female Genital Mutilation: A Guide to Laws and Policies Worldwide* (Zed Books 2000) (hereafter Rahman and Toubia, *Guide to Laws and Policies*).

sex, preserve virginity, and curtail infidelity on marriage. Some communities believe that cutting a woman's genitalia would reduce her sexual desire, thus ensuring that she conforms to the role expected of her as a wife and mother. De-emphasising a woman's sexual behaviour is believed to emphasise her re-productive role in producing the next generation.[8] A woman depends on mar-riage for economic and social survival, thus she is compelled to undergo FGM or she could be considered unmarriageable.[9] For other communities, FGM represents a rite of passage meaning that girls do not become women until their genitalia is cut or removed.[10] Other communities believe that women's genitalia are masculine and thus undergoing FGM emphasises their femin-inity. Anti-FGM scholar, Toubia, contends that strong belief systems predi-cated on preserving FGM create pressure from peers, family, and communities to undergo the practice.[11] All of the women who were interviewed identified that the purpose of FGM was to ensure that they are marriageable, to maintain a girl's virginity until marriage, and to ensure women's fidelity to their husband after marriage.

Women's experiences of their own sexuality is an area of limited research. According to Rahman and Toubia, available studies suggest that FGM inter-feres to some degree with women's sexual responses and indeed, the intention of FGM is to reduce women's sexual pleasure.[12] However, it is likely that women will have different experiences of their sexuality depending on a number of factors, not all of which relate solely to FGM. Scholars opine that FGM nega-tively impacts upon women's sexual experiences. Growing research shows that the practice does not necessarily eliminate sexual pleasure and climax.[13]

---

[8] Anthropologist Janice Boddy states that many Sudanese women regard FGM as an 'assertive, highly meaningful act that emphasises female fertility by de-emphasising female sexuality': Janice Boddy 'Womb as Oasis: The Symbolic Context of Pharaonic Circumcision in Rural Northern Sudan.' (1982) 9(4) American Ethnologist 682, 682.

[9] Women's dependence on maintaining the practice to ensure economic and social currency is ex-plored in Hanny Lightfoot-Klein and Evelyn Shaw, 'Special Needs of Ritually Circumcised Women Patients' (1991) 20(2) Journal of Obstetric, Gynecologic, & Neonatal Nursing 102 (hereafter Lightfoot-Klein and Shaw 'Special Needs').

[10] According to Marie Bassili Assaad, 'Female Circumcision in Egypt: Social Implications, Current Research, and Prospects for Change.' (1980) Studies in Family Planning 3. Some FGM-performing communities believe 'that a woman is not fully a woman until her ugly genitalia are removed' (ibid 6).

[11] Toubia, Call for Global Action (n 5).

[12] Rahman and Toubia, Guide to Laws and Policies (n 7).

[13] For academic research showing that women experience sexual pleasure after FGM see, A A Shandall, 'Circumcision and Infibulation of Females: A General Consideration of the Problem and a Clinical Study of the Complications in Sudanese Women' (1967) 5(4) Sudan Medical Journal 178; Asma El Dareer, Woman, Why Do You Weep? Circumcision and Its Consequences (Zed Press 1982) (here-after El Dareer, Woman, Why Do You Weep?); U Megafu, 'Female Ritual Circumcision in Africa: An Investigation of the Presumed Benefits Among Ibos of Nigeria.' (1983) 60(11) East African Medical Journal 793; Olayinka Koso-Thomas, The Circumcision of Women: A Strategy for Eradication (Zed Press 1987).

Empirical research into the sexual experiences of women who have undergone FGM challenges preconceived views that it curtails women's sexuality.[14] Malmström interviewed lower-class women about the practice in Egypt and found that women are angry at the accusation that FGM removed their sexuality and sexual pleasure.[15] Some interviewees argued that FGM heightens and makes their sexual experience holistic. Suggesting that women have not experienced the height of sexual pleasure leads to the contentious label of 'false consciousness' projected onto cut women by uncut women, which was met with fierce resistance. Sierra Leonean-American anthropologist, Ahmadu, asserts that many women, including herself, who had sexual experiences prior to FGM, experience either no difference or increased sexual pleasure following the practice.[16] The available research about women's sexual experiences after undergoing FGM appears to challenge leading anti-FGM narratives that the practice curtails *all* women's sexuality. Despite the competing narratives about whether FGM is performed to curtail a girl's or woman's sexuality or for other reasons, many of the women interviewed shared deeply traumatic stories of their experiences of FGM. Even if the practice did not have long-term effects on women's sexual experiences, FGM is likely to have had a profound effect on their mental health. Women's experiences of FGM were divided; some women stated that they did not have any recollection of FGM, whilst others described torturous pain associated with FGM when they were cut, when they consummated their marriage, and when they gave birth.

- People talk about their experience of being cut, from a young age being tortured in that way. When they can't even talk about it sometimes it can really torment.
- I have seen people who have been traumatised by the experiences they have had especially when they were giving birth or the night they got married. I have seen people like that who have talked about it and who have been affected and thinking I am not going to forgive my parents who did this. I have seen people like that. [FG1]

[14] Lightfoot-Klein and Shaw found that in some cases, infibulated women in Sudan reported pleasurable sex and orgasm: Lightfoot-Klein and Shaw, 'Special Needs' (n 9).

[15] Maria Frederica Malmström, 'The Production of Sexual Mutilation Among Muslim Women in Cairo' (2013) 3(2) Global Discourse 306. In Egypt FGM is medicalised thus the health complications are not usually as complex as when performed in the private sphere, often underground. Without clear public health problems, it can make it challenging to argue the practice should be prohibited when met with defiant views of women.

[16] Fuambai Ahmadu, 'Rites and Wrongs: An Insider/Outsider Reflects on Power and Excision' in Bettina Shell-Duncan and Ylva Hernlund, *Female 'Circumcision' In Africa: Dimensions of The Practice and Debates* (Lynne Rienner Publishers 2000) (hereafter Ahmadu, 'Rites and Wrongs'.

The interview participants described women as being traumatised by FGM. An interview participant from the Gambia explained that she assisted the community cutter and that she was even responsible for ensuring her own daughter was cut. The interviewee was due to take on the prestigious role of cutter in her community against her wishes.[17] She described the flashbacks[18] that she still experiences today. The interview participant fled the Gambia to Britain and applied for asylum in the UK.

INTERVIEWER: Do you remember when you were cut?
PARTICIPANT: Of course. I was seven. The flashbacks I am having now, it's not when they perform it to me. The flashback I am having is when I was holding the girls when they were cutting them. The screams that the girls do. I used to have it a lot. Sometimes I even scream and think there is blood all over my house, sometimes I will have the flashbacks that they are cutting someone. I used to have all the flashbacks even now. [P3, FGM-PCM, Gambia]

FGM can have lifelong consequences for some women and girls who suffer with the trauma of FGM years after the practice. The interview participant suffers with severe mental health consequences as a result of her role in assisting with the cutting of young girls in her community. The visceral image of blood, which formed part of her flashbacks, is reinforced in the next interview participant's quotation, as she describes the blood that poured from a woman's body after she consummated her marriage. A survivor of FGM of Somali heritage describes the long-lasting impact of FGM on her body and her life. As a result of experiencing physical complications following FGM, the woman suffered gravely as a child and then into adulthood as she is unable to have children.

I am survivor of FGM. I was cut when I was seven years old. For me I had problems after the FGM. At the age of 11 I got ill and the doctors thought I had a cyst but it wasn't a cyst so they realized it was my period. So, for me FGM problems started at age 11, after having so many operations from the age of 11 to 17 I got my period for the first time. So I came to the UK, I got married, I wasn't getting pregnant, I went to the gynecologist, I had the IVF

---

[17] For an exploration of FGM as an economic necessity see, Hilary Burrage, *Eradicating Female Genital Mutilation: A UK Perspective* (Routledge 2016).
[18] Flashbacks were a key theme of women's stories of being cut. Further research of the medical and psychological effects of living with FGM is clearly an area that needs exploring.

and I miscarried and at the end of that period of time I won't be able to have another IVF because of all the operations I had meant I couldn't have my own child. [P13, FGM-PC, *Somalia*]

A woman of Somali heritage linked the motivation for FGM to control a woman's sexuality with the long-term negative physical effects experienced as a consequence of the practice.

> From my culture, the main motivations [of FGM] are purely to keep the virginity, to protect the virginity to keep the family name intact. Because if you get married it's like the next morning parents from his side and your parents come to investigate that you were a virgin, which means you will be lying in a pool of blood and they will be celebrating the blood around your bed. As my cousin said, she was groaning like a wounded animal in a pool of blood and her mum and his mum [husband's mother] were dancing around their bed instead of helping her first. So you can see how deeply [engrained] the culture is. [P12, FGM-PCM and teacher, *Somalia*]

The interview participant describes her family celebrating the physical spectacle of her cousin having lost her virginity to her husband. The woman's body symbolises the pain and conflict of FGM and sexual relations upon marriage. The wife's virgin status is represented in the physical pain and blood that followed the consummation of marriage. Reaffirming the bride's virgin status reinforces the participant's family honour within the community. The quotation from the interview highlights in graphic detail the pain that women experience following FGM, which suggests that the practice is oppressive to girls' and women's sexuality. According to Western feminists who were at the forefront of the end-FGM campaign in the 1970s to the 1990s, a key motivation for FGM is to oppress girls' and women's agency over their sexuality and to reinforce women's sexual subjugation to men. A male with Ghanaian heritage in which FGM is performed[19] explained that the main motivation for FGM is to remove a woman's sexual feelings to ensure that she is faithful to her husband.

---

[19] Interviewing men from FGM-performing communities was a challenging task. Men would often refuse to be interviewed for research purposes and clearly felt deeply uncomfortable discussing a 'women's issue'. As a result, only two men were interviewed during the research. Whilst their attitudes are not representative of men's beliefs from FGM-performing communities, they do provide a unique insight into two men's views about FGM.

The reason behind it [FGM] is to stop promiscuity. The reason is to stop them having too much feeling for sex or something, you know, that's the main reason behind it, so they stay with their husband. The reason is for the woman not to be promiscuous, to be calm and be with one's husband, people who do that to their children, they want their children not to have too many feelings towards men so they will not be wayward. So if there is no feeling they will wait for marriage. [P14, FGM-PCM, *Ghana*]

Notably, the participant did not oppose the practice. The views of the male participant reflect the attitudes of many women participants who suggested that FGM is necessary to reduce a woman's sexual desire and pleasure. FGM is viewed as a means of maintaining power and control over a woman to ensure that she is faithful in marriage. Interviews with women who have undergone FGM show a divide in attitudes towards the practice; while some women oppose the practice, other women suggest that the practice has enhanced their sexuality. The divergence in attitudes also reflects the polarised debate between scholars as reported in the literature. There are three schools of thought that dominate the academic literature: scholars who oppose FGM and define it as an oppressive practice, scholars who do not support FGM but reject Westerners' portrayal of the practice as barbarous,[20] and scholars who argue FGM is a legitimate cultural practice embraced by women. Early Western feminist literature[21] on the eradication of FGM represents the practice as the

---

[20] Some Western scholars and African scholars have joined the largely universal condemnation of FGM, while criticising Western portrayal of FGM as a torturous practice. For example, see, Raqiya Haji Dualeh Abdalla, *Sisters in Affliction: Circumcision and Infibulation of Women in Africa* (Zed Press 1982); El Dareer, *Woman, Why Do You Weep?* (n 13); Kay Boulware-Miller, 'Female Circumcision: Challenges to the Practice as a Human Rights Violation' (1985) 8 Harvard Women's Law Journal 155; Isabelle R Gunning, 'Arrogant Perception, World-Travelling and Multicultural Feminism: The Case of Female Genital Surgeries' (1991) 23 Columbia Human Rights Law Review 189; Isabelle R Gunning, 'Uneasy Alliances and Solid Sisterhood: A Response to Professor Obiora's *Bridges and Barricades*' (1997) 47 Case Western Reserve Law Review 445; Isabelle R Gunning 'Women and Traditional Practices: Female Genital Surgery' in Kelly D Askin and Dorean Koenig (eds), *Women and International Human Rights Law*, Vol 1 (Transnational Publishers 1999) (hereafter Gunning, 'Women and Traditional Practices'); Alice Walker and Pratibha Parmar, *Warrior Marks: Female Genital Mutilation and the Sexual Blinding of Women* (Harcourt Brace 1993) (hereafter Walker and Parmar, *Warrior Marks*). Leading medical professionals have supported women affected by FGM and advocated for the elimination of FGM on an international level, see, Dorkenoo, *Cutting the Rose* (n 5); Nawal El Saadawi, *The Hidden Face of Eve: Women in the Arab World* (Zed Books 2007); Comfort Momoh (ed), *Female Genital Mutilation* (Radcliffe Publishing Ltd 2005).

[21] See, Fran P Hosken, *The Hosken Report: Genital and Sexual Mutilation of Females* (Women's International Network News 1979) (hereafter Hosken, *Hosken Report*); Mary Daly, *Gyn/Ecology: The Metaethics of Radical Feminism* (Subsequent edn, Beacon Press 1990) (hereafter Daly, *Gyn/Ecology*); Esther K Hicks, *Infibulation: Female Mutilation in Islamic Northeastern Africa* (Transaction Publishers 1996); Walker and Parmar, *Warrior Marks* (n 20).

sexual subordination and oppression of women.[22] Fran Hosken, one of the first Western FGM researchers, wrote that FGM represents 'the sexual castration of women'.[23] Western feminists have been heavily criticised for portraying African women as infantile beings who lack the autonomy and agency required to resist FGM.[24] There is a perception that African women are represented as passive cultural dupes whose sexual and reproductive functions are controlled by men without resistance. African-American academics[25] have attacked Western feminists for the colonialist and imperialist discourse[26] in constructing stereotypical images of helpless women denied the choice to not be mutilated. They accuse Western feminists of lacking an understanding of the non-Western meaning of women's bodies and sexuality and perpetuating an essentialist and ethnocentric view of women.[27] To suggest that women who

---

[22] Anti-FGM activism coincided with the movement for the liberation of women's sexual desire in the 1970s, when Western feminists discovered their own clitorises and redefined the parameters of sexuality. In viewing the clitoris as a powerful symbol of women's sexual liberation in the 1970s, FGM became a symbol of patriarchal oppression, because the clitoris had been mutilated in order to de-emphasise women's sexuality and emphasise their reproductive utility. The sharp contrast of FGM with women's sexual liberation of the 1970s perhaps incited the staunch criticism of Western feminists. See, Juliet Rogers, *Law's Cut on the Body of Human Rights: Female Circumcision, Torture, and Scared Flesh* (Routledge 2013) (hereafter Rogers, *Law's Cut on the Body*).

[23] Hosken, *Hosken Report* (n 21) 73. The earlier literature on FGM condemned the practice forcefully. Sociologist Elizabeth Moen argued that FGM is performed to control women's bodies and thus any movement concerned with liberating women must include the politics of FGM: Elizabeth W Moen, 'What Does "Control Over Our Bodies" Really Mean?' (1979) 2(2) International Journal of Women's Studies 129. Western radical feminist Mary Daly contends that the 'cultural' justifications for FGM, such as initiation into adulthood, serve as a smokescreen to perpetuate male control over women's sexuality: Daly, *Gyn/Ecology* (n 21).

[24] Moira Dustin, 'Female Genital Mutilation/Cutting in the UK: Challenging the Inconsistencies' (2010) 17(1) European Journal of Women's Studies 7. As early as the late 1970s, Marie Angelique Savane, President of the Association of African Women, published an article criticising cultural insensitivity and calling for Western feminists to reconsider their conceptions of women, women's oppression, and women's needs in light of cultural difference: Marie Angelique Savane, 'Why Are We Against the International Campaign?' (1978) International Child Welfare 40.

[25] See, Ahmadu, 'Rites and Wrongs' (n 16); L Amede Obiora, 'Bridges and Barricades: Rethinking Polemics and Intransigence in the Campaign Against Female Circumcision' (1997) 47 Case Western Reserve Law Review 275 (hereafter Obiora, 'Bridges and Barricades'); L Amede Obiora, 'The Anti-Female Circumcision Campaign Deficit' in Obioma Nnaemeka (ed), *Female Circumcision and the Politics of Knowledge: African Women in Imperialist Discourses* (Praeger Publishers 2005) 209; L Amede Obiora, 'A Refuge from Tradition and the Refuge of Tradition: On Anticircumcision Paradigms' in Bettina Shell-Duncan and Ylva Hernlund (eds), *Transcultural Bodies: Female Genital Cutting in Global Context* (Rutgers University Press 2007) 67; M A Ogbu, 'Comment on Obiora's *Bridges and Barricades*' (1997) 47 Case Western Reserve Law Review 411; Micere Githae Mugo, 'Elitist Anti-Circumcision Discourse as Mutilating and Anti-Feminist' (1997) 47 Case Western Reserve Law Review 461.

[26]. African women scholars who condemn FGM have challenged Western feminist discourse on FGM. For example, see the work of Sengalese political activist Awa Thiam: Awa Thiam, *Black Sisters, Speak Out: Feminism and Oppression in Black Africa* (Pluto Press 1986). Also, Obioma Nnaemeka (ed), *Female Circumcision and the Politics of Knowledge: African Women in Imperialist Discourses* (Praeger 2005), a volume of essays written by African women scholars.

[27] Chima Korieh, '"Other" Bodies: Western Feminism, Race, and Representation in Female Circumcision Discourse' in Obioma Nnaemeka (ed), *Female Circumcision and the Politics of Knowledge: African Women in Imperialist Discourses* (Praegar 2005).

belong to cultural groups that practise FGM are devoid of autonomy would deny them existing opportunities for choice. African-American legal scholar, Obiora, contends that overly simplistic representations of African women as cultural dupes make invisible women's own acts of agency and resistance in the context of FGM.[28] Women's acts of resistance in the context of FGM are rarely discussed within the literature. Philosopher, Meyers, contends that women exercise effective agency as *accommodators* and *resisters* of FGM and neither group can be presumed to enjoy greater autonomy than the other.[29] Meyers does not believe that autonomy can simply be determined by analysing the nature of resistance. Women can be seen as exercising effective agency in performing and preventing FGM. Indeed, many women interview participant's ascribe agency to themselves as perpetrators of FGM. It is important to address women's divergent attitudes towards FGM in order to acknowledge the rationale for the persistence of the practice.[30] Some women who were interviewed vigorously supported FGM on the basis that women's sexual desire is controlled while men's sexual pleasure is maintained. A participant in the focus group of Somalia heritage stated that she preferred Type I FGM as opposed to Type III FGM because Type I enhanced men's sexual pleasure while women's sexual gratification was limited in some cases.

> The sunna [Type I FGM] is totally different. The pleasure for men is still fine because the entrance is not affected so for him it's totally fine. However, with the women it depends on, it varies from one woman to the next. This feeling is not only clitoris based because it's still there. So she will still have some feeling. Some of them will have normal feeling, some women have partial feeling, some of them, it depends. [FG1]

When the focus group participants discussed sexual pleasure, their first observation was the sexual pleasure of men, then they focused on the impact of FGM upon women's sexual experiences, which varies between different women.

---

[28] L Amede Obiora, 'A Refuge from Tradition and the Refuge of Tradition: On Anticircumcision Paradigms' in Bettina Shell-Duncan and Ylva Hernlund (eds), *Transcultural Bodies: Female Genital Cutting in Global Context* (Rutgers University Press 2007) 71.

[29] Diana Tietjens Meyers, 'Feminism and Women's Autonomy: The Challenge of Female Genital Cutting' (2000) 31(5) Metaphilosophy 281, 470 (hereafter Meyers, 'Feminism and Women's Autonomy'.

[30] Scholars argue that it is arrogant of Western feminists to dismiss the consent of African women to undergo FGM as the product of false consciousness or to offer to change the mind of the 'Exotic Other Female' (Karen Engle, 'Female Subjects of Public International Law: Human Rights and the Exotic Other Female' (1991) 26 New England Law Review 1509) in a bid to "rescue Other women"; I Grewal, 'On the New Global Feminism and the Family of Nations: Dilemmas of Transnational Feminist Practice' in Ella Habiba Shohat (ed), *Talking Visions: Multicultural Feminism in a Transnational Age* (MIT Press 2001).

However, the interview participants appeared unconcerned with the detrimental impact that FGM might have upon their sexual experience and instead appeared to prioritise men's pleasure. Similarly, a woman from Zimbabwe who had undergone Type IV FGM, otherwise known as labia elongation[31], described her experience of FGM at the age of seven as well as the consequent physical pain that she endured in graphic detail. When reflecting on the motivations for the practice she stated that it is performed for the benefit of men's sexual pleasure.

When I was 7 years in Zimbabwe ... they would take us to a secluded place like near a river and then they would start pulling our clitoris and labia. It was elderly women in the neighbourhood who were specially trained to do that. They used a wild fruit which they first roasted in a high heat pan and then it became roasted and then they started grinding it to make it powder. Then after it is powder they mix it with cooking oil and then that's the herb that they used. They used their fingers to do that for girls whose girls clitoris was hard they used pegs ... they suffer from it because it resulted in them have cists ... then there are others who are having problems giving birth and sometimes they have to go surgery ... because it doesn't have anaesthetic for some young girls once you go there the next day you come back with a lot of pain, then you are start actually feeling the pain, a lot of pain. Some women get their genitalia swollen, some women react to the herbs. So, it gets abnormal, like they have a lot of infections the day after that cannot be easily infected, so you end up treating infection after infection ... The reasons were that we were supposed to prepare so that when men have sex with us they have their pleasure and then it was done because they said many young women who got

---

[31] Labia elongation is also referred to as labia stretching and is defined as Type IV FGM, 'all other harmful procedures to the female genitalia for non-medical purposes' according to the World Health Organization. See, World Health Organization 'Types of Female Genital Mutilation' (*WHO.int*) <https://www.who.int/teams/sexual-and-reproductive-health-and-research/areas-of-work/female-genital-mutilation/types-of-female-genital-mutilation> accessed 3 March 2021 (hereafter WHO, 'Types of Female Genital Mutilation'). In a paper by Dr Kenneth Kaoma Mwenda it is argued that the practice of labia elongation is customary in many parts of Africa and does not violate the rights of women unless a woman is coerced into the practice: Dr Kenneth Kaoma Mwenda, 'Labia Elongation under African Customary Law: A Violation of Women's Rights?' (2006) 10(4) The International Journal of Human Rights 341. Guillermo Martinez Perez, Conception Tomas Aznar, and Brigitte Bagnol conducted a systematic review of the evidence-based knowledge published on the health risks and benefits of labia elongation as informed by African female respondents who are insiders of the practice and found that there is pain at the beginning of the practice in failing to comply with principle health risks. However, there is evidence that the practice may benefit the sexual health and well-being of women who choose to undergo it: Guilermo Martinez Perez, Conception Tmoas Aznar, and Brigitte Bagnol, 'Labia Minora Elongation and its Implications on the Health of Women: A Systematic Review' (2014) 26(3) International Journal of Sexual Health 155.

married without doing that were returned back to their homes and rejected at the marriage age because that was not the norm ... [P2, FGM-PCM and NGO worker, *Zimbabwe*]

The woman's experience of FGM shows the inter-generational practice of FGM with elderly women performing FGM upon young girls to maintain the practice. The customary nature of the practice, performed without medical equipment, highlights the pain that a woman would experience when undergoing FGM. At the conclusion of the quotation, the woman explains that FGM is performed to enable a woman to marry. A man's sexual pleasure achieved through FGM is prioritised over a girl's right to bodily autonomy to *choose* to undergo such practices. A woman from an FGM-performing community stated that women undergo labia elongation to increase the sexual pleasure of men, which makes the women more desirable.

I know friends from Southern Africa who have gone through that [labia elongation] but you see the irony is they don't talk about it in a negative way. They are very proud of what they went through. They see it as a badge of honour. Some of them went through when they were a young age, others in their early teens. They talk about the whole process and they laugh about it. I am not sure if they were even aware that was abuse ... They all talk about it in a very positive way and they haven't experienced any pain with it. I am from West Africa and they are from South Africa and sometimes there is this banter because a lot of Western African men seem to be dating South African women and they say it's because of the labia elongation and that's why they like them. And this is how these conversations start out. So to them they have something the Western African women don't have which is why the Western African men are going to them ... I think it's more to do with the men. It's a discussion about how men find them attractive. Men enjoy having sex with them because of the way their clitoris looks or things like that. [P75, social worker, *West Africa*]

The interview participant states that women who have undergone type IV FGM experience elevated social status due to the increased sexual arousal of men stemming from women's elongated labia. Women participants accept that one of the motivations for FGM is the increased sexual pleasure of men. However, interview participants appear to accept this motivation without challenge rather than thinking critically about whether this is an acceptable reason for the persistence of FGM; some women reject FGM whilst others accept it without criticism. Whilst the control of a woman's sexuality is closely associated with oppressing a woman's sexual desire and enhancing a man's sexual pleasure, there are other motivations for FGM that indicate that the practice is performed to undermine a woman's sexuality, including the need to clean and purify a woman's body both physically and psychologically. Furthermore, cleanliness and purity also denote the virgin status of women, which is one of the primary reasons for performing FGM, to ensure that the girl is a virgin on marriage. Following interviews with lower-class women in Egypt, Malmström found that women believe they are neither clean nor pure if they have not been cut. In a research study conducted by anti-FGM NGOs and academics[32] among UK-based migrants from FGM affected countries living in Norfolk and Essex, women interviewees spoke about FGM being performed due to honour, history, and tradition and the importance of being 'clean' and 'protected' from having sex outside of marriage. Women of Somalia heritage in focus groups and interviews linked FGM to hygiene and virginity.

It [FGM] enhances the female aspect of the body or female psyche, or how she should be clean, pure woman that would be perfect when her husband would marry her. [P7, FGM-PCM, *Somalia*]

- I just want to add that there is a reason why it's a sunna [Type I FGM] and there's a big reason behind it. There's a bigger picture to it. The reason of why sunna is hygienic.
- Basically the Type I, the one that is encouraged, the clitoris, it needs to be not cut but blood needs to come out of it, they believe that blood inside that clitoris is not something that is pure and after that blood is drained out then it becomes nice and clean and pure. But the cutting behind it I think is taken out of proportion that it's being cut and all that. But the cutting is not part of the religion. They believe it will become elongated so at least it needs to be cut and then it will look nice. [FG1]

FGM is believed to be hygienic by making an unclean girl pure through undergoing FGM. The draining of the blood from the clitoris is believed to represent the drawing of impure and unclean parts of the body to fulfil notions of purity and cleanliness. FGM appears to be maintained due to cultural beliefs

---

[32] See, SB Gegzabheb, K Norman, N Otoo-Oyortey, '"Between Two Cultures": A Rapid PEER Study Exploring Migrant Communities' Views on Female Genital Mutilation in Essex and Norfolk, UK' (2016) FORWARD & National FGM Centre Report (hereafter Gegzabheb, Norman, and Otoo-Oyortey, 'Between Two Cultures'

that a female's genitalia is unclean until cut. The underlining premise is that a female's genitalia require alteration in order to be socially acceptable, which reinforces gender inequality and in its darker manifestation is a form of gender policing. Preserving the cleanliness and purity of a woman's body through FGM is believed to constitute feminine beauty. According to women interview participants, beauty is a prime driver for performing FGM. In the focus groups, women of Somali heritage, mainly elderly women aged over sixty, described FGM as a form of beautification. There was an exchange between a grandmother and granddaughter, which highlights that FGM is performed as a means of cleaning women's genitalia which in turn 'beautifies' their vaginas. The grandmother was responsible for having her granddaughter cut in Somalia before they resided in England and Wales.

- Grandmother: If I am being honest she said, I have three girls, when I was in Somalia, one died in infant age, the other two I did circumcision, I did pharaoni[33] because that was the fashion at that time and I believe still, I believe it still today that they were the best girls and I have never seen any problem with them, on their body also and their genital was beautiful for me like it has been. I believe that the age that the elder woman, of the elder woman my age, we are the same age who has not been circumcised, I believe that I have a beautiful more prettier vagina than them, those who have not been circumcised. I believe and I can demonstrate also that I am clean. I can show you, I can show you that I am clean. And the circumcision that I had was pretty and I am more, more pretty, I have more prettier vagina than those who have not had it. I was happy because I believe that when the woman who have not been stitched and has not been cut it was very, very ugly her vagina, I was happy then because I was having this pretty vagina after my circumcision.
- Granddaughter: In Somalia culture if the woman has a larger clitoris or things are too like messy they want it to be tidy and neat. I think, because me and my grandmother discussed this, and it's for the women's satisfaction.
- Interviewer: Was it painful?
- Grandmother: Very painful. It was very painful but it was something, which I wanted because I had to go through and I was waiting really to have it. [FG2]

---

[33] Pharaoni or pharaonic circumcision refers to Type III FGM, which is generally considered to be one of the most physically invasive Types of FGM. See, WHO, 'Types of Female Genital Mutilation' (n 31).

The grandmother and the granddaughter use similar language and narratives to Western women who advocate for cosmetic procedures and thus promote the beauty industry. Interview participants argued that FGM is liberating because it enhances the appearance of their genitalia and is carried out for 'women's satisfaction'. Type III FGM is described as 'fashion at that time' through enhancing the aesthetic appearance of a woman's genitalia. Although cultural norms dictate beautification practices, the participants frame FGM as stemming from a woman's individual choice to conform to aesthetic norms within their communities. Narratives of beautification and choice could be used to detract attention from the underlying dominant purpose of FGM, to control a woman's sexuality. However, some interview participants did not regard FGM as a means of exercising control of women's and girls' bodies. Even if participants defined FGM as a means of controlling girls' and women's sexuality, some still defended the practice because it is integral to their identity and sense of belonging. Cultural pressures to undergo FGM are implicit in the language used by the grandmother and granddaughter. The grandmother distinguishes between vulvas that are cut and are beautiful and those that are uncut and are in her words, 'very, very ugly'. Dualisms were described by participants: beautiful/ugly genitalia and clean/dirty genitalia. The fear of falling into the ugly/dirty category could result in the practice continuing amongst generations to come. As highlighted by the interview participants, women are the key gatekeepers to the practice of FGM. The grandmother ensured that her daughters were all cut, which reinforces the central role that women have in maintaining the practice. An interview participant of Somali heritage explains the central role of women, particularly grandparents, in maintaining FGM:

INTERVIEWER: Who decides whether a girl should be cut?

PARTICIPANT: Woman. Woman driven. Normally mothers who make the decision but if you are living in an extended family like Somali people do it's usually the grandparents and there is no way you are going to escape FGM if you have your grandparents in the house. Grandparents are held up high, whatever they say goes, they are extremely powerful, it's a status thing, it's a respectful thing. So whatever they say goes in the family. They actually even choose who married who. In my family, cousins marry cousins. They pair them up. [P12, FGM-PCM and teacher, *Somalia*]

The participant notes that grandparents are considered 'extremely powerful' and are given an elevated status in the community. Some grandparents, particularly grandmothers, use their position to enforce traditional practices onto the next generation of girls. Anti-FGM activist, Dorkenoo, contends that 'after the menopause patriarchal society has no need to control women's reproduction or sexuality as they can no longer bear children', as a result older women derive status and power within the family by performing the traditional practice on the younger generations.[34] Sierra Leonean-American anthropologist Ahmadu regards FGM as an empowering practice for women of all age groups, particularly grandmothers who control the practice and are given increased status in their community through maintaining the cultural practice upon the younger generation.[35] Western anthropologist Shweder equated FGM with power and capital amongst women on the basis that FGM is almost exclusively controlled, performed, and strongly upheld by women.[36] Another interview participant explained that women perform FGM because they fear the consequences of girl's not conforming to the practice which might result in them being ostracised from their community.

All FGM is driven by women because of protecting virginity. They are afraid to be segregated from the community. They are afraid to be talked about, because they would be talked about because they would say oh her girls are dirty, her girls go with boys easily, they are kind of sluts, Somalis won't want to marry a girl if they know she has not been cut. The rest will stay away from you. Some of the women don't want to cut their girls but they don't know where to go for help. If they want to talk to some professionals, but there is nothing here like that. If they are under pressure from the family side they will buckle under because there is no one to talk to about what's going on. [P12, FGM-PCM and teacher, *Somalia*]

The interview participant links not being cut with being branded dirty and not a virgin. The quotation reinforces themes of virginity and cleanliness that were highlighted by other interview participants. Fear of the social consequences of living a life uncut, such as social isolation because a girl is perceived to be dirty, ensures that women continue to perform FGM. Indeed, women might fear that ending FGM could jeopardise the promise of elevated social status

---

[34] Dorkenoo, *Cutting the Rose* (n 5) 49–50.
[35] Ahmadu, 'Rites and Wrongs' (n 16).
[36] Richard A Shweder, 'Moral Realism without the Ethnocentrism: Is it Just a List of Empty Truisms?' in Andreas Sajo (ed), *Human Rights with Modesty: The Problem of Universalism* (Martinus Nijhoff Publishers 2004) 100 (hereafter Shweder, 'Moral Realism').

when they enter the stage in life of grandparents. Arguably, FGM is not viewed as an empowering practice but rather a means of maintaining their limited social status in a patriarchal society. An interview participant describes the role of women and men in the family in maintaining FGM. Often FGM is viewed as a woman's issue but, as highlighted by the interview participant, men have a vital role in allowing the practice to continue.

INTERVIEWER: Who decides if a girl should be cut?
PARTICIPANT: I think it's mostly the grandparents. For me it was my step-mother. It is mainly the women of the family. Still we have this shadow of the men. Don't think the men are not involved with that. Because men are not saying no so they implicitly say yes because when a girl is cut they go out or they like just leave the place and so that's the way for them to agree because like I have my grandfather and he sat down everyone in the family and said you have seen I have got three girls they have been born in a certain way and I don't want anything done to them. So, I think men are implicitly guilty of the FGM even when it's carried out by females. [P9, FGM-PCM and midwife, *Mali*]

While women have an active role in organising and performing FGM, men are also involved in maintaining the practice. Often FGM is performed for the benefit of men, to ensure that girls are virgins and thus suitable for marriage. Men's failure to oppose the practice means that it is implicitly accepted and thus continues to persist. The interview participant explains that when her grandfather vocally opposed FGM, the practice ceased in the family. Whilst men also have a central role in defining and abandoning cultural traditions, it is important to acknowledge that women also have a vital role in encouraging family members to end the practice. Philosopher, Meyers,[37] emphasises the agency that women have when making courageous choices and persuading family members not to practice FGM (475). FGM as a means of controlling a girl's and woman's sexuality remains highly contested with some women vehemently opposing the control of female's sexuality as a motivation for the persistence of FGM. Women described other motivations for FGM, such as, the desire to maintain cultural traditions in migrant communities where they felt a loss of a tradition and a sense of belonging.

---

[37] See Meyers, 'Feminism and Women's Autonomy' (n 29).

Clash of Cultures: Maintaining Cultural Traditions in the UK

Interview participants identified the preservation of culture as a dominant motivation for continuing FGM. However, the cultural meanings ascribed to FGM vary between different individuals and communities. In some communities, FGM is performed as a rite of passage from childhood to adulthood.[38] FGM is believed to be a central cultural tradition to mark a girl becoming a woman. If a girl does not undergo FGM then she cannot perform the roles expected of her as a wife and mother and it is unlikely that she will be able to marry within her community. FGM is also regarded as a means of socialising girls to adopt cultural values and pass them on to the next generation. Communities that practice FGM affirm their relationship with the beliefs of the past by continuing the tradition over generations, thereby maintaining community customs and preserving their cultural identity.[39] It can also be a way for migrant groups to indicate their difference from Western culture. Cultural relativists often contend that the cultural traditions of migrant groups ought to be permitted within migrant communities rather than abandoned.[40] Attempts to criminalise cultural practices is often viewed as neo-colonial with Western powers oppressing migrant communities. However, some feminists view cultures as male dominated and cultural practices as male created for their own gains. Culture and religion are often the basis of criticism as domains of male domination and female subjugation.[41] Okin in *Is Multiculturalism Bad for Women?* argues sexist cultures that promote FGM as well as veiling, polygamy, and child marriage should become extinct:

> [people] *might* be much better off if the culture into which they were born were ... to become extinct (so that its members would become integrated into the less sexist surrounding culture).[42]

The notion of making a culture extinct in its entirety, rather than focusing on the problematic practices, could give rise to hostility and anger within cultural

---

[38] Gunning, 'Women and Traditional Practices' (n 20); Rahman and Toubia, *Guide to Laws and Policies* (n 7).

[39] Rahman and Toubia, *Guide to Laws and Policies* (n 7); Gegzabheb, Norman, and Otoo-Oyortey, 'Between Two Cultures' (n 32).

[40] Shweder, 'Moral Realism' (n 36).

[41] Eva Brems, 'Enemies or Allies? Feminism and Cultural Relativism as Dissident Voices in Human Rights Discourse' (1997) 19(1) Human Rights Quarterly 136.

[42] Susan Moller Okin, *Is Multiculturalism Bad for Women?* (Princeton University Press 1999) 22–23.

groups. However, distinguishing between culture as a whole and cultural practices is complicated given the deeply embedded cultural norms that are often unchallenged and normalised. A woman participant of Somali heritage described FGM as entrenched within her family for generations. She compared the decision-making process relating to FGM to deciding whether a child attends school to highlight the acceptability of the practice.

INTERVIEWER: Who decides whether a girl is cut?
INTERVIEWEE: Primarily the mum. Whether a child goes to school or not, this is not something that is discussed. Something like that it's natural. It's like I'm just going to get circumcised. [FG1]

An interview participant of Somali heritage describes the link between the persistence of FGM and feelings of loss and distance from their country of heritage. Maintaining a cultural practice becomes even more important in a 'foreign country' in which community members do not readily assimilate. FGM represents a sense of belonging to a community and kinship group in their country of heritage.

If you want to criminalise female circumcision, you could criminalise it but if a community want to keep continuing female circumcision and the reasoning is something along the lines of, we live in a foreign country and we want to keep our tradition alive and for us living in a foreign country is traumatic and we want to keep it for our own piece of mind, whatever reasons they give you, that could be deemed as a mental, a form of mental kind of coping mechanism. [P7, FGM-PCM, *Somalia*]

Intersectional issues of culture, belonging, and nationality are readily apparent within this powerful quotation. The interview participant describes community members' experience of being a migrant in a country in which they do not feel a sense of belonging. Migration into a 'foreign country' can result in a cultural clash, which leads to community members preserving their nationality and identity. There is a fear amongst migrants that when they migrate they are no longer culturally bound. In this context, FGM-performing communities hold onto the cultural practice of FGM as a means of maintaining their culture and identity in another country. FGM is described as an integral ritual underpinning the cultural identity of communities, which in turn is likely to be a significant barrier to encouraging communities to abandon FGM. This may partly explain the rationale for FGM continuing despite the practice being a criminal offence. A woman participant of Somali heritage explained the importance of maintaining kinship cultural values by performing FGM upon the next generation of children

INTERVIEWER: What reasons do people give for cutting girls in the UK?
PARTICIPANT: Because they still believe to continue and carry out the culture and because if they leave this they may think they are leaving something. So, they may feel it is still valued to be carried out, it's their duty and they are the person to pass it on to their children. So, it's like carrying out some values, that's what they believe [FG2]

The interview participant explains that one of the ways to maintain links with cultural traditions that are prevalent in their country of heritage is through ensuring the next generation undergo the same cultural practices as their kinship group. This creates a sense of shared identity and belonging. Whilst culture might appear static, a survivor of FGM originally from Sierra Leone, argues that culture is fluid and continues to evolve from one generation to the next.

We started campaigning about it but some of them are still in the denial stage saying that it's a culture, a tradition. I will argue with them, I will say culture, tradition, who made the culture and tradition, tradition didn't come from God, it's men that made the tradition, the culture, we can amend it. We can keep culture that is good for humans. Those traditions and cultures that are not good for human beings. I gave them an example I said before we used to have facial marks I say do you see people with facial marks [scarring] now. We need to change the cultural tradition. [P10, FGM-PCM and social worker, *Sierra Leone*]

The interview participant argues that FGM has greater potential to be abandoned because it is rooted in a cultural practice and culture is fluid and ever changing. To highlight her contention, she gives an example of facial scarring, a dominant cultural practice that has now been abandoned. However, the participant also identifies that attempts to challenge cultural practices can be met with suspicion and distrust. Confusion about where the practice stems from shows the deep-seated normalisation of FGM. When people understand that God does not sanction the practice, the participant argues that attitudes towards FGM change. According to women participants of Somali heritage, communities' cultural beliefs stem from a sense of belonging to a kinship group in their country of heritage, thus to change cultural practices, communities will need to feel a sense of belonging to culture in the UK.

- People who have been in these countries or in Europe it's not something they agree with, the majority. However, if people sometimes come fresh from Somalia in the rural villages they still practice and they still think it's a good idea. So, generally I think it depends on educational background and where they are from.
- I think it's the fact that people have migrated to Western countries where this thing isn't practised, it's something that is completely alien to the country that you're coming to so even though there weren't any laws against it until recently here, people just didn't practise it because you are trying to integrate into the society that you've come to live in.
- So, our parents and grandparents and great-grandparents came to live in Europe from Somalia they tried their best to try and integrate into the society that they were living in whether that's Holland, Denmark, Sweden, or here or whatever, so you are trying to integrate. And doing FGM isn't really integrating, it's going against the status quo of the country. So, I think religious put aside I think the fact that people migrated to Western countries is another reason why people have stopped. [FG1]

The interview participants drew a distinction between migrants who recently arrived in Britain and migrants that have been in Britain for a lengthy period and have assimilated into wider society. The participants believed education and assimilation are key to changing cultural practices and the abandonment of FGM. An interview participant highlights her own experience of assimilation and changing cultural attitudes in contrast to her mother who remains supportive of FGM.

For some reason I said if I ever have a baby girl she will be never ever touched. Her [my mother's] face dropped, like how dare you, her face dropped . . . I said I am not going to cut my girl and you have a face. So which one, she said people are going to talk about you, I said I don't care we are in Europe, who talks. [My mother said] Nobody is going to marry your girl, it's their job to find their own husband, not me, they will have freedom that I didn't have, I will make sure of that, they will marry whoever they want. She said 'oh my god you are becoming western.' I said it's not western its freedom which you took away from me. Freedom why they cut me this way, to protect my virginity. They cut to control your sexuality . . . I haven't heard anyone say I don't want cutting done. I haven't seen that. Parents still believe in FGM, my own sister does. [P12, FGM-PCM and teacher, *Somalia*]

The quotation shows that assimilation of the younger generation into British society results in a greater likelihood that FGM will be abandoned. The interview participant described Britain and Europe as a context in which there is no cultural pressure to perform FGM. However, the participant still experiences pressure exerted by her mother, who is eighty years old and has lived in America for thirty years. This highlights the older generations' resistance to abandoning the practice perhaps in order to maintain their limited control and power in the kinship groups. Whilst culture is a core motivation for the continuation of FGM, a religious belief in the practice also supports the continuation of FGM.

Religious Beliefs

Anti-FGM advocates rightly highlight that FGM is not condoned by any religion, yet many interview participants stated that religion is a motivation for performing FGM. Scholars are quick to note that FGM is a cultural, not a religious, practice due to fears that equating FGM with religion could lead to further entrenchment of the practice.[43] A historical fact that is often overlooked is that FGM predates the arrival of Christianity and Islam in Africa and is not a requirement of either religion. Today, FGM is practised by Jews, Christians, Muslims, and indigenous religious groups. However, FGM is often conflated with Islam in mainstream media, which can stir racist sentiments towards ethnic minority communities. While many scholars state that FGM is not a Muslim practice, the validity of this assertion is a theological debate within Muslim communities themselves. It is generally accepted amongst scholars that the Quran, the primary source for Islamic law, contains no explicit endorsement of FGM. However, debates focus on whether a hadith, which is a collection of the words of the Prophet Mohammed, implicitly supports FGM:

> There is a contested Hadith that addresses the practice of female genital cutting directly. It described Mohammed suggesting to a midwife that excision is 'allowed' but should not be 'overdone' because a more limited cutting 'brings more radiance to the face ... and is ... better for the husband' ... the *hadith*

---

[43] Rahman and Toubia, *Guide to Laws and Policies* (n 7).

is contested, however, because the relevant authority is obscure and its ge-
nealogy questionable.[44]

While the validity of this Hadith is highly contested within Muslim communities, some scholars and religious community groups have advocated for the
practice along religious lines. Scholars have attempted to establish that there
is no scriptural support for enforcing FGM. However, the absence of scriptural evidence does not necessarily undermine the religious motivation for
communities who continue to practise it.[45] Some interview participants stated
that FGM is an Islamic practice. It is clear from the interviews that religion
is important to women's identity, therefore linking religion to FGM results in
the continuation of the practice. Whether Islam requires FGM is a highly contested and debated question. Confusion surrounds the Islamic status of Type
I FGM in particular. Unlike the other types of FGM, Type I is often referred to
by interview participants as 'sunna'. Sunna means a practice that is 'advised' in
Islam, which shows the conflation of FGM and religion in the language used
to describe the practice.[46] An Imam explains the Islamic heritage of Type I or
sunna, which mirrors interview participant's descriptions about the contested
Islamic hadith.

> The sunna means acts saying deeds of the prophet of doing something that it
> is advised by the prophet ... Here's an example, he found the woman who was
> carrying out circumcisions in Medina. The verification of this is uncertain.
> My understanding was he said, let's leave something hanging out. He didn't
> speak in scientific terms, did he? He said it's allowed providing it's not cut all
> the way. He said leave something hanging out. [P45, Imam]

While the Hadith is contested by some religious scholars and anti-FGM advocates, it is clear from the interviews that the participants were aware of
the Islamic heritage of FGM. Interview participants who were supportive of
FGM or rejected the practice still recited the Hadith in the interviews to show
their religious knowledge. Women who supported the practice explained that

---

[44] Dorian Lambalet Coleman, 'The Seattle Compromise: Multicultural Sensitivity and
Americanization' (1998) 47 Duke Law Journal 717; Elizabeth Heger Boyle, Fortunata Songora, and
Gail Foss, 'International Discourse and Local Politics: Anti-Female-Genital-Cutting Laws in Egypt,
Tanzania, and The United States' (2001) 48(4) Social Problems 524 (hereafter Boyle, Songora, and Foss,
'International Discourse').

[45] Hope Lewis, 'Between Irua and "Female Genital Mutilation": Feminist Human Rights Discourse
and the Cultural Divide' (1995) 8(1) Harvard Human Rights Journal 1.

[46] Boyle, Songora, and Foss, 'International Discourse' (n 44).

religious observance is one of the motivations for performing FGM, which differs from the assertions of some academics. Women who conform to FGM due to a perceived religious motivation highlighted their agency in choosing to undergo FGM rather than being viewed as cultural dupes. Scholars contend that women can exercise agency in contexts that might be viewed as oppressive by Western feminists[47] when resistance is not visible.

- The sunna one is criminal. So, although we believe religiously sometimes it's advised, it is still illegal? I think that's wrong because people's religious values should mean more to the legal system than prettifying your [vagina]. I mean I know your self-image is a lot, your religious views are also a lot. In a way it is self-image anyway, because if you believe and that's your religion then doing it.
- The argument isn't whether this is a must or it isn't. The argument is that it's part of your religion if you want to do so, if you choose. The fact that the law is preventing you from practicing your religion if you want to do it. [FG1]

Boyle, Songora, and Foss argue without empirical evidence that most communities that practise Islam do not perceive FGM as a religious requirement, whilst this might be true, there are Muslims who link FGM and Islam together.[48] When women became aware that all types of FGM are a criminal offence, they forcefully opposed criminalisation because, as they argued, the law infringes upon a woman's right to practise their religion. Women resisted anti-FGM norms and representations of women as victims by emphasising their agency to consent to FGM.[49] Obiora highlights the importance of communities recapturing and controlling the representation of FGM as a means of resisting Western dominant narrative.[50] Obiora argues, 'women's control over rituals can be located as a source of strength and power ... acting as a religious

---

[47] Anthropologist Saba Mahmood in her book *The Politics of Piety*, explores women's agency within the cultural and ethnographic context of the grassroots women's Islamic piety movement in Cairo, Egypt. Mahmood contends that agency can be de-linked from enacting or subverting norms and associated with the choice of Muslim women to uphold patriarchal practices through their actions. In upholding inherently patriarchal norms, women realise the divine path set out in religious texts for themselves. Saba Mahmoud, *The Politics of Piety: The Islamic Revival and the Feminist Subject* (Princeton University Press 2011) (hereafter Mahmoud, *Politics of Piety*).

[48] Boyle, Songora, and Foss, 'International Discourse' (n 44).

[49] Parallels can be drawn with academics' critiques of a public discourse of victimhood projected upon women that uphold cultural or religious practices. See, Meyers, 'Feminism and Women's Autonomy' (n 29); Meyda Yegenoglu, *Colonial Fantasies: Towards a Feminist Reading of Orientalism* (Cambridge University Press 1998); Sirma Bilge, 'Beyond Subordination vs. Resistance: An Intersectional Approach to the Agency of Veiled Muslim Women' (2010) 31(1) Journal of Intercultural Studies 9; Mahmoud, *Politics of Piety* (n 47).

[50] Obiora, 'Bridges and Barricades' (n 25).

counterbalance to the secular male power'.[51] Rather than the law operating as an effective tool of advocacy to change attitudes and beliefs towards FGM, the law could encourage communities to reinforce FGM. It is important to acknowledge the religious underpinning of FGM in order to effectively advocate for the abandonment of FGM. Indeed, women who rejected FGM appeared more likely to reject the contested Hadith and instead defined the practice as emanating from culture rather than religion.

It's clear that it's [FGM] something to do with tradition and nothing to do with religion ... [P1, FGM-PCM, *Somalia*]

Whilst many women defined FGM as a cultural rather than religious practice, women interview participants were aware of the contested Hadith and some women regarded FGM as a religious practice. Attempting to change religious beliefs is a further challenge for the anti-FGM movement. However, it is important to identify that religion is a motivation for the persistence of FGM for some individuals and families and therefore 'religion' is an additional obstacle to the end-FGM movement. The final theme that was prevalent in interviews with women was their fear of abandoning FGM and the social sanctions that might follow for failing to conform to the practice. For example, interview participants stated that if they did not undergo FGM it would mean that they are unable to marry and could be socially ostracised from their families and communities. Breaking taboos, such as FGM, can result in significant social costs for many girls and women. Instead, FGM is performed to maintain social order and continuity.

Transgressing Social Norms and Breaking Taboos

Another explanation for the persistence of FGM is the social pressure to conform to a long-standing practice. In communities where most women are cut, family, peers, and community members create an environment in which the practice of FGM is performed due to social conformity, norms, and expectations. The pervasive nature of the practice creates a perception of acceptance and normality. In these circumstances, abandoning FGM and transgressing social norms could carry significant social costs. The persistence of the practice is maintained due to fears that individuals might be isolated from their

---

[51] ibid 303.

family and community as well as fearing the prospects of living a life unmarried. Believing that FGM is necessary for social and kinship homogeneity ensures the continuity of the practice. According to Gunning, the consequences of abandoning FGM can include isolation from family, friends, and the community to being outcast and viewed as dangerous or dirty for not undergoing FGM.[52] A survivor of FGM from the Gambia explains that failing to undergo FGM has a significant impact on girls' and women's roles in their families and communities.

> Before they cut you, if you cook, people will not eat it because they will say this is the food of someone who is not cut. So, the food is not clean. People should not eat it. That can even lead you to tell them to hurry for the ceremony to take place to be cut, so you have space in the community. [P3, FGM-PCM, *Gambia*]

Uncut women are punished for not conforming to FGM by preventing them from performing a key aspect of their gender role, for example, cooking for the family. The social costs of being uncut reinforce cultural pressures of continuing FGM. The cultural myth that uncut women are unhygienic, dirty,[53] and could contaminate the food is a form of social control, gender policing, and in its darker manifestation, a hidden form of social violence. Given the dire consequences of not being cut, women interview participants of Somali heritage argued that girls request to be cut to ensure that they are socially accepted.

- Sometimes she is looking forward to this thing being done because otherwise her classmates will tease her if she hasn't got FGM and she's dirty. They find her dirty if she is uncut. If the girl is uncut they will tease her otherwise.
- So, if your friends are circumcised before you and you haven't been done yet they will tease you. So, basically it's for your own benefit to get cut in some cases.
- I should be ashamed if I am not cut. That social stigma. Society feeds that idea that she should get cut otherwise no one will marry you. Then if she does get cut, psychologically she is sound. The day that she does not get [FGM] she might feel like, why am I not normal. I want to be just like the other girls. [FG1]

---

[52] Gunning, 'Women and Traditional Practices' (n 20) 659.
[53] In this chapter, women interview participants stated that FGM is performed to ensure that a girl or woman was clean. There are broader links between the control of sexuality and the need to ensure cleanliness to allow a girl or woman the ability to perform her gender role in the family.

- You know back home this is something every girl has to go through and if the girl will not go through to her circumcision it was really bad for her. Stigmatising, teasing by all the other family, also stigmatised by other families and neighbours and so she said every girl was expecting this, especially when there was circumcision of pharaoni[54] and the sunna one.
- Because the worst thing is if we are not circumcised how can we be in the society and live with integrity? [FG2]

Interviews with women from FGM-performing communities show that the social pressure to undergo FGM remains immense for some girls from a young age, which leads girls to request FGM. The stories of participants reiterate scholars' writings that young girls approaching adolescence and under the pressure of peers ask their parents to have FGM performed on them.[55] An interview participant of Somali heritage describes FGM as a marker by which you are either part of the community or you are not. Undergoing FGM allows girls and women to perform their ascribed role in their communities as wives and mothers, which gives them a sense of belonging and identity.

> If you want to get married or if you want to have a life, or take part in society then you get it [FGM] done. If you don't want to take part in society then you don't get it done. [P5, FGM-PCM, *Somalia*]

The interview participant highlights that a woman who is uncut is unable to marry and has no role in her community. She is isolated from her family because her transgression of a deeply held cultural norm is likely to threaten the cohesion of their community. Clare Chambers criticises the privileging of autonomy and choice in contexts where women's decisions are constrained and women do not have any reasonable alternative.[56] Women are often expected to choose between undergoing FGM or being isolated from their family and community. In such cases, how can women's choices truly be considered free? A woman's *consent* to FGM is neither real nor viable when an individual is coerced to make choices that might disadvantage her. A Nigerian and British woman who was the first generation of her family not to undergo FGM explains

---

[54] Type III FGM.

[55] See, Hanny Lightfoot-Klein, *Prisoners of Ritual: An Odyssey into Female Genital Circumcision in Africa* (Haworth Press 1989); Nahid Toubia, *Female Genital Mutilation: A Call for Global Action* (RAINBO 1995); Tamar Diana Wilson, 'Pharaonic Circumcision under Patriarchy and Breast Augmentation under Phallocentric Capitalism: Similarities and Differences' (2002) 8(4) Violence Against Women 495.

[56] Clare Chambers, *Sex, Culture, and Justice: The Limits of Choice* (Penn State Press 2008).

that she is seen as 'Western' or 'modern', which means that she is viewed as sexually promiscuous. FGM is performed to control a girl's and woman's sexuality, therefore if the individual is not cut she is 'free' to disregard other social and cultural norms linked to virginity and fidelity.

> Because we are not cut, they speak to us like we are so western, we are modern, we are cheap, they think because we haven't had that kind of training or that background, they think oh you are loose women, definitely, they think that, loose women. You've got no sexual respect. When actually you've got people who have been cut that are really promiscuous. Being cut didn't make a difference to their sexual behaviour. It depends on how they've been cut. For some, sex is painful. [P6, FGM-PCM, *Nigeria*]

The quotation shows that uncut women are dismissed as modern, cheap, and loose. The remarkable aspect of the passage is that the interview participant does not challenge or criticise the gendered norms of virginity and chastity associated with FGM. Instead, she reinforces these norms by arguing that uncut women are as 'pure' as cut women. The abuse that an uncut woman receives reinforces the cultural and traditional status quo of performing FGM. An uncut woman is viewed as a target for abuse because she has rejected social and cultural norms that have continued for generations. The abuse uncut women experience could result in silencing other women who might have otherwise argued against FGM.

Conclusion

Women's lived experiences of FGM transcend a monolithic condemnation of FGM. Rather than presenting themselves as victims or cultural dupes, the interview participants highlighted their agency as accommodators or resisters of FGM. Women's stories vary from deeply traumatic experiences to women who argued that FGM beautifies and purifies a girl's genitalia. Regardless of whether women support or oppose FGM, the motivations for the practice appear broadly similar, a desire to control a girl's and woman's sexuality. Even if the practice is performed to make a girl's genitalia clean and pure, the underlying rationale is that a girl's uncut genitalia is abnormal and requires intervention and modification, which is a form of gender policing. The cultural rationale underpinning FGM as a means of continuing an inter-generational practice to show kinship loyalty in migrant communities is a significant driver for the performance of FGM. Encouraging greater assimilation into dominant Western society could assist with the abandonment of FGM. However, societal narratives depicting FGM as a barbaric practice are likely to hinder attempts to encourage the assimilation of migrant communities because they might feel under threat by hostile mainstream narratives about FGM. Whilst FGM is depicted as a cultural practice, it has deeply entrenched roots in religion beliefs, which is contrary to anti-FGM advocacy that stresses FGM is not mandated by any religion. Many women who were interviewed linked their religious beliefs in Islam to the continuation of FGM, arguing that it is a religious imperative. In doing so, many women opposed the criminalisation of FGM, which they argue constitutes a restriction on people's freedom to practise religion. Opposing a cultural *and* religious practice is likely to be an additional barrier to the anti-FGM movement and as such, further advocacy will be required to encourage the elimination of a deeply held religious practice for some individuals. The social pressure to continue to perform FGM is enormous for many women who were interviewed. The fear of transgressing social norms and abandoning FGM results in the practice being maintained. Without undergoing FGM, many girls and women are unable to perform their expected gender roles, such as marrying, because they are seen as unclean. When faced with the realistic prospect of social sanctions or even ostracisation from one's community, abandoning FGM does not appear to be a realistic prospect. One must question whether consent to undergo FGM, even as an adult woman, is free and unrestricted in a context which privileges FGM and other patriarchal norms. FGM was described by some women as a practice that causes life-long consequences; some women described the flashbacks and vivid recollections of the trauma that they endured as a child. Whilst some women might not have experienced adverse consequences following FGM, many have endured torturous treatment that has had a profound impact upon their lives. No girl or woman should experience an assault on their genitalia regardless of the cultural underpinnings of the irreversible practice. The risks of later harm caused to their physical and mental wellbeing are sufficiently serious to justify a blanket prohibition on FGM through the law.

2

Criminalising Female Genital Mutilation

Introduction

The evolution of FGM legislation in the UK has had a lengthy and tortured history.[1] FGM was first made a specific criminal offence in the UK under the Prohibition of Female Circumcision Act 1985 (the 1985 Act) with a maximum penalty of five years. This was repealed and replaced by the Female Genital Mutilation Act 2003 (FGM Act 2003) in England, Wales, and Northern Ireland, increasing the maximum penalty to fourteen years' imprisonment and the Prohibition of Female Genital Mutilation (Scotland) Act 2005 in Scotland. Under the 1985 Act and now the FGM Act 2003, a person is guilty of an offence if they excise, infibulate, or otherwise mutilate the whole or any part of a girl's or woman's labia majora, labia minora, or clitoris.[2] The FGM Act 2003 was further amended by the Serious Crime Act 2015 to address lacunas and loopholes in the legislation in England, Wales, and Northern Ireland. Further amendments were made to Scottish law, which introduced Female Genital Mutilation Protection Orders (FGMPOs) into law in Scotland.[3] The consent of the complainant is not a defence; no one can consent to FGM under the law. Despite FGM becoming a criminal offence in 1985, there has only been one conviction for FGM as recent as February 2019 and there have been several failed prosecutions for FGM.[4] The first FGM conviction and three failed

---

[1] For a comprehensive overview of the end FGM campaign in the UK from a social, legal, and political perspective, see, Hillary Burrage, *Eradicating Female Genital Mutilation: A UK Perspective* (Routledge 2016). For an overview of the development of anti-FGM laws in England and Wales see, Ruth Gaffney-Rhys, 'From the Offences Against the Person Act 1861 to the Serious Crime Act 2015—the Development of the Law Relating to Female Genital Mutilation in England and Wales' (2017) 39(4) Journal of Social Welfare and Family Law 417.

[2] The Prohibition of Female Circumcision Act 1958, s 1(1)(a) (hereafter the 1985 Act) and the Female Genital Mutilation Act 2003, s 1(1) (hereafter the FGM Act 2003).

[3] The Female Genital Mutilation (Protection and Guidance) (Scotland) Act 2020 amended the Prohibition of Female Genital Mutilation (Scotland) Act 2005 in Scotland.

[4] According to CPS data in 2018–19, the CPS does not collate formal statistics for FGM. In 2018–19, two defendants were prosecuted for FGM; one was convicted and the other acquitted. There were no prosecutions for breach of a FGMPO. See, Crown Prosecution Service, 'Violence against Women and Girls crime report 2018–2019'. According to CPS data in 2017–18, since 2010 the CPS received

Female Genital Mutilation. Charlotte Proudman, Oxford University Press. © Charlotte Proudman 2022.
DOI: 10.1093/oso/9780198864608.003.0003

prosecutions[5] are explored in further detail, which highlights the common barriers to prosecuting cases of FGM, such as the difficulty in gathering medical evidence to confirm that FGM has been performed.

The efficacy of FGM laws is contested in a context where there has only been one conviction for FGM.[6] FGM is an unusual crime in that it ordinarily involves the criminalisation of a girl's family members. Victims are often too young to report the crime or they fear that their parents or family members could be imprisoned. Indeed, there is limited available research about the impact of the law on changing deeply held attitudes and beliefs towards FGM. The impact of the law is unclear, thus it is unknown whether the law actively deters families from continuing the practice or whether the criminalisation of FGM results in the practice being performed underground. Interviews with women from FGM-performing communities and professionals who work with communities and are responsible for designing and enforcing the law show the divergent attitudes and beliefs towards the criminalisation of FGM. Women's attitudes ranged from supporting the eradication of FGM to other women who advocated FGM for adult women. Women and professionals both described the impact of the criminalisation of FGM on the dynamics of FGM, which appear to have changed to prevent the practice from being detected and perpetrators from being prosecuted. In order to evade the law, for example, interview participants suggested that girls are now cut at a younger age to prevent professionals from identifying that FGM has been performed and to prevent girls from reporting FGM. Changes to the dynamics of FGM suggest that the law has had a significant impact upon the practice but it has thus far failed to eliminate FGM.

---

thirty-six referrals, of which thirty-three did not proceed to charge due to insufficient evidence to provide a realistic prospect of conviction. See, Crown Prosecution Service, 'Violence against Women and Girls crime report 2017–2018'. Of the remaining three cases, two cases were charged with FGM (one in 2017–18) and acquitted at trial; and one case was charged as child cruelty in 2017–18 and the judge ordered an acquittal. There were no prosecutions for breach of FGMPOs.

[5] It is unknown precisely how many prosecutions there have been for FGM; however, the three most high-profile prosecutions that failed are explored in more detail.

[6] Whilst this book focuses on a British overview of FGM legislation and social impact, see other studies that explore a European perspective: Helen Baillot and others, 'Addressing Female Genital Mutilation in Europe: A Scoping Review of Approaches to Participation, Prevention, Protection, and Provision of Services' (2018) 17(1) International Journal for Equity in Health 21; Els Leye and Jessica Deblonde, 'Legislation in Europe Regarding Female Genital Mutilation and the Implementation of the Law in Belgium, France, Spain, Sweden and the UK' International Centre for Reproductive Health (ICRH) (2004); Els Leye and others, 'An Analysis of the Implementation of Laws with Regard to Female Genital Mutilation in Europe' (2007) 47(1) Crime, Law and Social Change 1.

Evolution of a Specific Criminal Offence for FGM

The Prohibition of Female Circumcision Act 1985

The impetus for introducing criminal legislation in 1985, which specifically criminalised FGM, was increasing international pressure to criminalise FGM. Another impetus for the legislation were emerging concerns that FGM was being performed in England by migrants who moved from the Horn of Africa in the 1970s and 1980s to England and continued to practise FGM. FGM became a matter of public concern in the early 1980s after a Malian child died from the practice in England.[7] There were also reports of FGM being carried out in private health clinics and on the medical black market in the UK.[8] FORWARD, an anti-FGM NGO, was proactive in highlighting the prevalence of the practice. In the early 1980s, NGOs and a few committed politicians launched a legislative campaign to pass the first legislation prohibiting FGM.[9] This resulted in a number of legislative changes to end FGM in the 1980s.

On 16 July 1985, the 1985 Act was introduced to the House of Lords by Wayland Yong, 2nd Baron Kennet. The 1985 Act applies to the UK as a whole. The purpose of the initial legislation in 1985 was to ensure that FGM was a criminal offence and that there was no ambiguity about the criminal status of the practice, thus ensuring that the UK's international obligations to end violence against women and girls was complied with. As Baroness Trumpington stated in a House of Lords debate in 1985, 'the whole purpose of the Bill is to make the law crystal clear'.[10] Arguably, FGM was already a criminal offence under other offences, for example actual bodily harm or grievous bodily harm. Criminologist Juliet Rogers analysed parliamentary debates about FGM and argued that hyperbole language and images of tortured girls were convened to legitimise the production of law.[11] Rogers explains that the stories highlighted during debates about the criminalisation of FGM were infused with notions of loss of girls' and women's freedom and loss of their sexuality.[12] Political debates

---

[7] Efua Dorkenoo, *Cutting the Rose: Female Genital Mutilation: The Practice and its Prevention* (Minority Right Publications 1994).

[8] Moira Dustin and Anne Phillips, 'Whose Agenda Is It? Abuses of Women and Abuses of "Culture" in Britain' (2008) 8(3) Ethnicities 405 (hereafter Dustin and Philips, 'Whose Agenda Is It?').

[9] Adwoa Kwateng-Kluvitse, 'Female Genital Mutilation and Child Protection' in Comfort Momoh (ed), *Female Genital Mutilation* (Radcliffe Publishing 2005).

[10] Prohibition of Female Circumcision Bill, HL Deb 18 June 1985, vol 465, cols 207–24 <https://api.parliament.uk/historic-hansard/lords/1985/jun/18/prohibition-of-female-circumcision-bill> accessed 4 March 2021 (hereafter Prohibition of Female Circumcision Bill, HL Deb).

[11] Juliet Rogers, *Law's Cut on the Body of Human Rights: Female Circumcision, Torture, and Scared Flesh* (Routledge 2013) (hereafter Rogers, *Law's Cut on the Body*) 4.

[12] ibid.

gave politicians the opportunity to publicly condemn the practice as barbaric and send a clear message to the public that FGM will not be tolerated. Debates in the Houses of Parliament in the 1980s were emotionally charged and aroused provocative images. As Baroness Masham of Ilton stated in the House of Lords during a debate on FGM[13] recorded in UK *Hansard* in 1985:

> My Lords, it has been said over and over again that all noble Lords who have taken part in these states of the Prohibition of Female Circumcision Bill are against this cruel and mutilating practice and this has also been stressed by the noble Lord, Lord Hatch of Lusby, tonight. Many people are amazed that your Lordships are still discussing this horrific custom, which appalled most people in Britain when they realized it was practiced here even though by a small minority of people.

The horrific single image of the torturous practice of FGM is invoked time and time again during political debates. FGM is described as a 'cruel and mutilating practice' and a 'horrific custom', which justified the need for law. The intersection of racist, patriarchal, and static representations of African women are often used in legislative efforts to criminalise FGM.[14] Rogers concluded that the instigation of anti-FGM law suffered from an urgency that accompanied demands to prevent child abuse, which was at the expense of consultation with communities who would be affected by the law and evidential facts of the harm caused to girls than the imagined harm invoked by stories of mutilation.[15] Stereotypical perceptions of women of colour as aggressive and immune to the effects of violence have prevented women of colour from receiving equal treatment in the criminal justice system.[16] Racist narratives accompanying legislation may have the unintended consequence of ethnic minority women feeling disempowered and reluctant to cooperate with the police to address cases of FGM.[17] Baroness Gaitskell said in the House of Lords recorded in the UK *Hansard* debate on 10 November 1983:[18]

---

[13] Prohibition of Female Circumcision Bill, HL Deb (n 10).

[14] Rogers, *Law's Cut on the Body* (n 11).

[15] ibid 7, 24.

[16] See, Linda L Ammons, 'Mules, Madonnas, Babies, Bathwater, Racial Imagery and Stereotypes: The African-American Woman and the Battered Woman Syndrome' (1995) 5 Wisconsin Law Review 1003; Nathalie J Sokoloff and Ida Dupont, 'Domestic Violence at the Intersections of Race, Class, and Gender Challenges and Contributions to Understanding Violence against Marginalized Women in Diverse Communities' (2005) 11(1) Violence Against Women 38 (hereafter Sokoloff and Dupont, 'Domestic Violence').

[17] Sokoloff and Dupont, 'Domestic Violence' (n 16).

[18] Prohibition of Female Circumcision Bill, HL Deb (n 10).

I am absolutely thrilled that the noble Lord, Lord Kennet, has this wonderful Bill in this country. After all, we can be kind and welcome people from other countries, but we must not import primitive and ignorant cruelties and practices just because some other countries have them. It has been a pleasure to read this Bill and to learn how much we have been doing in order to get rid of some of the practices we have heard about.

The excerpt from Baroness Gaitskell's speech highlights that FGM discourse plays a role in the polarisation between 'us'—freedom in the West—and 'them'—victims of oppressive cultures/religions.[19] FGM legislation legitimised the role of the British state in enforcing British values and norms upon migrant communities. The anti-FGM campaign can be seen as stirring racist sentiments due to its polemical nature and hysterical and ethnocentric tone in comparison with other campaigns against violence against women, for example domestic violence and rape that are not considered 'traditional' or 'cultural' issues.[20] According to African-American legal scholar, Isabelle Gunning, Western concern for FGM can be 'perceived as only thinly disguised expressions of racial and cultural superiority and imperialism', which can lead to racist assumptions of cultural and religious groups.[21] Indeed, the public representation of violence in cultural groups is pervasive and inherent. The rhetoric about anti-FGM has the unintended consequence of reinforcing this ignorant representation of communities.[22]

Interviews were conducted with House of Lords Peers who were instrumental in the criminalisation of FGM in 1985. It was apparent from the interviews that Peers' political elite or establishment status has meant that they lack knowledge and understanding about FGM and the communities subject to the law. The language used by the political elite during debates shows their devaluation of ethnic minority communities and the marginalisation of their sexual victimisations.[23] The political elites' lack of education about FGM could partially explain the failure of law enforcement agents' implementation of

---

[19] Moira Dustin, 'Female Genital Mutilation/Cutting in the UK: Challenging the Inconsistencies' (2010) 17(1) European Journal of Women's Studies 7 (hereafter Dustin, 'Challenging the Inconsistencies').

[20] ibid.

[21] Isabelle R Gunning, 'Arrogant Perception, World-Travelling and Multicultural Feminism: The Case of Female Genital Surgeries' (1991) 23 Columbia Human Rights Law Review 189 (hereafter Gunning, 'Arrogant Perception').

[22] Chapter Three explores whether there is a link between anti-FGM narratives and wider racism.

[23] Kimberle Crenshaw, 'Mapping the Margins: Intersectionality, Identity Politics, and Violence against Women of Color' (1991) 43(6) Stanford Law Review 1241 (hereafter Crenshaw, 'Mapping the Margins').

anti-FGM laws. A Member of the House of Lords described his reluctance and embarrassment in debating FGM in Parliament in the early 1980s.

> You would understand that this isn't my favourite subject. It's not something that I'd even heard of … I was only too glad to get rid of the whole subject quite honestly. When you had to deal with it the whole time and it was on the television and one's friends revelled in this mockery that went on. But there we are, we are grown up people [laughs]. [P21, Member of the House of Lords, M]

It appears that FGM was not prioritised as a practice that required eradication perhaps because it did not impact upon the lives of mainstream society. Instead the participant said he was only 'too glad to get rid of the whole subject'. FGM-performing communities were distanced from designing and enforcing the law; instead it was imposed upon them by an elite who were embarrassed and disinterested in the subject. A Member of the House of Lords explained that politicians were disinterested in FGM because it was not a part of 'their' culture or identity.

> There was a generation of the Lords who viewed it is a barbaric practice but didn't particularly care about it because it wasn't part of their culture … there are still some people who don't want to know about those things because they are unpleasant and distasteful to them, but this is a matter of personal temperament, isn't it. [P25, Member of the House of Lords, F]

The ethnocentric tone of politicians of 'us' and 'them' is a form of cultural imperialism. The polemic nature of anti-FGM discourse can lead to racist assumptions of cultural and religious groups.[24] Politicians' ignorance and disinterest in FGM could be a barrier to effectively implementing anti-FGM laws. Furthermore, politicians' marginalisation of FGM-performing communities from the consultation process is likely to represent a hurdle to the law being effective from a grass-roots level.[25] A Member of the House of Lords explained the lack of consultation process with FGM-performing communities.

---

[24] Gunning, 'Arrogant Perception' (n 21).

[25] The Home Affairs Select Committee's report into FGM in 2016 recommended that the government establish an advisory panel of FGM campaigners who should be consulted before any major policy decisions are taken; the panel can advise on policy decisions and communicating them to communities: House of Commons Home Affairs Committee, 'House of Commons Home Affairs Committee: Female Genital Mutilation: Abuse Unchecked' (Ninth Report of Session 2016–17) (2016) 27 (hereafter House of Commons Home Affairs Committee, 'Abuse Unchecked').

We never met any of the people who felt it was something that should be done. We were told it was custom and it was a habit and they were doing it because of protecting them from intercourse, having too many boyfriends. But we never met any of the people. We met the people who were campaigning against it. [P26, Member of the House of Lords, F]

Politicians only consulted with selective anti-FGM campaigners who reaffirmed politicians' preconceived views about FGM and thus supported criminalisation. The bias of the consultation process is a form of discrimination against marginalised communities. This could have solidified community objections to anti-FGM legislation. A Member of the House of Lords who was involved in criminalising the practice in the 1980s explained that she encountered a backlash from women who supported the practice.

I remember the first day I was there [in Parliament] and I came out of the Chamber and there were black ladies there and they took one look at me and they shook their fists at me. And they said, 'don't think you're going to stop it dear, if you try and stop it we will do it on the kitchen table.' Just like that. Two great big black ladies who had been listening in the gallery and were associated with their tribes. They are not a bit interested in the law in this country. They are just interested in getting these poor girls under the knife, really. So that rather shook me. [P25, Member of the House of Lords, F]

The political elite projected narratives of barbarism upon migrant communities when they had no understanding and knowledge of FGM. The participant described visceral images of savages shaking their fists and threatening to cut girls on the kitchen table. Dominant, abusive images of children being subjected to violating treatment suppresses alternative narratives that contrast with rhetoric describing the practice as child abuse. Laws and policies designed to prevent FGM without consultation with FGM-performing communities could have created anger and resentment against anti-FGM laws rather than encouraging the abandonment of FGM. As in UK Parliamentary debates, FGM was portrayed by Swiss MPs as a threat to the Swiss nation but female genital cosmetic surgery (FGCS) performed in Swiss clinics as a signifier of 'swissness'.[26]

---

[26] Dina Bader and Veronique Mottier, 'Femonationalism and Populist Politics: The Case of the Swiss Ban on Female Genital Mutilation' (2020) Nations and Nationalism.

The Female Genital Mutilation Act 2003

Whilst FGM was criminalised in 1985, it was again resurrected as an issue of public concern in the 1990s following the failure of the state to secure a prosecution or conviction for FGM. Anti-FGM NGO, FORWARD, continued their campaign work, putting pressure on the government to make FGM a political priority. Political pressure mounted following a report produced by the All-Party Parliamentary Group on Population Development and Reproductive Health in 2000 that argued for legislative and policy change in a bid to tighten the law and prevent loopholes.[27] The legislation was introduced as a Private Members Bill by Ann Clwyd, former Labour MP for Cynon Valley. As a result, the FGM Act 2003 was introduced and it replaced the 1985 Act. The FGM Act 2003 changed the wording of the practice in legislation from 'circumcision' to 'mutilation' to achieve clarity and send a strong message.[28] The FGM Act 2003 also made it a criminal offence to perform FGM in the UK or abroad,[29] to assist a girl to mutilate her own genitalia in the UK or abroad,[30] and to assist a non-UK person to carry out FGM outside the UK on a UK national or permanent UK resident.[31] The Act also increased the maximum sentence to fourteen years' imprisonment.[32] There was no meaningful debate about adult women's ability to consent to FGM nor the exemption for performing a procedure that is 'necessary for mental and physical health'. The changes in legislation do not differentiate between FGCS and FGM.

Almost ten years after the introduction of the FGM Act 2003 there had still not been a conviction for FGM. In 2013 FGM became a highly politically charged issue on the agenda leading to further legislative change to encourage a prosecution for FGM. Survivors of FGM and anti-FGM NGOs[33] mobilised in

---

[27] See debate about the current state of the criminal law on FGM; HL Deb 23 March 2000, vol 611, cols 402–04 <https://api.parliament.uk/historic-hansard/lords/2000/mar/23/female-circumcision#S5L V0611P0_20000323_HOL_38> accessed 4 March 2021.

[28] Rogers, *Law's Cut on the Body* (n 11).

[29] FGM Act 2003, s 1.

[30] ibid s 3.

[31] ibid s 4.

[32] ibid s 5.

[33] The late Efua Dorkenoo was a renowned anti-FGM activist. She had dedicated her life's work to campaigning against the practice. Survivors Leyla Hussein and Nimco Ali, founders of the NGO Daughters of Eve, are two high profile anti-FGM activists. They gained public notoriety in 2012 after sharing their own stories and demanding legal and policy change in England. Leyla Hussein presented BAFTA-nominated Channel 4 documentary *The Cruel Cut*. The Home Affairs Select Committee's report into FGM notes that funding is required to support campaigners such as Leyla Hussein as they can reach out to communities to bring back information and intelligence to the police resulting in prosecutions: House of Commons Home Affairs Committee, 'Abuse Unchecked' (n 25). In 2019, Leyla Hussein and Nimco Ali were awarded OBEs for their anti-FGM campaign work.

2013 to start a high-profile movement in England that would put FGM on the political agenda. Women challenged the taboo of FGM by sharing their stories in public, often evoking an emotional response. The faces and names of young women of colour were published on the front page of mainstream newspapers, as they vividly described their stories of FGM. Newspapers the *Guardian*[34] and the *London Evening Standard*[35] launched anti-FGM media campaigns in 2014 raising public awareness of the practice. A sizeable movement of leading figures emerged. Responding to a public outcry that there had still not been one conviction for FGM, the House of Commons Home Affairs Committee launched an inquiry into FGM in 2014. The inquiry examined why FGM continued and what action is needed to protect girls at risk of FGM. Witnesses who had undergone FGM and professionals who worked with those affected by FGM gave evidence at the inquiry. The Committee published a report on 3 July 2014. It recommended a national action plan, which would involve 'strengthening the law on FGM, principally to ensure the safeguarding of at-risk girls, but also to increase the likelihood of achieving successful prosecutions'.

The House of Commons Home Affairs Committee inquiry into FGM made comparisons between the approaches adopted in the UK and in France throughout their report. France is often held up as a leading example with over 40 trials and 100 people, including parents and children, having been convicted for FGM since 1979.[36] In France there is no specific legislation criminalising FGM, instead perpetrators are prosecuted for crimes such as bodily harm and child cruelty.[37] There is no need to establish who performed FGM, instead parents can be prosecuted for failing to protect their children from FGM. If FGM is identified, professionals are required to report cases to the police; failing to do so could result in prosecution. Children up to around the age of

---

[34] The *Guardian* Global Media Campaign to end FGM ran from May 2014 to September 2015 and its budget was $1 million. The focus of the campaign was initially to accelerate the end of FGM in the UK and it later expanded its focus to other countries. The aim is to ensure FGM remains high on the social and political agenda.

[35] The *Evening Standard* commenced a campaign to end FGM in Africa on 9 October 2014, which involved spreading stories of change, supporting media campaigns, and organising events, as well as working on programmes abroad: Anna Davis, 'New Campaign to End Female Genital Mutilation in Africa' *Evening Standard* (London, 9 October 2014) <https://www.standard.co.uk/news/london/new-campaign-to-end-female-genital-mutilation-in-africa-9784134.html> accessed 4 March 2021.

[36] Ascertaining the correct statistics for prosecutions and convictions for any country is challenging due to different reports giving different numbers. See, Anika Rahman and Nahid Toubia, *Female Genital Mutilation: A Guide to Laws and Policies Worldwide* (Zed Books 2000) (hereafter Rahman and Toubia, *Female Genital Mutilation: Guide*); John Litchfield, 'The French Way: A Better Approach to Fighting FGM?' *Independent* (London, 15 December 2013).

[37] For an overview of the French context from lawyer, Linda Weil-Curiel who was responsible for prosecuting a significant number of FGM cases, see Chapter 8 of Hilary Burrage, *Female Mutilation: A Global Journey behind the Curtains of the Horrifying Worldwide Practice of Female Genital Mutilation* (New Holland Publishers 2016).

six have regular physical health examinations.[38] Girls at risk of FGM will sometimes undergo medical examinations annually, especially when they return from trips abroad. The system is largely mandatory, as social security benefits can be dependent upon participation in health screening. There appears to be no political will to adopt a similar mandatory health check system in the UK. The Committee did not recommend introducing comparable measures.

During the House of Commons Home Affairs Committee Inquiry on 21 March 2014, the Director of Public Prosecutions, Alison Saunders, announced the first prosecution for FGM only hours after she gave oral evidence before the Inquiry.[39] A British-Somali doctor, Dr Dhanuson Dharmasena of Whittington Hospital, North London, was charged with re-infibulating[40] a Somali-born British patient after she gave birth. Hasan Mohamed, the woman's husband, was charged with intentionally encouraging an offence of FGM and aiding, abetting, counselling, or procuring Dr Dharmasena to commit an offence. The case was unusual, as the complainant[41] gave evidence on behalf of the defendants. The case was a media spectacle with daily reports about the trial. On 4 February 2015 the jury found the defendants not guilty after only thirty minutes of deliberation. The judge criticised the Whittington Hospital for failing to have appropriate support structures in place for medical practitioners treating women who had undergone FGM.

The government responded to growing public, political, and media pressure[42] by hosting the first Girl Summit, co-hosted by UNICEF, on 22 July

---

[38] Helen Baillot and others, 'Tackling Female Genital Mutilation in Scotland: A Scottish Model of Intervention' (2014) Scottish Refugee Council; Helen Baillot, 'Addressing Female Genital Mutilation in Europe: A Scoping Review of Approaches to Participation, Prevention, Protection, and Provision of Services' (2018) 17(1) International Journal for Equity in Health 21.

[39] The case generated significant media attention.

[40] Re-infibulation is a criminal offence under the FGM Act 2003. It has no health benefits and involves resuturing of incised scar tissue resulting from infibulation often after delivery of a baby. There are no statistics on the prevalence of re-infibulation. For more information about re-infibulation see, Gamal I Serour, 'The Issue of Reinfibulation' (2010) 109(2) International Journal of Gynecology & Obstetrics 93; Rebecca J Cook and Bernard M Dickens, 'Special Commentary on the Issue of Reinfibulation' (2010) 109(2) International Journal of Gynecology & Obstetrics 97.

[41] The complainant in the case did not make a complaint about FGM. A midwife working with the doctor referred the case to the police.

[42] Anti-FGM campaigner Muna Hassan, a member of anti-FGM campaign group Integrate Bristol, told the then Prime Minister David Cameron to 'grow a pair' on Newsnight in 2014 as she encouraged the government to make FGM a political priority. Hassan, along with five other members of Integrate Bristol, took a *Guardian*-supported petition with over 230,000 signatures to the former Secretary of State for Education, Michael Gove MP, requesting him to ensure schools teach about the risks of FGM and he agreed to email information about FGM to schools. See, Corrinne Jones, 'Interview: Muna Hassan: "One of Us Mentioned Vaginas and Michael Gove Went Really Red!"' *Guardian* (London, 14 December 2014) <https://www.theguardian.com/world/2014/dec/14/muna-hassan-faces-of-2014-one-of-us-mentioned-vaginas-and-michael-gove-went-really-red> accessed 4 March 2021.

2014.[43] The Summit aimed at mobilising domestic and international efforts to end FGM and child, early, and forced marriage within a generation. The government used the Summit as an opportunity to make legislative and policy announcements. It pledged to establish a dedicated anti-FGM Unit, which became the National FGM Centre,[44] to provide outreach work, resources for frontline staff, and funding for national FGM prevention programmes.[45] Internationally, the UK launched a £35 million programme to tackle FGM globally.[46] Subsequently, the government launched the 'Girl Generation' in October 2014 supported by the Department for International Development (DFID), funding grassroots initiatives globally designed to eliminate FGM.[47] The Department for International Development has continued to fund anti-FGM projects committed to ending FGM abroad.[48] However, Nafisa Bedri and Tamsin Bradley caution that if the numerous programmes funded by DFID are not shaped by grass-roots experiences of FGM and specifically by local change agents, there is a real danger that this opportunity will fail.[49] In presenting the viewpoints of local activists and community groups in the UK and Sudan, they argue that an overreliance on a constructed image of a suffering FGM victim makes it difficult for local activists' nuanced representations of FGM to be heard.

The Serious Crime Act 2015

The government's next step was to introduce further legislative change.[50] On 9 December 2014, the government responded to the House of Commons Home Affairs Committee report on FGM and proposed to introduce five legislative

[43] For more information see, Home Office, 'Girl Summit 2014' (Archived) <https://www.gov.uk/government/topical-events/girl-summit-2014> accessed 4 March 2021 (hereafter Home Office, 'Girl Summit 2014').

[44] The centre is run by Barnardos charity with government funding. There are concerns each year that the National FGM Centre will struggle for funding and may not be able to continue to operate.

[45] <https://www.gov.uk/government/topical-events/girl-summit-2014> accessed 4 March 2021.

[46] <https://www.gov.uk/government/news/uk-to-help-end-female-genital-mutilation> accessed 4 March 2021.

[47] For more information see, Home Office, 'Girl Summit 2014' (n 43).

[48] In 2018, the Department for International Development announced £50 million of new funding to end FGM abroad. See, DFID 'Ending FGM: UK Aid Makes Largest Ever Investment' (*DFID In the News*, 23 November 2018) <https://dfidnews.blog.gov.uk/2018/11/23/end-fgm-female-genital-mutilation-uk-aid-makes-largest-ever-investment/> accessed 4 March 2021.

[49] Nafisa Bedri and Tamsin Bradley, 'Mapping the Complexities and Highlighting the Dangers: The Global Drive to End FGM in the UK and Sudan' (2017) 17(1) Progress in Development Studies 24.

[50] For a discussion and critique of the five key legislative changes see, Nkumbe Ekaney and Charlotte Proudman, 'FGM and the Serious Crime Act 2015' (*Family Law Week*, 15 July 2015) <https://www.familylawweek.co.uk/site.aspx?i=ed145848> accessed 4 March 2021.

changes. However, the government did not adopt the other proposed non-legislative changes such as mandatory training for frontline professionals, increased funding for grassroot NGOs working with women and girls and introducing FGM as an educational requirement within schools. Instead, the government chose to enact further legislation focusing on punitive sanctions. The Serious Crime Act 2015 was enacted, which gave rise to amendments to the FGM Act 2003 involving: the inclusion of extra-territorial acts, the anonymity of complainants, an offence of failing to protect a girl from FGM, frontline professionals have a duty to notify the police of FGM, and FGMPOs.

1. Offence of Female Genital Mutilation: Extra-Territorial Acts

The FGM Act 2003 originally criminalised acts done by UK nationals or permanent UK residents to girls or women who are UK nationals or permanent UK residents. Perpetrators and victims who were merely habitually resident in the UK were not covered by the legislation. The Bar Human Rights Committee noted in its report on FGM that 'the UK's legal obligations extend to all children within its jurisdictions—therefore UK organisers of such mutilations should face prosecution, irrespective of the child's status'.[51] The Serious Crime Act 2015 amended sections 1–3 of the FGM Act 2003 to apply to habitual residents. There are a range of factors to consider when determining if a person is habitually resident in the UK, including the length of presence in UK, reason for visiting the UK, intended duration of stay, and their ties to the UK. The amendments do not, however, protect those who are temporarily based in the UK. For example, no provision is made for a woman who travels to the UK for a short period, visits a National Health Service doctor who discovers that the woman has been subjected to FGM, and intends that her daughter(s) should also be subjected to the procedure and then returns to her country of heritage a few days later.

2. Anonymity for Complainants of Female Genital Mutilation

The FGM Act 2003 now provides lifetime injunctions prohibiting the publication of any matter that could lead the public to identify the alleged victim of an offence.[52] This measure was introduced to encourage the reporting of FGM offences without fear of identification. Given the familial nature of

---

[51] Bar Human Rights Committee. 'Report of the Bar Human Rights Committee of England and Wales to the Parliamentary Inquiry into Female Genital Mutilation' (2014) 3.
[52] Pursuant to FGM Act 2003, s 4A. The power to waive the restrictions is limited to the circumstances necessary to allow a court to ensure that a defendant receives a fair trial (ECHR, art 6) and to safeguard freedom of expression (ECHR, art 10).

FGM, it is likely that any defendants in a criminal case would be related to the complainant, therefore the complainant would probably be inadvertently identified.

3. Offence of Failing to Protect a Girl from Female Genital Mutilation

A person is liable for an offence if they are responsible for a girl under the age of sixteen when FGM is performed.[53] The term 'responsible' covers two groups of people. First, a person who has 'parental responsibility' for the girl and has 'frequent contact' with her; and, second, any adult who has assumed responsibility for caring for the child in the manner of a parent, for example, grandparents who might be caring for a child during the school holidays. There are two possible defences. The first is that the defendant did not think that there was a significant risk of the child being subjected to FGM and could not reasonably have been expected to be aware that there was any such risk. The second defence is that the defendant took reasonable steps to protect the child from being subject to FGM. The wide drafting of the defences could prove a challenge to implementation. Academics Christou and Fowles argue that this amendment to the law can be seen as an example of the presumption of innocence having changed and the burden of proof shifting to the parents to prove their innocence where the child has been cut.[54] They also argue that the offence recognises that the continuation of FGM is based on parental choices and if FGM has been performed on a child their parents have fallen below the standard expected of reasonable parents. The offence also sends a clear message to parents that they could be prosecuted if they perform FGM. Parents might even use the law as an advocacy tool to argue for the elimination of FGM in a context of community and familial pressure. Christou and Fowles contend the offence does not necessarily disproportionately target women or mothers of girls; instead it can apply to any person, whether a parent or other person with parental responsibility for the child.[55] Indeed, the failed prosecutions show that it is mainly fathers who are prosecuted but expectations that a mother is responsible for FGM might have contributed to their acquittal.

4. Duty to Notify Police of Female Genital Mutilation

There is now a duty on persons who work in a 'regulated profession' in England and Wales, namely healthcare professionals, teachers, and social care workers,

---

[53] Pursuant to FGM Act 2003, s 3A.

[54] Theodora A Christou and Sam Fowles, 'Failure to Protect Girls from Female Genital Mutilation' (2015) 79(5) The Journal of Criminal Law 344.

[55] ibid.

to notify the police when, in the course of their work, they discover that an act of FGM appears to have been carried out on a girl who is under eighteen. The term 'discover' would refer to circumstances where the girl discloses to the professional that she has been subject to FGM, or where the professional observes the physical signs of FGM. This offence does not apply to girls or women who might be at risk of FGM or cases where professionals discover that a woman who is eighteen or over has been subjected to FGM.

This provision was subject to a government consultation process in 2014 and many professionals objected to the proposals.[56] Further research is required to ascertain whether professionals are reporting cases to the police and whether this information has been useful intelligence for the police. The obligation on public sector professionals to enforce the criminal law highlights the changing role of professionals as they are entrusted with maintaining law and order.[57] Sokoloff and Dupont contend that there has been an overreliance on law enforcement to deal with social problems of ethnic minority communities, which has led to consequences of increased surveillance, removal of children by the state, and prosecution.[58] This could create tensions for migrant women who need the state's protection from abuse, whilst state intervention also increases their vulnerability.[59]

The British Association of Social Workers released a statement in response to the consultation, warning 'against blurring the boundaries between social work and other agencies such as the police and health'.[60] The offence shows the extension of the boundaries of the criminal law to the extent that professionals ordinarily outside of the criminal justice system, such as medical practitioners, are now responsible for implementing the law. It is likely that ethnic minority women, particularly women without immigration status, are seeking support from professionals who work outside of the law because they do not want to face criminal sanctions.

Amasanti, Imcha, and Momoh oppose the introduction of this offence, as they are concerned that it will drive the practice underground.[61] There is a

---

[56] See, the British Medical Journal rapid response section of the website for medical practitioner's attitudes towards the reform: 'Improve Reporting of Female Genital Mutilation, MPs Tell Doctors' BMJ (18 March 2015) <https://www.bmj.com/content/350/bmj.h1467/rapid-responses> accessed 7 March 2021.
[57] David Garland, The Culture of Control: Crime and Social Order in Contemporary Society (University of Chicago Press 2001).
[58] Sokoloff and Dupont, 'Domestic Violence' (n 16) 55.
[59] Sokoloff and Dupont, 'Domestic Violence' (n 16).
[60] British Association of Social Workers, 'FGM: Social Workers Should Not Take on the Role of the Police' (11 February 2015) <https://www.basw.co.uk/media/news/2015/feb/fgm-social-workers-sho uld-not-take-role-police> accessed 7 March 2021.
[61] Maria Luisa Amasanti, Mendinaro Imcha, and Comfort Momoh, 'Compassionate and Proactive Interventions by Health Workers in the United Kingdom: A Better Approach to Prevent and Respond

strong medical lobby that opposes this duty on frontline professionals as they argue that women will be less inclined to seek out support from professionals for fear of criminal sanctions. They argue that legal action could result in the 'double victimisation' of the girl or woman, as a victim and a subject within the criminal system, rather than providing girls or women with the support they require. Given that frontline professionals now have a duty to report cases of FGM, professionals have argued that they require training in FGM to ensure that they properly understand their duties and the potential liabilities.[62] Indeed, research conducted by Mills[63] found that there was a gap in midwives' knowledge and understanding of FGM with 10.6% stating that they had no formal training for FGM and 62.5% said they had no specialist FGM service within their health board.

Professionals have suggested that the mandatory duty to report cases of FGM should be revised to report FGM to social care rather than the police. In response to the article about mandatory reporting, Dixon, Shacklock, and Leach argue that mandatory reporting could reduce trust in medical professionals.[64] Treating FGM differently from other safeguarding issues risks 'perceptions of discriminatory judgements and cultural bias'. Dixon and others argue that despite efforts to educate, the impact of legislation has been disappointing.[65] Research found that 'the impact of these legislative and reporting requirements on the trust needed for community members to seek to consult health services was identified as an important area for further research' as well as a potential downfall of the current legislation.

Karlsen and others conducted five focus groups with ethnic Somalis living in Bristol during 2018 to ascertain their attitudes towards FGM safeguarding as adults or children.[66] They found that government priorities to support those

---

to Female Genital Mutilation?' (2016) 13(3) PLOS Medicine 1; Sarah M Creighton and others, 'Tackling Female Genital Mutilation in the UK' (2019) 15 BMJ 364.

[62] Sarah M Creighton and others, 'Multidisciplinary Approach to the Management of Children with Female Genital Mutilation (FGM) or Suspected FGM: Service Description and Case Series' (2016) 6(2) BMJ 1.

[63] Emma Mills, 'UK Midwives' Knowledge and Understanding of Female Genital Mutilation' (2018) 28(4) MIDIRS Midwifery Digest 491.

[64] Sharon Dixon, Joy Shacklock, and Jonathan Leach, 'Tackling Female Genital Mutilation in the UK: Female Genital Mutilation: Barriers to Accessing Care' (2019) BMJ 364.

[65] Sharon Dixon and others, 'Female Genital Mutilation in the UK—Where Are We, Where Do We Go Next? Involving Communities in Setting the Research Agenda' (2018) 4(1) Research Involvement and Engagement 1.

[66] See the original research report, which found that women believed that the mandatory reporting law meant that healthcare professionals prioritised extracting information over giving medical care. Participants felt that Somalis were treated like criminals during FGM safeguarding and that the current policies were racist: Saffron Karlsen and others, 'When Safeguarding Becomes Stigmatising: A Report

who have had FGM are being undermined by their own approaches to protect those considered at risk. Approaches to FGM safeguarding were based on out-dated stereotypes and inaccurate evidence which encouraged health service providers to see every Somali parent as a potential perpetrator of FGM as such they had become fixated on FGM. Participants described feeling stigmatised and traumatised by their experience, which undermined their trust in health services resulting in a reluctance to seek care. The authors criticise the statutory approaches to end FGM which are currently ill-conceived and heavy-handed. Whilst healthcare approaches are subject to criticism, much of their policies stem from the criminalisation of FGM and the need to end the practice.

Aside from the criticism made by scholars about this legal provision, it could be deficient in a number of other respects. First, there appears to be a contradiction in legislation in that FGM is a criminal offence according to the FGM Act 2003 for adults and minors and consent is not a defence, and yet professionals are not under a duty to report cases of adults who have undergone FGM. If there was a duty to notify police of FGM even when the woman is an adult, this could lead to a conviction of 'failing to protect a girl from risk of FGM'. For example, if a healthcare professional discovers that a British-born woman of eighteen years old or more has been subjected to FGM, her parents could be guilty of an offence of failing to protect her from FGM. However, under the section 5B offence, a professional has no duty to report the offence, thus leading to no prosecution. Second, frontline professionals are not under a duty to report cases in which vulnerable girls and women of any age are at risk of FGM. Therefore they might escape receiving appropriate support from the police in terms of protection because professionals have no duty to report cases involving adult women to the police. The Home Affairs Select report into FGM recommended that the government set out the sanctions that may apply when a professional has failed to meet their duty, which should range from compulsory training to a criminal offence for intentional or repeated failures.[67]

5. Female Genital Mutilation Protection Orders
FGMPOs were also introduced in Schedule 2 of the FGM Act 2003. An order can be made to protect either a girl or woman at risk of FGM without immediate

---

on the Impact of FGM-Safeguarding Procedures on People with a Somali Heritage Living in Bristol' University of Bristol (2019).

[67] House of Commons Home Affairs Committee, 'Abuse Unchecked' (n 25) 27.

criminal sanctions for parents.[68] FGMPOs are modelled on Forced Marriage Protection Orders introduced by the Forced Marriage (Civil Protection) Act 2007. The terms of such an order can be broad and flexible and enable the court to include whatever terms it considers necessary and appropriate to protect the girl. These include, for example, provisions requiring a person to surrender his or her passport. Breach of the order is a criminal offence.

Criminalising A *Cultural* Practice

The historical background of FGM policy shows that the law has been perceived as one of the most effective means to end FGM, which perhaps best explains the number of legislative amendments since 1985. Certainly, politicians have emphasised the need to convict people for FGM. The law is generally considered an important institution to maintain social control within society. The criminal law is used to prohibit behaviour that is either a serious wrong against an individual or society as a whole.[69] In criminalising certain actions, the law steers people's behaviours.[70] However, there are tensions that emerge as a direct result of criminalising FGM, which is perceived by some individuals and communities to be a cultural practice. It is acknowledged that generally debates about FGM often proceed from a universal standpoint that the practice should be prohibited through law. The criminalisation of FGM is justified on the basis that FGM is generally considered a cruel and barbaric practice. Such hyperbolic language is reiterated in parliamentary debates, case law, and in the media.[71]

FGM has been a site of tension between international human rights proponents, cultural relativists,[72] and feminists. The fundamental premise of universal human rights is that rights and rules are universally valid across all societies

---

[68] Samantha Bangham, 'Re E (Children) Female Genital Mutilation Protection Orders) [2015] EWHC 2275 (Fam)' (*Family Law*, 29 July 2015) <http://www.familylaw.co.uk/news_and_comment/re-e-children-female-genital-mutilation-protection-orders-2015-ewhc-2275-fam#.Vvp52MdBDdk> accessed 5 March 2021.

[69] See, Andrew Ashworth and Lucia Zedner, *Preventive Justice* (Oxford University Press 2014).

[70] Nicola Lacey, 'Community, Culture and Criminalisation' in Rowan Cruft, Matthew H Kramer, and Mark R Reiff (eds), *Crime, Punishment, and Responsibility: The Jurisprudence of Antony Duff* (Oxford University Press 2011) 292.

[71] Sensationalised narratives have been accused of targeting vulnerable and marginalised groups who could have been persuaded to abandon the practice with active community engagement.

[72] According to Awa Thiam, cultural relativism gained trajectory during the twentieth century, as it was used to support anti-colonialist movements in the non-Western world: Awa Thiam, *Black Sisters, Speak Out: Feminism and Oppression in Black Africa* (Pluto Press 1986).

on the basis of human dignity.[73] A conflict emerges when international human rights laws are set up to protect both the cultural group's right to sovereignty in maintaining tribal group practices, such as FGM, and a woman's right not to be violated.[74] FGM is an example of this conflict. Cultural relativists criticise international human rights for excluding the concerns of cultural groups whilst feminists argue women are marginalised by international human rights norms.[75] Feminists and cultural relativists each want human rights to account for gender or culture.

From a cultural relativist perspective[76] there are often tensions in determining the types of behaviours that ought to be criminalized, particularly when criminal offences impact disproportionately upon marginalised groups in society.[77] Religious clothing, religious education, and family law for minority groups have become increasingly heated within popular discourse and public life. It is noteworthy that a specific criminal offence was introduced to criminalise FGM, while there is no legislation criminalising other cultural and traditional practices. For instance, there is evidence that South Asian communities practice discrimination on grounds of caste in the UK and yet there is no legislation prohibiting this caste-based discrimination despite efforts to introduce laws.[78] The core reason for the focus on FGM, forced marriage, honour killings, and women's Islamic dress to the exclusion of other cultural practices is that government public policy and legal judgment has focused on gendered violence within Muslim communities.[79] Kandala and Komba examined anti-FGM laws across the world and argued that in the majority of national jurisdictions, FGM is already an offence, for example under grievous bodily harm laws, which then begs the questions, why is specific legislation required to outlaw FGM?[80] Furthermore, Dustin contends that some campaigners and service

---

[73] Jack Donnelly, 'Cultural Relativism and Universal Human Rights' (1984) 6(4) Human Rights Quarterly 400.

[74] Robin Cerny Smith, 'Female Circumcision: Bringing Women's Perspectives into the International Debate' (1991) 65 Southern California Law Review 2449.

[75] Eva Brems, 'Enemies or Allies? Feminism and Cultural Relativism as Dissident Voices in Human Rights Discourse' (1997) 19(1) Human Rights Quarterly 136.

[76] Cultural relativist scholars are often criticised for upholding culturally reductive theories which perceive FGM as purely a cultural trope. This supports the emergence of racialised interpretations in which whole cultures are rendered backward or barbaric.

[77] Will Kymlicka, Claes Lernestedt, and Matt Matravers, *Criminal Law and Cultural Diversity* (Oxford University Press 2014) (hereafter Kymlicka, Lernestedt, and Matravers, *Cultural Diversity*).

[78] Annapurna Waughray, 'Caste Discrimination: A Twenty-First Century Challenge for UK Discrimination Law?' (2009) 72(2) Modern Law Review 182.

[79] Dustin and Philips, 'Whose Agenda Is It?' (n 8).

[80] Ngianga-Bakwin Kandala and Paul Nzinga Komba, 'Compatibility between National FGMs and International Human Rights Law' in *Female Genital Mutilation around the World: Analysis of Medical Aspects, Law and Practice* (Springer 2018).

providers show that there has been a disproportionate emphasis on securing a prosecution rather than education and awareness-raising measures which has been an unproductive focus, particularly with the low numbers of prosecutions and convictions for FGM.[81] Whilst legislation that criminalises violence against women and girls is imperative to deter such behaviour and bring perpetrators to justice, it is important that a critical lens is applied to legislation to analyse its intent and outcome.

Scholars argue that the link between cultural diversity and criminal law cannot be overlooked.[82] There is much debate about whether cultural practices should be exempt under criminal laws or whether individuals should be permitted to put forward a cultural defence or mitigation.[83] One might argue that cultural groups should have a defence to criminal offences that prohibit behaviours that are sacred to their identity[84] whilst others, particularly feminists, contend that a so-called 'cultural evidence' has been used to justify violence against women and girls in courts[85] to their detriment. Those that might claim the law ought to make provision for a religious or cultural defence could seek to prove that religion and culture can deeply influence an individual's thoughts and behaviour in ways that mean individuals are 'less legally blameworthy' or culpable.[86] Someone who is deeply embedded in a minority culture may feel morally compelled to act in a certain way, which could excuse or mitigate the crime.[87] Other influences such as poverty or family breakdown could influence individuals' behaviours, for example, a victim of a poor upbringing may be viewed as less culpable of committing crime.[88] Applying the same principle to cultural influences, culture may have influential explanatory potential.[89] The problem with a cultural defence is that it stereotypes entire cultural groups as responsible for abusing women, which stirs racist discourse and anti-immigration rhetoric.[90]

---

[81] Moira Dustin, 'Culture or Masculinity? Understanding Gender-Based Violence in the UK' (2016) 24(1) Journal of Poverty and Social Justice 51.

[82] Kymlicka, Lernestedt, and Matravers, *Cultural Diversity* (n 77).

[83] ibid.

[84] Richard A Shweder, 'Moral Realism without the Ethnocentrism: Is It Just a List of Empty Truisms?' in Andras Sajo (ed), *Human Rights with Modesty: The Problem of Universalism* (Martinus Nijhoff Publishers 2004) 65.

[85] Alice J Gallin, 'The Cultural Defense: Undermining the Policies against Domestic Violence' (1993) 35 Boston College Law Review 723 (hereafter Gallin, 'The Cultural Defense').

[86] Kymlicka, Lernestedt, and Matravers, *Cultural Diversity* (n 77) 3.

[87] ibid.

[88] Nicola Lacey, *Unspeakable Subjects: Feminist Essays in Legal and Social Theory* (Bloomsbury Publishing 1998).

[89] Sokoloff and Dupont, 'Domestic Violence' (n 16).

[90] ibid; Gallin, 'The Cultural Defense' (n 85).

Dustin asks why violence against American and European women is *not* seen as a cultural issue but instead an aberration of the individual man, while violence against African, Arab, and Asian women is viewed as intrinsic to their culture and identity, which in turn is linked to racism.[91] The behaviour of cultural groups is perceived as more culturally determined than that of the dominant culture.[92] The powerful West is seen as having no culture but the universal culture of civilization.[93] Black and Asian activists have campaigned for honour killings and forced marriage to be viewed as forms of violence, not culturally specific practices.[94] This could prevent the link between gender-based violence and culture. Scholars struggle to achieve a balance between the impact of culture and tradition on violence and how patriarchy operates differently in diverse cultures.[95] Rather than viewing FGM as culture, one might argue that it should be viewed as a patriarchal traditional custom in the context of colonialism and economic exploitation of marginalised communities. If the practice was viewed through a non-cultural, gender-based violence lens, there would be an argument for not introducing a specific criminal offence for FGM, but instead allowing it to be captured by other criminal laws.

Mestre and Johnsdotter provide an overview of criminal court cases involving FGM in the European Union and note that a-typical FGM court cases make unfair court cases which can cause further harm that is avoidable if professionals were better trained with cultural expertise or if experts were involved in FGM cases to provide much needed input.[96] France is the only country in the world to have secured over 100 convictions[97] for FGM.[98] Winter reviews FGM prosecutions in France and states that cases that have gone to trial have usually resulted in one of the two following cultural defences being raised.[99] The first is: 'these poor illiterate Africans don't know any better' ploy,

---

[91] Dustin, 'Challenging the Inconsistencies' (n 19) 9.
[92] Sokoloff and Dupont, 'Domestic Violence' (n 16).
[93] ibid.
[94] Erica Burman, 'Engendering Culture in Psychology' (2005) 15(4) Theory & Psychology 527.
[95] Sokoloff and Dupont, 'Domestic Violence' (n 16).
[96] Ruth M Mestre i Mestre and Sara Johnsdotter, 'Court Cases, Cultural Expertise, and "Female Genital Mutilation" in Europe' (2019) Cultural Expertise and Socio-Legal Studies (Studies in Law, Politics, and Society Series) 78.
[97] Rahman and Toubia, *Female Genital Mutilation: Guide* (n 36).
[98] A significant number of convictions were allegedly secured in one case involving a cutter whose notebook was found, which contained the contact details of parents whose children had been cut. As a result, the children's parents were found by police and criminalised. The penal code in France does not explicitly refer to the criminalisation of FGM, rather it refers to the criminalisation of intended bodily harm causing mutilation, which can result in a term of imprisonment of ten years or up to twenty years for cutting a girl under the age of fifteen and thus it is wide in nature in contrast to Britain which has a specific criminal offence for FGM.
[99] Bronwyn Winter, 'Women, the Law, and Cultural Relativism in France: The Case of Excision' (1994) 19(4) Signs: Journal of Women in Culture and Society 939, 948– (hereafter Winter, 'Women, the

where lawyers and defendants maintain immigrant communities were ignorant of the laws in France.[100] Lawyers have been accused of reinforcing negative stereotypes of immigrant communities to their immediate advantage but
to the communities' long-term disadvantage.[101] The second defence strategy
is that perpetrators of FGM are acting according to their cultural traditions,
which they feel carry the weight of a law that they are bound to obey.[102] In this
way, FGM is not mutilation or the subjection of women to a patriarchal practice, instead it is culturally acceptable because it allows girls to become women
and members of a cultural group in which they can marry and reproduce.
Cultural defences for the crime of FGM that have been used in France have yet
to be adopted in criminal trials in the UK. Even so, it is unlikely they would be
successful given the public's strength of feeling towards FGM.

A number of complexities have arisen through the implementation of law
and policy designed to prosecute parents and perpetrators of FGM. The criminalisation of FGM raises acute problems that do not always exist for other
criminal offences. One of the most obvious is that the offender is likely to be a
parent or relative of the woman or girl and the victim is unlikely to view their
relatives as criminals.[103] Since 2015, parents can be prosecuted for failing to
protect their children from FGM[104] even if they were not responsible or involved in the organisation of FGM. Criminal trials in the UK have resulted in a
general perception that fathers are absolved of responsibility because the practice is believed to be dominated by mothers. FGM is perceived as a 'woman's
issue' because it is usually performed by a female cutter. Struggling to show that
FGM has been performed *at all* or that a father is responsible for the practice
results in a number of competing challenges to the prosecution and conviction of FGM cases. Indeed, all of the prosecutions of fathers for FGM failed,
whilst there has only been one successful conviction for FGM and that was of
a mother. Meanwhile, prosecuting mothers could result in them being *double
victimised*, first as victims of FGM and second as perpetrators.

FGM is a unique crime that is controlled by women and performed by
women upon girls. The practice stems from gender inequality. Women who are

---

Law and Cultural Relativism'). Whilst the academic paper is now dated in that it was published in 1994
the case examples remain relevant in highlighting the use of cultural defences in FGM trials.

[100] ibid. The article provides a thorough exposition of the impact of FGM trials in France.
[101] ibid.
[102] ibid; Kymlicka, Lernestedt, and Matravers, *Cultural Diversity* (n 77).
[103] Dustin and Philips, 'Whose Agenda Is It?' (n 8).
[104] Pursuant to FGM Act 2003, s 3A, a criminal offence of failing to protect a girl from female genital
mutilation.

responsible for performing FGM have ordinarily been cut themselves as children. Girls are socialised to adopt cultural values and pass them on to the next generation. In a context of patriarchy, women are often the foot holders of patriarchy in that they gain currency and power through performing FGM upon the next generation. It is often assumed that because women perform FGM, they are solely culpable. FGM is not performed for the 'benefit' of women. The most dominant motivation for FGM is to control women's and girl's sexuality, to prevent premarital sex, preserve virginity, and curtail infidelity on marriage. Other motivations include custom and tradition, social pressure, and religion.[105] The meanings attached to women's sexuality depend on the community performing the practice. In patriarchal communities, a family's or clan's honour depends on a girl's and woman's virginity and chastity.[106] It is thought that cutting a woman's genitalia would reduce her sexual desire, thus ensuring that she conforms to the role expected of her as a wife and mother.[107] De-emphasising a woman's sexual behaviour is believed to emphasise her reproductive role in producing the next generation.[108] Women's dependence on marriage for economic and social survival could result in duress to undergo FGM.[109] Victims of FGM are often punished twice; first, as victims of the practice; and second, as mothers who fail to protect their daughters from FGM. There are a number of challenges in prosecuting and convicting perpetrators of FGM who are mothers and themselves victims of the practice, particularly in a context in which they have little agency to resist FGM. Some anti-FGM campaigners argue against prosecuting mothers for FGM and instead contend that the focus should be on education initiatives to change mindsets.[110]

Women and girls experience multiple layers of vulnerabilities not only as victims of FGM but also on grounds of class, race, poverty, and immigration

[105] Rahman and Toubia, *Female Genital Mutilation: Guide* (n 36). Note that FGM is a cultural, not a religious practice. The practice predates the arrival of Christianity and Islam in Africa and is not a requirement of either religion.

[106] ibid.

[107] Nahid Toubia, 'Female Genital Mutilation' in Julie Peters and Andrea Wolper (eds), *Women's Rights, Human Rights: International Feminist Perspective* (Psychology Press 1995).

[108] Janice Boddy, 'Womb as Oasis: The Symbolic Context of Pharaonic Circumcision in Rural Northern Sudan' (1982) 9(4) American Ethnologist 682; Olayika Koso-Thomas, *The Circumcision of Women: A Strategy for Eradication* (Zed 1987).

[109] Hanny Lightfoot-Klein and Evelyn Shaw, 'Special Needs of Ritually Circumcised Women Patients' (1991) 20(2) Journal of Obstetric, Gynecologic, & Neonatal Nursing 102.

[110] For an overview of criticisms towards the criminalisation of FGM in the UK and the need for community-led educational information programmes supporting FGM-performing communities, see, Marge Berer, 'The History and Role of the Criminal Law in Anti-FGM Campaigns: Is the Criminal Law What Is Needed, At Least in Countries Like Great Britain?' (2015) 23(46) Reproductive Health Matters 145; Marge Berer, 'Prosecution of Female Genital Mutilation in the United Kingdom: Injustice at the Intersection of Good Public Health Intentions and the Criminal Law (2019) 19(4) Medical Law International 258.

status.[111] These inequalities shape women's relationship with the criminal justice system, which can serve to inadvertently disenfranchise women rather than empower them. Cultural and class inequalities can impact upon the enforcement of the law when immigrant women in particular have limited access to resources. Some women and girls might experience cultural and language barriers, which present as structural problems where their vulnerabilities are reinforced through prosecution.[112] Women of colour have experienced at first hand the effect of overzealous state intrusion in their lives: police surveillance, incarceration, and removal of children from their care.[113] FGM legislation can be seen as legitimising the role of the British state in enforcing ethnocentric values and norms upon migrant communities, particularly mothers who are entrusted with producing the next generation. Communities have attempted to resist and evade the law by performing FGM underground and continuing their tradition upon the next generation. In this way, FGM can be viewed as a means for migrant groups to indicate their difference from Western culture. Indeed, a common issue that has arisen in criminal cases since 2015 is the poor medical evidence available to prove to a criminal standard that Type IV FGM[114] has been performed because it is difficult, if not impossible, to detect upon a girl's genitalia. The efficacy of FGM laws is challenged and there might be a legitimate argument to consider, namely that the law is a hinderance to furthering the elimination of FGM. African-American legal scholar, Gunning, notes that the development of human rights laws needs to be the result of multicultural dialogue and consensus and the implementation of laws must favour education rather than punishment.[115]

Four FGM Trials

Despite the ever-changing dynamic of the law, there has only been one conviction for FGM as recently as 2019, whilst other prosecutions for FGM have failed. The media reported widely about three failed prosecutions before the first conviction was secured in 2019. Political and media pressure continued to mount after three FGM trials collapsed and those trials will be investigated

---

[111] Jennifer C Nash, 'Re-thinking Intersectionality' (2008) 89(1) Feminist Review 1.
[112] Crenshaw, 'Mapping the Margins' (n 23).
[113] Donna Coker, 'Crime Control and Feminist Law Reform in Domestic Violence Law: A Critical Review' (2001) 4(2) Buffalo Criminal Law Review 801.
[114] Type IV is the least physically invasive type of FGM.
[115] Gunning, 'Arrogant Perception' (n 21) 193.

further herein. It has become a matter of public importance in bringing a perpetrator to justice to show that the law is effective. The criminal law is used to deter people from the commission of a criminal offence due to the punitive and often draconian penalties that follow. It was therefore presumed that a conviction would send a strong message to communities that sympathise with FGM, notably that the practice will not be tolerated and they could be prosecuted. Whilst evidence suggests that FGM is prevalent in the UK, no one had been brought to justice for FGM prior to 2019. The same question was asked time and time again, by politicians, the media, and survivors, why has there not been a criminal conviction for FGM since 1985? There is a raft of obstacles that makes prosecuting and convicting cases of FGM exceedingly difficult.

On 11 February 2019, a girl's mother was convicted for FGM upon her daughter whilst the girl's father was acquitted of FGM-related offences. On 22 March 2018, a father was found not guilty of arranging FGM on his daughter. On 22 February 2018, a father was found not guilty of child cruelty in respect of arranging FGM upon his daughter. On 4 February 2015, Dr Dhanuson Dharmasena and the complainant's husband were acquitted of FGM-related offences upon a patient following the birth of the complainant's child. Exploring the prosecutions in more detail shows that the relationship between FGM and the law is complex. The trials do not represent 'conventional' FGM cases, which are highlighted in the media, such as where wider family and community members are involved in continuing FGM on the next generation. The motivations for performing FGM varied in the trials, from punishing the complainant to witchcraft. There were clashes in cultural understandings of FGM during the trials. It was said during the trials that FGM is controlled and performed by women to the exclusion of men. Such a simplistic understanding of FGM often ignores the fact that FGM is performed for the benefit of men to control girls' and women's sexuality.[116] Meanwhile, medical practitioners struggled to identify that FGM had been performed on a girl's genitalia, particularly when Type IV FGM was alleged.

Punishing a Child's Mother: The First Conviction for FGM

Headline news on 1 February 2019 read: 'Ugandan mother becomes first person in Britain to be convicted of FGM for mutilating her daughter, three, as her bizarre witchcraft kit including a cow's TONGUE and frozen limes is

---

[116] Rahman and Toubia, *Female Genital Mutilation: Guide* (n 36).

revealed.'[117] The mother was convicted for performing FGM upon her daughter and for failing to protect her daughter from FGM.[118] The girl's father was acquitted. It was a landmark case; the first case of FGM in which the perpetrator was convicted by jury.[119] The media narrative had a self-congratulatory tone for *finally* bringing a perpetrator of FGM to justice. The case was presented as a triumph for the British justice system, which reinforced the significance of the law. The exaggerated language and imagined visceral image of an abused girl helped legitimise the law against FGM, such as mother 'convicted for mutilating her daughter'. The mother was sentenced to ten years' imprisonment.[120] The maximum sentence was fourteen years under the FGM Act 2003. Anti-FGM campaigner, Dr Leyla Hussein OBE, said that she had mixed emotions about the conviction, 'We are sending out a strong message that children now come first ... However, the sad thing is we could have helped that mother. That could have easily been me because 17 years ago I did not understand that FGM was wrong.'[121] The Metropolitan Police lead on FGM, Inspector Allen Davies, said 'FGM is still happening across London and the UK, behind a cloak of secrecy ... The young victims often have no way to speak out or may not even know what is happening to them. We really need information from people in communities who know FGM is happening, which young people are at risk, and who is doing the cutting.'[122] The narrative is clear, the conviction is a pivotal moment for the anti-FGM movement in publicly highlighting the serious sanctions for continuing the practice; however, law enforcement agents still lack intelligence about FGM cases and education is needed to change attitudes and beliefs towards FGM.

The presentation of the case in the media was simplistic and superficial. There were visible layers of vulnerabilities in the mother's background that were not highlighted in the media. The mother appeared to have little education; she lived in a marginalised immigrant community from Ghana; she was

---

[117] Richard Spillett, 'Ugandan Mother Becomes First Person in Britain to Be Convicted of FGM for Mutilating her Daughter, Three, as her Bizarre Witchcraft Kit, Including a Cow's TONGUE and Frozen Limes, is Revealed' *Daily Mail* (London, 1 February 2019) <https://www.dailymail.co.uk/news/article-6656933/Mother-three-year-old-girl-person-guilty-FGM-Britain.html> accessed 5 March 2021.

[118] ibid.

[119] It is understood that at the time of the trial, the three-year-old girl was subject to care proceedings and was residing in foster care. Care proceedings were ongoing during the criminal trial.

[120] Two further years were added to the mother's sentence for the possession of indecent images of a child, publishing videos of sexual activity with animals, and possessing extreme pornographic images.

[121] Hannah Summers and Rebecca Ratcliffe, 'Mother of Three-Year-Old is First Person Convicted of FGM in UK' *Guardian* (London, 1 February 2019) <https://www.theguardian.com/society/2019/feb/01/fgm-mother-of-three-year-old-first-person-convicted-in-uk> accessed 5 March 2021 (hereafter Summers and Radcliffe, 'First Person Convicted of FGM').

[122] ibid.

caring for both her daughter and son as a single parent; and the photographs of the family home appeared to reflect the family's low socio-economic status and likely deprivation. The case was described as a conventional FGM case but in fact it had all the hallmarks of being an outlier. The parents are not from FGM-performing communities. The mother had not undergone FGM. FGM is usually performed within tightly bound kinship groups to maintain cultural norms. The motivation for FGM in this case was allegedly witchcraft[123] rather than one of the prevalent motivations such as the control of a girl's sexuality or the continuation of a kinship tradition. Whilst witchcraft and other forms of (so-called) honour-based violence overlap with FGM, such as forced marriage or child marriage, it is rare that FGM is performed *because* of witchcraft.

The girl allegedly referred to the person who cut her as a 'witch' with 'silver hair'.[124] Whilst the parents were on bail during the police investigation, the police found evidence of witchcraft throughout the property, including spells aimed at silencing professionals involved in the case. For example, spells were found written inside forty frozen limes and two ox tongues with screws embedded in them with the aim of silencing the police, social workers, and lawyers.[125] A jar was found with a picture of a social worker covered in pepper behind the toilet and another spell was hidden under the bed. Spells read, 'shut up' and threatened to 'freeze your mouths'.[126]

Photographs of screws in the ox tongue depicted a savage attack using brutal tools on a sensitive part of the anatomy. The scenes of witchcraft reflected imagined brutal images of FGM. FGM discourse alongside violent images creates a universal, singular, and monolithic portrayal of FGM based on a cruel image of a girl being held down and cut.[127] The images and discourse of the practice performed in this case reinforced stereotypes of imagined FGM: the girl being held down and cut in the kitchen, blood pouring from the helpless girl's body, and the abusive mother motivated by witchcraft. The credibility of the mother was likely diminished after the jury heard that the mother dabbled

---

[123] Links between witchcraft and FGM have never been made in the popular press prior to this case.

[124] In addition, it was reported that the police were unable to confirm whether the mother or a cutter had carried out FGM on the girl, yet the mother was still convicted of performing FGM. Lizzie Dearden, 'FGM Conviction: Mother of Girls, 3, Becomes First Person Found Guilty of Female Genital Mutilation in UK' *Independent* (London, 1 February 2019) <https://www.independent.co.uk/news/uk/crime/fgm-first-uk-conviction-mother-three-year-old-female-genital-mutilation-witchcraft-london-a8758641.html> accessed 5 March 2021 (hereafter Dearden, 'Mother of Girls'). According to the *Guardian*, the mother denied cutting her daughter stating, 'someone who would cut a child's private parts, they're not human. I'm not like that', Summers and Radcliffe, 'First Person Convicted of FGM' (n 121). The girl and her brother's stories changed and were contradictory.

[125] Summers and Radcliffe, 'First Person Convicted of FGM' (n 121).

[126] Dearden, 'Mother of Girls' (n 124).

[127] Rogers, *Law's Cut on the Body* (n 11).

in witchcraft. Whilst engaging in witchcraft is not a criminal offence and bears no relevance to whether the mother performed FGM, witchcraft dominated headlines and no doubt skewed the perception of the jury towards the mother.

The mother was found guilty of FGM at the Old Bailey whilst her partner was acquitted of FGM-related offences.[128] Popular myths that FGM is a practice dominated by women could have contributed to the girl's father being acquitted of FGM-related offences despite the father being in the mother's presence at the time the girl was cut.[129] The judge hearing the criminal case in the Old Bailey, Justice Philippa Whipple, remarked that, 'this is a significant and lifelong burden for her [the girl] to carry. You betrayed her trust in you as her protector.'[130] The judge's comments are infused with notions of loss of a girl's and woman's freedom and loss of their sexuality.[131] The mother was punished for cutting her daughter and for failing to conform to societal expectations of motherhood. As FGM is defined as child abuse, the state might place children who have been cut or are at risk of FGM in foster care.[132] It is surprising that the father was not convicted of failing to protect his daughter from FGM because he had parental responsibility for her and he was caring for the girl at the time along with the mother. His status as a man and a father is likely to have reinforced a perception that he was not involved in the cutting of the girl's genitalia.[133] FGM performed upon a girl's genitalia is seen as a private practice controlled by women. Such a simplistic narrative ignores the power that men hold in FGM-performing communities in reinforcing the practice. The discourse excludes the core motivation for FGM: to curtail a woman's and girl's sexuality for the benefit of men, largely for their future husbands. FGM discourse propagated in the media often conveys a simple message: the act is abusive and perpetrators need to be brought to justice. The media rarely acknowledges the complexities of the practice and the vulnerabilities of the families involved.

---

[128] The father pleaded guilty to two charges of possessing indecent images of a child and two charges of possessing extreme images showing sexual activity with animals and was sentenced to eleven months in prison, although he had already served his time on remand. The Home Office was due to decide whether it would allow the father to continue residing in the UK or whether he would be removed to his country of heritage.

[129] Summers and Radcliffe, 'First Person Convicted of FGM' (n 121).

[130] 'First Person to be Convicted for Female Genital Mutilation in the UK Jailed' (*Newstalk*, 8 March 2019) <https://www.newstalk.com/news/woman-jailed-female-genital-mutilation-835605> accessed 5 March 2021.

[131] See Rogers for an analysis of parliamentary discourse on FGM: Rogers, *Law's Cut on the Body* (n 11).

[132] Dustin and Philips, 'Whose Agenda Is It?' (n 8).

[133] As shall be shown later in the chapter, the other failed prosecutions indicate that the fathers were depicted as absolved of responsibility due to their gender and role in the family.

A Public Relations Disaster: The First Failed Prosecution

There have been a handful of failed prosecutions that have hit the headlines. The first FGM prosecution was a public relations disaster for the (former) Director of Public Prosecutions, Alison Saunders. The lawyer of Dr Dhanuson Dharmasena, the defendant, referred to the case as a *show trial*.[134] Saunders was under immense pressure to prosecute a case of FGM. Four days before Saunders gave oral evidence to the Home Affairs Select Committee's Inquiry into FGM on 25 March 2014,[135] the Crown Prosecution Service (CPS) confirmed the first prosecution for FGM. Dr Dhanuson Dharmasena, a doctor at the Whittington Hospital, was prosecuted for performing FGM upon a patient during childbirth. Hasan Mohamed, the complainant's husband, was prosecuted for encouraging FGM upon the complainant. The jury acquitted the doctor and the complainant's husband within thirty minutes.

The trial was a media frenzy with daily news reports each day. There were a number of anomalies that made this case an outlier. It did not represent a 'conventional' FGM case in which FGM was performed underground on a young girl from a family and community which support the practice. The prosecuting lawyer described the case as a far cry from the stereotype of the 'back street clinic'.[136] FGM is usually portrayed as being performed on a helpless child outside of the purview of authorities underground. FGM is rarely depicted as being performed upon an adult woman in a hospital during childbirth. In this case, the mother left Somalia during the civil war in the 1990s and settled in Britain where she met her husband and married. She underwent de-infibulation[137] in 2011, a reversal of the FGM procedure, which suggests that she might have been opposed to FGM. The prosecution accused the mother's husband of encouraging the doctor to re-infibulate the woman after giving birth by re-closing the introitus.[138] The doctor put one stich (less than 1 cm) in the woman's genitalia to stop the woman bleeding after the birth. In an unusual turn of events, the complainant gave evidence on behalf of the defence,

---

[134] 'Doctor is Cleared After UK's FGM Prosecution Amid Claims of "show trial"' *Evening Standard* (London, 5 February 2015) <https://www.standard.co.uk/news/crime/doctor-cleared-after-uks-first-fgm-prosecution-amid-claims-of-a-show-trial-10024336.html> accessed 5 March 2021 (hereafter 'Doctor is Cleared' *Evening Standard*).

[135] <https://www.independent.co.uk/news/uk/politics/britain-s-first-ever-prosecution-female-genital-mutilation-announced-political-reasons-expert-suggests-9215293.html> accessed 12 May 2021.

[136] 'Doctor is Cleared' *Evening Standard* (n 134).

[137] For more information about de-infibulation see, Sara Johnsdotter and Birgitta Essén, 'Deinfibulation Contextualized: Delicacies of Shared Decision-Making in the Clinic' (2020) Archives of Sexual Behavior 1.

[138] For more information about re-infibulation see, Gamal I Serour, 'The Issue of Reinfibulation' (2010) 109(2) International Journal of Gynecology & Obstetrics 93.

supporting both her husband and the doctor. The woman actively supported the defendants during the case.

The surgical procedure after just giving birth could arguably constitute 'mutilation' for the purposes of the FGM Act 2003 unless a defence applied.[139] The mother's consent to FGM is immaterial under the FGM Act 2003. Even if a literal interpretation of the law meant that the doctor's act constituted a criminal offence, this case was a far cry from the intention of Parliament to criminalise cases of FGM, thus the jury acquitted the defendants. There are an array of problems in the interpretation, application, and purpose of FGM offences.[140] However, the failed prosecution shows the complexity of prosecuting cases of FGM. In this case there were questions asked about whether the complainant was complicit in the act, whether the act performed constitutes FGM, and the impact of prosecuting poorly chosen cases on the end-FGM movement. The impact of the case appeared to be significant for the complainant and potentially the Somali community. The complainant was given anonymity and therefore her identity was concealed from the public. However, her husband was a defendant in the case and his identity was made public, which in turn makes the complainant's identity known within their community. A woman of Somali heritage from the same community as the complainant spoke about the impact of the failed prosecution upon the complainant:

INTERVIEWER: What effect do you think prosecutions will have on FGM?
PARTICIPANT: Probably close down conversation. We all know who the lady is who they tried to prosecute her husband, everybody knows all the stress she went through, she lost loads of weight, she was really upset, she became depressed because she just gave birth and she had a small child. Her husband is up on charges and it was hanging over her head for a really long time even though it only took half an hour for them to say not guilty. So, there was all this lead up and she felt all this pressure to be a witness. I don't know anyone who would be willing to talk to the police. And everybody knows who she is even though she didn't have her name in the press, everybody knows who she is ... everyone knows everyone's business. [P5, FGM-PCM, *Somalia*]

---

[139] For example, the surgical operation was performed by a medical practitioner upon a girl or woman during labour or when she had just given birth for purposes connected with the labour or birth (see FGM Act 2003, s 1(2)).
[140] Genital piercing performed upon a woman's and girl's genitalia might also constitute Type IV FGM yet there are no prosecutions for such cases, despite the prevalence of genital piercings across the country. This is explored further later in the book.

The participant explains the detrimental impact of the case on the woman's emotional and physical well-being. At the time of the trial, the complainant had just given birth to a child and she was in an enduring relationship with her husband who was facing serious criminal charges of up to fourteen years' imprisonment. As a result of the high-profile nature of the first prosecution, the interview participant speculates that attempts to change attitudes and beliefs in the community towards FGM will be suppressed for fear of prosecution. Rather than changing cultural practices, the law could have the opposite effect, as communities oppose and resist the law because of the negative consequences of criminalisation upon families and communities.[141] In the failed prosecution case, the prosecution cross-examined the complainant on the basis that she was complicit in FGM being performed after childbirth. A criminal lawyer described the cross-examination of the complainant by the prosecution in the courtroom.

> The crown [the CPS] had to cross-examine the victim of FGM ... That was unattractive and not only did she cross-examine but she cross-examined rather aggressively which was quite extraordinary ... She was basically suggesting that this woman had been complicit in her own reinfibulation. Not nice. The other thing that, that revealed was an undercurrent of racism. Oh, you're from Somalia therefore you must be in favour of FGM. Not taking into account individuality, the effect of living in the West. I thought that was unattractive. [P46, Lawyer, M]

In the courtroom, the CPS drew on cultural and racist stereotypes of women from FGM-performing communities being complicit in their own abuse due to pervasive cultural pressures that make them cultural dupes. Parallels can be drawn with the first prosecution of FGM and the trials of FGM in France. Winter contends that lawyers in FGM trials in France reinforce negative stereotypes of immigrant communities to their advantage, arguing that they are illiterate Africans who do not know any better or that they act according to their cultural traditions that carry the weight of the law in their communities.[142] The cultural narratives that play out in the courtroom discriminate against ethnic minority women and girls who are described as passive victims, while defendants are dehumanised as savages or beasts. Racist narratives

---

[141] Gabriele Marranci, 'Multiculturalism, Islam and the Clash of Civilisations Theory: Rethinking Islamophobia' (2004) 5(1) Culture and Religion 105.
[142] Winter, 'Women, the Law and Cultural Relativism' (n 99)

depicted in court and later reported in the media could deter women and girls from reporting cases of FGM to the police.

Unlike other criminal offences, prosecuting cases of FGM raises unique problems that makes convicting perpetrators of FGM challenging. A key barrier to prosecuting and convicting cases of FGM is the familial and community nature of the offence. When women and girls are faced with a choice of giving evidence against their family and community and being socially ostracised or refusing to give evidence and remaining within their kinship group, many individuals understandably choose the latter. The perpetrator is usually related or known to the girl who has been cut. In circumstances that require victims to give evidence against family or community members, it is unlikely that they will support the prosecution of perpetrators of FGM. A CPS employee who has worked on cases of FGM explains the challenges of encouraging women and girls to give evidence in FGM cases against their family and community members.

> We've had victims come and say they won't give evidence against their family or community. All we can do is risk assess the best I can ... Victims are scared. They don't want their parents to go to prison ... Obviously the more serious allegation the more I would consider a witness summons and actually taking people in and turning them hostile, but that's the last resort because people are so adamant that they don't want to give evidence in a lot of cases and the difficulty is you have got to be sure you don't completely alienate them from the criminal justice system so they don't report again. [P70, CPS Worker, F]

Coercing victims to give evidence against their family and community could re-victimise and re-traumatise them. Acting contrary to the complainant's wishes could further alienate community members from engaging with the criminal justice system. Women are usually presented as victims of FGM (Dustin and Phillips 2008). However, women who refuse to cooperate with law enforcement agents and continue the practice of FGM could be depicted as a threat to Western civilisation and women's freedom. The impact of women's refusal to cooperate is particularly relevant here, as the first FGM complainant gave evidence in support of the defendants. The woman was initially presented as a victim of FGM but when she refused to cooperate she was presented as a victim of cultural pressure. However, one might expect women who support FGM to be presented as dangerous threats to the West because their 'choice' to adopt FGM could be perceived as a personal (and potentially political) choice. The enforcement of cultural changes through the law is rarely successful and more often dangerous.[143] Rather than changing cultural practices, the law could have the opposite effect, as communities oppose and resist the law by reinforcing the practice. The challenges in prosecuting cases of FGM are highlighted in each FGM case.

The Bristol Case: The Second Failed Prosecution

The next failed prosecution also garnered significant media coverage. Again, the case was presented in the media without nuance. It was alleged that a taxi driver of Somali heritage told a passenger[144] that FGM was performed on his daughter. The defendant denied that he told the passenger that his daughter had undergone FGM. On 22 March 2018, the judge hearing the case, Julian Lambert sitting in Bristol Crown Court, halted the trial after ruling that the defendant had no case to answer due to insufficient evidence.[145] The defendant said the case put 'intolerable pressure upon him and his family'. There was no cogent medical evidence to support the CPS case that FGM had been performed.

Similar to the other cases of FGM, this case also contrasted with the conventional depictions of FGM. First, the defendant was the child's father. Yet it is women who are portrayed as controlling and defending FGM, perhaps making it more challenging to prosecute a child's father. Second, the defendant was charged with child cruelty rather than FGM due to Type IV FGM[146] allegedly being performed. It therefore remains unclear whether Type IV FGM constitutes FGM for the purposes of section 1 of the FGM Act 2003. Third, the case reinforces the tenuous nature of gathering evidence in cases of FGM. In this case medical evidence did not support the assertion that FGM had been performed. Many of the themes in this case overlap with other criminal cases of FGM.

It was reported that the defendant argued that FGM is traditionally a woman's role. Therefore, even if his daughter had been cut, and he argued that

---

[143] ibid.

[144] The passenger was a man of Somali heritage who also worked for the Bristol anti-FGM charity, Integrate UK.

[145] Steven Morris, 'UK FGM Trial: Father Says Failed Case Put Intolerable Pressure on Him' *Guardian* (London, 23 February 2019) <https://www.theguardian.com/society/2018/feb/23/uk-fgm-trial-father-failed-case-intolerable-pressure> accessed 4 March 2021.

[146] See the introduction to the book which sets out the four types of FGM. Type IV FGM is considered the least physically invasive type of FGM. For more information see, Sarah M Creighton and Deborah Hodes, 'Female Genital Mutilation: What Every Paediatrician Should Know' (2016) 101(3) Archives of Disease in Childhood 267.

she had not been cut, he would not have been involved in FGM. The conventional perception of the practice is that women are responsible for ensuring FGM is performed upon the next generation. It was argued that the defendant could not have been responsible for FGM as a man, and the child's father, he would not be involved in FGM. However, the motivations for the practice are reported to be complex but one of the core motivations is to control women's and girl's sexuality for the benefit of men.[147] Indeed, it was claimed that the defendant had said to the taxi passenger that FGM was done 'so women don't feel sexy all the time'.[148] This rhetoric relates to broader understandings about FGM, namely that it is performed to ensure their sexuality is curtailed for men. In this case, the father allegedly claimed a lack of knowledge about FGM.[149] This is somewhat surprising given that his wife had undergone FGM as a child. The evidence against the defendant was tenuous as it rested upon one disputed conversation with a taxi passenger who also worked for an anti-FGM charity. Gathering robust evidence is a key barrier to prosecuting FGM cases.

The father was charged with child cruelty rather than FGM-related offences due to the child allegedly having undergone Type IV FGM, which is the least physically invasive type of FGM. A safeguarding doctor examined the girl and found a small lesion that could represent FGM whilst other medical opinions differed, noting that FGM could not be physically detected. The defence argued that there was no proof that Type IV FGM, which includes pricking, piercing, and cauterising, is being performed in the UK. The evidence was deemed by the judge as 'troubling'. Anti-FGM charity, Integrate UK, said 'We understand that there is a trend now to subject girls to less physically invasive FGM ... so that it can be said that there has been a "procedure" but it is less harmful or detectable by medics.[150] Some believe that this is not FGM. Whatever the injury, this is harmful, physically and emotionally, and it is FGM. We must stop it.'

Type IV FGM is difficult to detect because it does not necessarily involve the removal of healthy genitalia tissue. It can therefore be challenging to ascertain whether any abnormality in the genitalia area is a result of FGM or a birth

---

[147] A study of FGM in Egypt found that FGM continues due to deeply embedded attitudes about tradition, cleanliness, and virginity followed by men's wishes, aesthetic factors, marriage, and religious factors: Ghada F Mohammed, Magdy M Hassan, and Moustafa M Eyada, 'Female Genital Mutilation/Cutting: Will it Continue?' (2014) 11(11) The Journal of Sexual Medicine 2756.

[148] Geoffrey Bennett, 'Bristol Dad Accused of Having Daughter "Cut" in Female Genital Mutilation Procedure Found NOT Guilty' BristolLive (Bristol, 22 February 2022) <https://www.bristolpost.co.uk/news/bristol-news/live-bristol-dad-trial-child-1232470> accessed 5 March 2021.

[149] The father said FGM is against the Koran and he claimed to have heard men at meetings discuss FGM but did not pay attention due to lack of interest: ibid.

[150] Anecdotally, evidence suggests that families are cutting their children younger to evade detection and prevent prosecution.

defect. Type IV FGM is defined by UNICEF[151] as all other harmful procedures to the female genitalia for non-medical purposes, for example, pricking,
piercing, incising, scraping, and cauterization.[152] Pricking or nicking involves
cutting to draw blood, but no removal of tissue and no permanent alteration
of the external genitalia. This case was prosecuted under child cruelty criminal offences. It therefore remains unclear whether Type IV FGM constitutes
'mutilation' under section 1 of the FGM Act 2003. This question arose in the
first family law case concerning FGM in care proceedings in the family jurisdiction[153] when the former president of the Family Division, Sir James
Munby, stated that all types of FGM, including Type IV, constitute mutilation.[154] However, the former president deferred to the criminal courts to determine whether Type IV constitutes 'mutilation' under the FGM Act 2003. The
former president of the Family Division noted the inadequacies of available
expert medical evidence in FGM cases. The case shows the acute difficulties of
finding medical professionals who are trained to deal with cases of FGM and
the challenges of physically identifying that Type IV FGM has been performed.
It remains unclear whether Type IV constitutes mutilation for the purposes of
section 1 of the FGM Act 2003. The prosecution of this case for child cruelty
rather than FGM suggests that it is not covered in the FGM Act 2003.

Tensions were heightened at the conclusions of the case. There was an alter-
cation between a supporter of the father and an anti-FGM Integrate UK worker
outside of court. The case highlights the clash in attitudes between anti-FGM
campaigners supporting the prosecution of FGM cases and community members who resent the involvement of the criminal justice system in their lives
as well as the media representation of their community as 'mutilators'. There

[151] UNICEF, 'Female Genital Mutilation/Cutting: A Statistical Overview and Exploration of the
Dynamics of Change' (2013) UNICEF (hereafter UNICEF, 'Dynamics of Change').
[152] Controversially, Type IV FGM or 'symbolic circumcision' has been proposed as an alterna-
tive to more severe forms of cutting in both African and other countries where FGM is performed.
L Amede Obiora, 'Bridges and Barricades: Rethinking Polemics and Intransigence in the Campaign
Against Female Circumcision' (1997) 47 Case Western Reserve Law Review 275; Doriane L Coleman,
'The Seattle Compromise: Multicultural Sensitivity and Americanization' (1998) 47 Duke Law Journal
717; American Association of Pediatrics, 'Policy Statement: Ritual Genital Cutting of Female Minors,
American Academy of Pediatrics' (2010) 125(5) Pediatrics 1088 ; UNICEF, 'Dynamics of Change'
(n 151).
[153] B and G (Children) No 2 [EWFC] 3. For a summary of the case see, Charlotte Proudman, 'In the
Matter of B and G (Children) (No 2) [2015] EWFC 3' (Family Law Week, 2015) <https://www.family
lawweek.co.uk/site.aspx?i=ed142550> accessed 5 March 2021.
[154] The president of the Family Division, Sir James Munby, found that all types of FGM including
Type IV constitute 'significant harm' within the meaning of Children Act 1989, s 31. The president reiterated at [68] that 'any form of FGM constitutes "significant harm" within the meaning of sections
31 and 100'. He cited Baroness Hale of Richmond in Re B (Care Proceedings: Appeal) [2013] UKSC 33,
[2013] 2 FLR 1075 [185], 'that any form of FGM, including FGM WHO Type IV, amounts to "significant
harm" ' [67].

is a stark divide between FGM-performing communities and anti-FGM campaigns, rather than bridging the gap and encouraging mutual cooperation to eliminate the practice.

Injustice for a Victim of FGM: The Third Failed Prosecution

One month after the Bristol prosecution failed, there was a third unsuccessful prosecution of FGM in the Old Bailey, London. On 22 March 2018, a solicitor of West African heritage was cleared of arranging FGM to be performed on his daughter on two occasions between 2010 and 2013 with a razor at the family home in South London.[155] The girl alleged that on each occasion she was made to lie on a mat in the hallway of her home, naked from the waist down as her father encouraged the cutter to mutilate her.[156] It was alleged that FGM was performed as a form of punishment for stealing money from the family home.[157] At the time of the case, the girl was age sixteen and living with FGM.

Similar to the other FGM cases, this is an unusual case. It does not represent a conventional FGM case as, according to the girl, the practice was not performed for cultural or traditional reasons but rather to inflict punishment. Parallels can be drawn between this case and the first conviction for FGM. In the first conviction for FGM, the mother was allegedly motivated to perform FGM because of witchcraft. In this case, FGM was allegedly performed to punish the girl for stealing money. In both cases, the father was on trial and in both cases the father was acquitted. The defence barrister highlighted that the dominant motivations for performing FGM do not apply in this case. The barrister defending the father suggested that FGM was 'predominantly perpetrated by female cutters on women' for reasons including 'purification, honour and social acceptance'.[158] These motivations are not compatible with a case in which punishment is the alleged rationale and the alleged perpetrator is male and Catholic. The failed FGM prosecutions show that jurors (who reflect public attitudes) often have preconceived views that FGM is performed by women to control a girl's or woman's sexuality. If the case does not fit within these rigid preconceptions, there is doubt as to whether FGM has been performed. Yet the reasons for FGM vary within each community that performs

---

[155] Alexandra Topping, 'UK Solicitor Cleared of Forcing Daughter to Undergo FGM' *Guardian* (London, 22 March 2018) accessed 5 March 2021.
[156] ibid.
[157] ibid.
[158] ibid.

FGM. To prosecute a case of FGM, the prosecution has to show more than medical evidence that the girl has been cut, it also seems that it needs to present the case as 'conventional' FGM. The perpetrator must ideally be the mother and the purpose must relate to the control of a girl's or woman's sexuality or other 'conventional' motivations for FGM. In this case the girl had been cut yet the parent's knowledge of the cutting was unclear in the media reporting of the trial. Leethen Bartholomew, head of the National FGM Centre, said 'While we respect the decision of the jury, it is important to remember that someone did carry out female genital mutilation on the victim almost a decade ago. The effects of FGM have a lifelong impact on survivors, both physically and psychologically, so it is vital support is in place for her for as long as she needs it.' In this case the girl had been cut as a child and no one had been brought to justice for FGM.

The prosecution cases before the courts highlight that FGM cases are diverse in nature. There are several barriers to prosecuting cases; the main barrier is the difficulty in gathering evidence. As a result, cases that are more unusual might be more likely to come to the attention of authorities than cases where FGM is performed within communities that support the practice. Exploring women's attitudes towards the criminalisation of FGM assists in understanding support and opposition for a criminal law aimed at eliminating the practice. Furthermore, FGM-performing communities' awareness of a zealous approach to criminalising FGM may have resulted in the dynamics of the practice changing to prevent detection and prosecution; for example, the practice continues but becomes more entrenched underground. The changing dynamics of FGM highlight the additional barriers that the law will need to overcome to further the prosecution of FGM cases.

Conclusion

The criminalisation of FGM gained traction in Britain in the 1980s, which resulted in FGM legislation being introduced in 1985 and further amended in 2003 and then 2015. The amendments to the legislation were a response to increasing public and political pressure for a prosecution and conviction for FGM. However, there are multiple barriers to detecting and prosecuting cases of FGM, which perhaps explains the failed prosecutions and single conviction for FGM, despite criminalising the practice in 1985. The four criminal trials described in this chapter appear to represent outliers rather than 'conventional' FGM cases. The cases that were brought to trial in part failed because they could be distinguished from the public's perceptions of traditional or conventional FGM cases, which acted as barriers to the prosecution securing a conviction. In many of these cases, the girl's father was prosecuted, whilst FGM was presented by the defence as a 'woman's issue'. Medical practitioners were unable to conclusively show that FGM had been performed due to the difficulty in detecting FGM on the girl's anatomy. The motivations for FGM further reinforce the exceptional nature of the cases, such as punishment or witchcraft, rather than to control a girl's or woman's sexuality or as a rite of passage.

FGM-performing communities are often marginalised from mainstream society and the criminal justice system. The interviews with women participants show the divide between women who oppose the practice and women who support or sympathise with FGM. Indeed, some women shared a commitment to pursuing the practice even though FGM is a criminal offence. The majority of women interview participants rejected defining FGM as child abuse due to concerns that this could result in communities being branded barbaric. The impact of the criminalisation of FGM is contested. It is unclear whether it has deterred the practice but it has changed the nature of FGM. Given the increased emphasis on prosecuting cases of FGM, the dynamics of the practice have changed in order to reduce the likelihood that FGM will be detected. As such, FGM is likely to be performed underground, outside of the purview of law enforcement agents, for example by performing FGM abroad or performing Type IV FGM, which is more difficult for medical practitioners to detect.

3

The Barriers to Criminalising FGM

Introduction

Since FGM was criminalised in 1985, there has only been one conviction for the practice as recently as 2019. FGM continues to persist in the UK despite the criminalisation of FGM. The reasons for the continuation of FGM are complicated. There are various barriers to the criminalisation of FGM, which make the picture complex. In this chapter, the obstacles and potential for the implementation of anti-FGM laws are explored in more detail. Whilst there is sensitisation to FGM in Western culture and through the law, the top-down approach to ending FGM has meant that anti-FGM initiatives, including legislation, rarely filter down to migrant communities who are often marginalised from mainstream society. Following interviews with women from FGM-performing communities, it is suggested that many families are not aware that FGM is a criminal offence. The key challenge is educating FGM-performing communities about anti-FGM laws to ensure that the law is effective in deterring FGM.

A further barrier to the efficacy of anti-FGM laws is FGM-performing communities' sympathetic attitudes towards the practice and opposition to the criminalisation of FGM. Women's attitudes towards anti-FGM laws are reported to be complex and largely dependent on whether the practice is performed on adult women, which some women perceived as more permissible, than when performed on girls under the age of consent. At present, FGM is defined in law as oppressive for both girls and women and is therefore prohibited. Indeed, family and community pressures to conform to the practice could undermine or vitiate women's consent to FGM. Women from FGM-performing communities argued that they ought to be permitted to exercise their agency to choose to undergo FGM rather than the law infantilising them. A core theme throughout the chapter is communities' resistance to dominant anti-FGM discourses, namely that FGM is a barbaric practice performed by abusive families.

Female Genital Mutilation. Charlotte Proudman, Oxford University Press. © Charlotte Proudman 2022.
DOI: 10.1093/oso/9780198864608.003.0004

An additional obstacle to the elimination of FGM is the contentious label of FGM as child abuse. Some women from FGM-performing communities expressed anger towards a blanket description of parents as mutilators and torturers. Labelling FGM as child abuse could be counterproductive when the practice is often understood by community members as safeguarding children from the dire consequences of living a life uncut. This chapter explores whether there is a relationship between the hyperbole anti-FGM discourse and racism in wider society. Rather than anti-FGM laws encouraging cooperation between community members and law enforcement, it could have encouraged further hostility as communities are under increasing surveillance from the police.

As the pressure to convict perpetrators of FGM increases, there is evidence to suggest that the dynamics of FGM are changing to enable FGM-performing communities to continue FGM whilst evading detection. FGM continues to be performed in ways that make detection less likely. The changing dynamics of FGM are analysed in further detail, for example, performing FGM on girls who are under the age of twelve months, cutting girls abroad, medical practitioners performing FGM underground in the UK, and changing the type of FGM to the least physically invasive, which makes detecting FGM more challenging. It is important to consider whether the fluidity of the practice could make the criminalisation of FGM ineffective. As will become apparent, introducing a law to criminalise FGM is insufficient in ending a culturally embedded practice. The barriers to eliminating FGM and criminalising perpetrators are significant and deeply entrenched.

Awareness Raising: Anti-FGM Laws

The end-FGM movement has expended significant resources in raising awareness of FGM laws within FGM-performing communities. Whilst FGM is firmly on the political agenda and has been covered in the media, many women who were interviewed, particularly first-generation migrant women, stated that they were unaware that FGM is a criminal offence. Larsson and others[1] conducted a pilot study in London in 2018 exploring attitudes towards FGM in men and women accessing FGM clinical services. Of the fifty-one women and

---

[1] Martina Larsson and others, 'An Exploration of Attitudes towards Female Genital Mutilation (FGM) in Men and Women Accessing FGM Clinical Services in London: A Pilot Study' (2018) 38(7) Journal of Obstetrics and Gynaecology .

three men who took part in the surveys, 89% of participants thought that FGM should be stopped, 72% said they were aware that FGM is illegal in the UK, and 15% reported that FGM causes no danger or were unaware of any danger caused by FGM to women's health. The study demonstrates the opposition to FGM by the majority of participants, but also a lack of knowledge about the legal and health consequences. Indeed, a likely barrier to criminalising FGM is a lack of education about the practice of FGM and anti-FGM laws. Criminal offences can act as a deterrent, but if individuals are unaware that FGM is a criminal offence, it is likely that the law has limited impact. Whilst FGM remains prevalent in some families and communities, the practice is rarely discussed in the private sphere because the practice is embedded in secrecy and taboo. Even when FGM is discussed it is rarely challenged, which makes changing attitudes and beliefs towards the practice arduous. An interview participant of Somali heritage, who was not cut, bravely chose to speak publicly about the practice, thereby shattering taboos and breaking social stigma, which allowed girls at the interview participant's school to be educated about FGM.

For me I couldn't understand why coming from a Somali background I had never heard of the practice before. No one wants to talk about it, no one wants to talk about it in the Somali community, no one wants to talk about it outside, no one wants to talk about it at government and policy level ... I know one of the main reasons why girls in my year group and the year above and below me discussed FGM was because we kind of made it normal to discuss FGM. It lost that kind of cultural fear. It's a shame to talk about it. [P8, FGM-PCM, *Somalia*]

Education is a powerful tool that can make a private practice public by discussing it openly with other pupils. Feminist movements have worked for decades to bring the private into the public, to make the personal political.[2] Once FGM is put on the political agenda and is freely discussed and debated, the practice loses its symbolic cultural value, as it is reinterpreted in the public sphere as a practice rooted in violence rather than status. A survivor of FGM who also works as a teacher explains that education is imperative in order to change attitudes and beliefs towards FGM, which are embedded in cultural norms.

---

[2] See feminist scholars' work on making the private, public, Catharine A MacKinnon, *Toward a Feminist Theory of the State* (Harvard University Press 1989); Charlotte Bunch, 'Women's Rights as Human Rights: Toward A Re-Vision of Human Rights' (1990) 12(4) Human Rights Quarterly 486.

It's [FGM is performed] out of ignorance, lack of education, it's out of a lot of things and it's merely cultural. Culture is like a cancer you can't take it out. It's too hard to take it out. [P12, FGM-PCM and teacher, *Somalia*]

The participant highlights the difficulties of changing cultural traditions that have been continued through generations. Interviews with women from FGM-performing communities and professionals show that relying solely on the law to change attitudes and beliefs towards the practice is unlikely to result in the abandonment of FGM. The law cannot change attitudes and beliefs if communities are unaware that FGM is a criminal offence. Lack of public awareness about anti-FGM laws could be a contributing factor to the persistence of FGM. During the focus groups, interview participants of Somali heritage shared their lack of knowledge about the legal status of FGM; they attempted to defer to the interviewer to seek clarification about anti-FGM laws.

We are saying there should be more awareness from the government rather than penalizing the people because some of them are not aware of even whether Type I is illegal. They think only Type III is illegal and some of them don't even know what FGM is. [FG1]

Lack of education about anti-FGM laws could partly explain why the law has limited impact in deterring FGM.[3] Having listened to the voices of women, it appears that the marginalisation of FGM-performing communities from mainstream society means there is a gap between legislation on the statute book and communities' understanding of the law. Indeed, qualitative research in respect of FGM-performing communities in the UK published in 2018 found that it was difficult to generalise about awareness and perceptions of the UK law on FGM.[4] Some believed that the law deters FGM whilst others confirmed that people continued the practice underground. The main obstacle to the law ending FGM was a perception that the long-standing cultural and traditional practice is more important than the law. The government has not prioritised and invested in nearly enough education at a grassroots level to help educate FGM-performing communities about the legal status of FGM. There

---

[3] A study exploring FGM prevention programmes in Europe found that in several countries there were gaps in professional knowledge and participation for FGM, see, Victoria Murray 'Women's Legal Landmarks: Celebrating the History of Women and Law in the UK and Ireland' [book review] (2019) 53(3) The Law Teacher 395.

[4] Brown E and C Porter, 'The Tackling FGM Initiative: Evaluation of the Second Phase (2013–2016)' Options UK (July 2016) (hereafter 'Brown and Porter, The Tackling FGM Initiative').

needs to be a holistic education and public health approach to tackle FGM in the UK rather than focusing largely on the criminalisation of FGM. Instead, there needs to be more active dialogue within communities using a non-punitive approach.

Professionals who work directly with FGM-performing communities stated that many communities are not aware that all types of FGM are a criminal offence. A Peer in the House of Lords who was responsible for designing and introducing the initial legislation in 1985 believed that introducing a specific criminal offence of FGM would generate publicity and communities and mainstream society would become aware about the practice and the criminal consequences of FGM.

> I suppose what it [the law] has done is to generate a lot of publicity and to have alerted the population in general to something, which makes it simply awful for those young girls who suffer this abuse for cultural reasons. [P21, Member of the House of Lords, M]

The law increased public awareness of FGM. However, it appears that media reporting about anti-FGM laws in the mid- to late 1980s did not permeate migrant communities. Without raising awareness of anti-FGM laws in society at large, including in communities that perform FGM, many people would be unaware of the introduction of criminal sanctions. A Peer in the House of Lords involved in implementing the Prohibition of Female Circumcision Act 1985 stated that there were no implementation plans for the legislation. Instead, the law was introduced by the government as a symbolic act to show that FGM is a human rights violation, but it did not address the implementation of the law.

> We really didn't have any plans as far as I can remember of putting the legislation into practice. I have no idea if it was implemented. Nobody wanted to do it of course. [P24, Member of the House of Lords, F]

The House of Lords Peer states that there were no implementation plans, which could explain why the first prosecution took thirty years; the law was introduced in 1985, the first prosecution was in 2015, and the first conviction was in 2019. Another Peer in the House of Lords stated that measuring the efficacy of law is an almost impossible task. There is limited evidence to show that the law is a deterrent and, as a result, the numbers of cases of FGM have decreased.

I think one of the most disappointing things about the law is that we haven't had one prosecution. What we will never know is whether the law has had a deterrent effect. We will just never know or understand that. I don't think there is any way we can. There's part of me that would love to think, yes, we haven't got prosecutions because the law was working well. [P22, Member of the House of Lords, F]

There was consensus amongst professionals that anti-FGM laws are unlikely to be effective in deterring FGM because the law has not been enforced. A police officer working with FGM-performing communities highlighted the issues raised by women from FGM-performing communities, namely that many communities lack knowledge about the status of FGM laws. First-generation migrants are often isolated from mainstream society where anti-FGM discourse dominates.

I think there are all sorts of problems that surround that law and the major one is that I think still in this day and age the isolated nature of ethnic communities that practice FGM means that they may well not be aware of the FGM laws ... I don't think enough work has been done to engage communities and let them know how very wrong it is in terms of the law ... I give presentations to community groups and they are still surprised and shocked that it's against the law. [P66, police officer, M]

The police officer's views reinforce the top-down approach of implementing anti-FGM legislation, which was echoed by Peers in the House of Lords. The law has yet to filter down to migrant communities at a grassroots level who are marginalised from mainstream society. The challenge is educating communities about anti-FGM laws when NGOs have limited resources to run community engagement programmes. An employee of a local authority explains the need for community programmes educating women about FGM in order to close the gap between government directions about FGM and communities' beliefs about FGM laws.

At the moment there's a big gap there. Centrally, the government issued all these directives but then it's not giving much thought on how this should be directed to communities, because some community groups aren't even funded, but they do community engagement work and they are not always the best people to do that work because they themselves might have certain views about it, the procedure. [P20, local authority employee, F]

It is unlikely that the law can have a deterrent effect when community members are unaware that FGM is a criminal offence. African-American legal scholar, Gunning, advocated for education and community awareness-raising rather than punitive criminal strategies, which she believed would be more effective in changing attitudes and beliefs in the long term.[5] During interviews with medical practitioners, they described attempts to educate patients from FGM-performing communities about the law. They tried to use the law as an advocacy tool to encourage FGM-performing community members to abandon the practice. Two medical practitioners explained that they use the law to deter women and their family members from performing FGM by highlighting the criminal consequences of imprisonment.

> We had a clinic last week. Seven new [FGM] patients and we had discussions about the law in this country and the law in their country of origin and as is often the case, there are laws criminalising FGM in their country of origin. Somalia is a classic example, it's [FGM] been criminalised since 1946 but people don't adhere to the law. So, the challenge for me is to say, actually in your country you may have a law and no one listens to that law. It's a corrupt approach to that law but in this country the law is here and we will use it. [P39, Consultant Obstetrician and Gynaecologist, F]
>
> I am asking everyone that I see, I am giving them [anti-FGM] passports, it's called an opposing statement [about FGM], it comes in 11 languages. It's there to take abroad when they travel to show to their family members and it states what FGM is, the penalty for it and how they can make contact to get help if required. So that's part of the work that I do. It is just part of the UK initiative. What I do is, I read it with them … I will still give her a Somali copy so that she can take that and give it to others, she can give it to family members. [P33, midwife, F]

Professionals encouraged women from FGM-performing communities to use their knowledge of the law as a bargaining tool to negotiate with family members abroad and persuade them to abandon FGM.[6] In circumstances where

---

[5] Isabelle Gunning, 'Women and Traditional Practices: Female Genital Surgery' in Kelly D Askin and Dorean M Koenig, *Women and International Human Rights Law* (Transnational Publishers 1999) (hereafter Gunning, 'Women and Traditional Practices').

[6] Parallels can be drawn with the literature on forced marriage where academics argue that the law against forced marriage was used as a bargaining chip to persuade family members not to force them into marriage; see, Charlotte R Proudman, 'The Criminalisation of Forced Marriage' (2012) 42 Family Law 460; Ruth Gaffney-Rhys, 'The Development of the Law Relating to Forced Marriage: Does the Law Reflect the Interests of the Victim?' (2014) 16(4) Crime Prevention & Community Safety 269. For example, women and girls could argue that if they are forced into marriage, their families could be subject to criminal sanctions, which might deter families from arranging the marriage.

girls and women support the elimination of FGM, the law can act as a deterrent in encouraging the abandonment of FGM. A London Assembly Member who works with FGM communities at a grassroots level raising awareness about FGM explained that a girl used the law to negotiate with her parents to encourage them to abandon the practice due to an economic impact of loss of their social benefits.

> This young girl last year told me, mum and dad you are not to mutilate us because you will lose your child benefit and she said none of us have been cut. Those parents know their children have an insight into the world that it is now and they have linked it to an economic factor. I mean not only would they lose their child benefit they would lose their children. [P29, London Assembly Member, F]

In this case, the girl used economic resources provided by the state as a bargaining chip to negotiate with her parents to ensure that she was not cut and none of her sisters were cut. Financial social benefits were given more weight in negotiation than criminal sanctions. Indeed, in research undertaken by anti-FGM NGOs and academics, Norman and others found that community members were becoming more aware of the law, which was seen as a powerful instrument in preventing FGM in the UK and abroad.[7] Education is a key factor to raising awareness about anti-FGM laws and eventually eliminating the practice. Professionals experience regular challenges in educating communities about anti-FGM laws. However, when communities are aware of anti-FGM laws, the law can be used as an advocacy tool to encourage communities to abandon the practice.

Women's Attitudes towards Criminalising FGM

FGM-performing communities' supportive or sympathetic attitudes towards FGM are relevant considerations when exploring the reasons for the continuation of the practice. Indeed, entrenched attitudes in support of the practice from within FGM-performing communities could partially explain why the practice persists. Furthermore, communities often oppose the criminalisation

---

[7] Kate Norman and others, 'FGM is Always with Us: Experiences, Perceptions, Beliefs of Women Affected by Female Genital Mutilation in London: Results from a PEER Study' Options Consultancy Services Ltd (2009) (hereafter Norman and others 'FGM is Always with Us').

of FGM for a variety of reasons and as such they might be reluctant to report cases of FGM to professionals due to fear that family members could be prosecuted. Interviews with women from FGM-performing communities showed that women were divided in their attitudes towards the criminalisation of FGM. Some women supported the continuation of FGM and therefore opposed the criminalisation of the practice. However, the majority of women believed that FGM should be a criminal offence when performed on children, but not when performed on adult women. The argument against performing FGM on children was that they are unable to give informed consent.[8] However, there was a divergence in attitudes amongst a vocal minority in the focus groups who believed that the law should allow parents to decide whether their child undergoes FGM:

INTERVIEWER: Should female circumcision be a criminal offence for children whose parents consent on their behalf?

FOCUS GROUP PARTICIPANTS:

- I think it should be the same as cosmetic surgery. If it's the child who wants to get it done and they need parental consent as long as it's coming from the child.
- If you truly believe in it and you've got it done [the mother has been cut] and it's your kid, then you shouldn't be penalized for it and there are not a lot of bad effects of sunna [type I]. It's not like back in the days where the girl can't have kids or it will block the blood and stuff, it is just a little cut. [FG1]

The second participant in the focus group described how important it is for mothers to ensure that their daughters undergo FGM, particularly if the mother had herself undergone FGM. The underlying reason appears to be that the family hold strong views in favour of FGM and wish to continue the practice on the next generation, thus the law has no role in prohibiting families from electing that their children undergo FGM in accordance with their beliefs. Furthermore, there was a general view that Type I FGM is not physically invasive in contrast to Type III and therefore, from a public health perspective, the practice should not be criminalised.[9] Whilst women on the whole supported the proposition that FGM should be a criminal offence for children, they were divided as to whether FGM should be criminalised for adult women.

---

[8] Interview participants did not provide any further reasons for their argument that FGM should not be performed on children other than a blanket response that children cannot consent to FGM because of their age.

[9] See introduction to the book for an overview of the different types of FGM.

The majority of women interviewed argued that adult women exercise their agency and *choose* to undergo FGM. They claim that the law should not override their ability to *choose* FGM by defining them as victims or cultural dupes and therefore the practice should not be prohibited for adult women, as explained by an interview participant:

INTERVIEWER: Do you think that we should criminalise adults who consent to undergo FGM?

INTERVIEWEE: I don't believe it. It's their choice. If they are an adult it's their choice. I do believe the government has the right to protect children but adults who choose that [it] is freedom [of choice], similar to cosmetic. [P1, FGM-PCM and NGO worker, *Somalia*]

There are growing numbers of scholars who contend that some women exercise agency and *choose* to undergo FGM.[10] Feminist scholars are divided as to whether agency is realised when women engage in acts of resistance or whether agency is realised in acts of accommodation.[11] Scholars argue that the process of women *choosing* to participate in cultural practices and then taking steps to make this a reality is a form of *action* and a means of expressing their *agency*. While the action may appear oppressive from a Western feminist standpoint, women make decisions based on structural and identity factors. Women's experiences of intersectionality including gender, race, and class all impact upon the different choices that women make. In seeking to promote a woman's identity and sense of belonging, some women argue for the continuation of FGM. Participants in the focus group in London explained that FGM for adult women should be permitted.

- It [FGM] shouldn't be criminalised it's her *choice*. When she sees that it's [vulva] open and has not been touched and she wants to really cut it, she has to be allowed.
- If people want to have FGM and they are 18 and above they want to then that's their *choice*, they have to realise the problems it's going to cause and they have to pay for it, it should not come out of the NHS pocket.

---

[10] For a discussion about women's agency to choose FGM see, Diana Tietjens Meyers, 'Feminism and Women's Autonomy: The Challenge of Female Genital Cutting' (2000) 31(5) Metaphilosophy 281.

[11] For a political and theoretical overview about whether agency is realised when women engage in religious practices that might be viewed as subordinate, political scientist and anthropologist Saba Mahmood researched Muslim women's attainment of religious piety in Egypt: Saba Mahmood, *Politics of Piety: The Islamic Revival and the Feminist Subject* (Princeton University Press 2005).

- When we are coming here to England when the child reaches 18 years they have their *choice*, their parents cannot say anything, nobody can tell them to do anything, they have their own *choice* and they are *free* to, so why this girl who is 18 years should be criminalised because she is doing her *choice*, the *choice* has been started with everything. [FG2] [Emphasis added]

It appears that the participants have adopted the language of *choice* which is often part of Western discourse used in contexts where cosmetic surgery or other forms of body alteration are supported. However, the Western rhetoric of choice and freedom is used to support FGM for cultural reasons. Arguments based on religion or culture are subjective and sometimes dismissed by narratives of cultural traditions oppressing women. In fact, the rationale for undergoing FGM is rarely mentioned, instead, the focus is on 'choice' and 'freedom' without any exploration of what these principles mean in practice for women seeking to undergo FGM. In contrast, other women interviewed, mainly in one-to-one interviews rather than in focus groups, argued that the family and community pressure to conform to cultural expectations can significantly undermine or even vitiate women's free and full consent to FGM. As a result, some women argued for the criminalisation of FGM. They believed that family and community pressures to conform to cultural expectations undermine women's consent to FGM:

There's so much pressure in the family, there's so much pressures in the community that they don't have any choice. [P9, FGM-PCM and midwife, *Mali*]

The implication in this quotation is that outside pressure will invalidate women's consent to FGM. African-American academic Gunning[12] argued that cultural pressure undermines women's consent to FGM due to fears of severe cultural and familial sanctions for not conforming to FGM. Philosopher Chambers argues that women's choices are often constrained in oppressive contexts, for example, a woman might fear not undergoing FGM because her family could ostracise her and she could find herself economically deprived.[13] The criminalisation of FGM remains a contested issue with women from FGM-performing communities who participated in interviews and focus groups. Women's attitudes towards the criminalisation of FGM appeared to depend upon whether they supported the practice.

---

[12] Gunning, 'Women and Traditional Practices' (n 5).
[13] Clare Chambers, *Sex, Culture, and Justice: The Limits of Choice* (Penn State Press 2008).

Questioning the Universal Label of Child Abuse

FGM is defined as child abuse.[14] As a result of defining FGM as child abuse, serious criminal sanctions are imposed to ensure that perpetrators are imprisoned and children are put into state care, away from their parents. The physical and psychological harm that women describe experiencing as children suggests that the practice is a form of child abuse. Rogers contends that anti-FGM laws and child abuse terminology is less based on evidence but on imagined harms invoked by stories of mutilated girls; Rogers and Werbner argue that these visions of cultural brutality being inflicted on girls reinforce racist narratives.[15] Scholars who advocate a cultural relativist perspective to FGM object to framing FGM as an abuse of human rights and the rights of the child.[16] Legal scholar, Gunning, says that describing black parents as 'mutilators' or 'torturers' of their own children, 'wittingly or unwittingly represents African adults as either monsters or as ignoramuses who do not appreciate the welfare consequences of their own child-rearing customs'.[17] Defining FGM as a human rights violation produces 'racist visionaries' of mothers as child abusers.[18] Producing visions of brutal and barbaric cultural practices being inflicted on

---

[14] Statements issued by the government related to FGM usually confirm that FGM is child abuse, see eg House of Commons Home Affairs Committee, 'House of Commons Home Affairs Committee: Female Genital Mutilation: Abuse Unchecked' (Ninth Report of Session 2016–17) (2016) (hereafter House of Commons Home Affairs Committee, 'Abuse Unchecked'); The Secretary of State for the Department of Health, 'The Government Response to the Ninth Report from the Home Affairs Select Committee Session 2016–17 HC 390: Female Genital Mutilation: Abuse Unchecked' (2016). Furthermore, public bodies responsible for safeguarding children such as the NSPCC define FGM as child abuse: NSPCC, 'Female Genital Mutilation (FGM)' <https://www.nspcc.org.uk/what-is-child-abuse/types-of-abuse/female-genital-mutilation-fgm/> accessed 7 March 2021.

[15] Juliet Rogers, *Law's Cut on the Body of Human Rights: Female Circumcision, Torture, and Scarred Flesh* (Routledge 2013) 24 (hereafter Rogers, *Law's Cut*); Pnina Werbner, 'Folk Devils and Racist Imaginaries in a Global Prism: Islamophobia and Anti-Semitism in the Twenty-First Century' (2013) 36(3) Ethnic and Racial Studies 450 (hereafter Werbner, 'Folk Devils'). However, there is rarely any acknowledgment from scholars who criticise defining FGM as child abuse that the brutal descriptions of FGM are provided by survivors of FGM, as they outline their own stories of FGM and the impact that undergoing the practice has had upon their lives.

[16] For example, Kay Boulware-Miller, argues that, 'to challenge female circumcision as a violation of the rights of the child suggests that women who permit the operation are incompetent and abusive mothers who, in some ways, do not love their children': Kay Boulware-Miller, 'Female Circumcision: Challenges to the Practice as a Human Rights Violation' (1985) 8 Harvard Women's Law Journal 155, 166 (hereafter Boulware-Miller, 'Female Circumcision'). Anthropologist Richard A Shweder, contends that defining FGM as child abuse has significant implications for branding FGM-performing communities as barbaric, 'the alarming claims and representations by anti-FGM advocacy groups (images of African parents routinely and for hundreds of years disfiguring, maiming and murdering their female children and depriving them of capacity for a sexual response) have not been scrutinised with regard to reliable evidence': Richard A Shweder, 'What About "Female Genital Mutilation"? And Why Understanding Culture Matters in the First Place' (2000) 129(4) Daedalus 209, 212 (hereafter Shweder, 'Female Genital Mutilation').

[17] Gunning, 'Women and Traditional Practices' (n 5).

[18] For a thorough description of 'racist visionaries' see, Werbner, 'Folk Devils' (n 15).

helpless girls feeds deep-seated fear and racism displaced onto ethnic minority communities. As early as the 1990s, practitioners noticed emerging tensions and conflicts in defining FGM as child abuse.[19] Within FGM-performing communities, FGM is often considered an act of love, while the law defines FGM as child abuse. Women participants' responses highlighted their polarised views towards labelling the practice 'child abuse'. Defining FGM as child abuse results in many parents being defined as child abusers, which many parents and children do not identify with. Many women, including women who oppose FGM, believe that the practice is performed to safeguard children from the dire consequences of living a life uncut and it is not performed with the intention of harming their children. An interview participant who has not been cut defines FGM as child abuse because it involves the mutilation of genitalia tissue of a child who cannot consent to the practice.

> I think with children it's a form of child abuse, removing something from their bodies. If a mother decided to cut off the tip of her child's finger it would be a complete national outrage, because oh my god she mutilated her child. Whether it's her genitalia, her ear, her finger, no child should have anything removed ... no one spoke about it [FGM] but now they have actually acknowledged it as a form of abuse. It has a lot to do with the language that is used to support FGM as a cultural factor but now people often use the word child abuse and that change in language has made them see it for what is was. [P8, FGM-PCM, *Somalia*]

The interview participant criticises the cultural discourse that is used to support and legitimise FGM. Instead the participant compares the cutting of genitalia to the cutting of a finger or another part of the anatomy. The narrative used by the interview participant mirrors the rhetoric of wider society, policymakers, and the media all of whom define FGM as child abuse, usually without robust engagement with FGM-performing communities who often resist this dominant narrative. As identified in the book, women's experiences of FGM vary significantly. While women describe graphic and traumatic stories of being cut, some women refuse to define the practice as child abuse because it labels unwitting parents as abusers.[20] As highlighted above, the majority of

---

[19] See Efua Dorkenoo, *Cutting the Rose: Female Genital Mutilation: The Practice and its Prevention* (Minority Rights Group 1994); Comfort Momoh, *Female Genital Mutilation* (Radcliffe Publishing 2005).

[20] It is important to note that women's experiences of gender, race, and class are likely to impact upon their experiences of FGM and their attitude as to whether FGM is defined as child abuse. Due to time constraints, I was unable to explore these overlapping issues.

women opposed FGM if it is performed upon children, yet the vast majority of women refused to define FGM as child abuse. Participants, particularly in the focus group, explained that FGM is an act of love because families or communities perform FGM to protect children from the social sanctions of failing to conform to FGM.

> It's also seen as your kid will never get married. You don't want shame for your kid so this is sort of an act of love. You want the best for your kid at the end of the day. [FG1]

As described by the participant in the focus group, the negative social and cultural consequences that ensue when FGM is rejected include shame, social and cultural isolation. Families fear that if FGM is not performed they will suffer social sanctions, which justifies the continuation of FGM. Some families might regard not performing FGM as a form of child abuse. Academics have opined that the sanctions for not conforming to a deeply entrenched cultural and traditional practice could result in women's ostracisation from their family and communities, leaving them with no reasonable alternative but to continue performing the practice on the next generation.[21] Many women distinguished FGM from child abuse on the basis that the parents did not intend to harm the children, instead they intend to perform FGM for the benefit of the child. In the interview excerpt below, a survivor of FGM who opposed the continuation of FGM stated that parents continue FGM to protect children not to cause them harm.

> Parents love their children and they do what they think is best and if you think my child is never going to get married and they are going to be ostracised from society and all they've got to do is go through a bit of pain for a few weeks, you do what you think is best for them. [P5, FGM-PCM, *Somalia*]

FGM was framed by many interview participants as a practice integral to the identity of women and the continuation of kinship groups that remain bound by the continuation of traditions. The significance attached to FGM highlights that FGM represents important issues such as cultural belonging, nationality, and even religion in migrant communities. Rather than defining FGM as child abuse, women described the practice as a form of protection for the child and community because it protects girls from social sanctions for transgressing

---

[21] See, Gunning, 'Women and Traditional Practices' (n 5).

the norms associated with FGM.[22] A grandmother who arranged to have her granddaughter cut explained as follows:

When I was doing [FGM] to my granddaughter I was doing [it] because I was doing it to protect her by her not been stigmatised or stereotyped by her peers. I was also protecting the family integrity and the family dignity and I was doing something good for her. [FG2]

The language of child protection resembles Western narratives of the safeguarding of children from harm and child abuse. Communities use similar language of child protection, which is used strategically in the end-FGM campaign. Adopting Western rhetoric is an effective advocacy tool because it reinforces the permissibility of FGM using familiar language, which permeates the public sphere and people readily identify with it. There is no empirical evidence to show that defining FGM as child abuse can have a material impact on changing communities' attitudes and beliefs towards FGM. Participants in the focus group argued that child abuse is a loaded term that is projected onto migrant communities by wider society which creates hostility and resentment.

- Interviewer: Do you think female circumcision is a form of child abuse?
- Participant: I don't believe it's child abuse. If you are looking from the outside in you'll think it's child abuse. If I look from the parent's view it's not child abuse. When I think of child abuse I think of paedophilia. I think of you know sexual abuse to young children by people who they trusted. But this is our culture. But people outside will still see it as child abuse because you didn't grow up in that kind of environment so I understand when people say it's a child abuse because you are abusing the child, you are hurting them. There's a lot of things that parents do out of love that still hurt the child. Like for me to this age I am still scared of vaccinations but they do it for my own good. You will see a lot of babies who have got their ears pierced. And there's no real health benefit to ear piercing.
- Also the child abuse is not just physical, it's to do with neglect, you know emotionally bullying the child or something, mentally, demoralizing them and everything else.

---

[22] Women who defined FGM as a form of child protection reiterated cultural relativist arguments that kinship group rights to practice their culture should be permitted and not prohibited. See, Shweder, 'Female Genital Mutilation' (n 16).

- I feel like FGM isn't what child abuse is defined as today. I think FGM is, like I said, parents wishing the best for their child. Again parents know more than the child obviously. They know that maybe there's health benefits involved. No parent today would completely mutilate their child and stitch them up.
- Child abuse is also a term people have familiarised themselves with the moment they come to like Western countries, especially in this country, no one used to use the term child abuse in our community. Whether you hit a child or you circumcise a child it wasn't child abuse.
- Our whole community who are doing this, they can't all be abusers, they can't all be crazy. [FG1]

Interview participants rejected the label child abuse. Given the negative connotations associated with child abuse, such as paedophilia, the term generated hostility and resistance, which in turn is likely to impact on the end-FGM campaign in the long term. A participant in the focus group stated, 'our whole community who are doing this, they can't all be abusers, they can't all be crazy', which showed the rejection of the term as well as the normalisation of the practice within some communities. Participants argued that parents have a right to determine the cultural traditions that their child practices without state intervention.[23] Scholars[24] have argued that defining FGM as a violation of the rights of the child suggests that parents are abusive and barbaric, which ignores a family's right to cultural autonomy and results in communities being marginalised from mainstream society. It is clear from the interviews with FGM-performing communities that defining FGM as child abuse could have the unintended consequence of stirring hostility and resistance towards efforts to eliminate FGM. Rather than deterring FGM, the label child abuse could result in antipathy towards efforts to abandon FGM, including the criminalisation of FGM. Communities might be less willing to engage in anti-FGM campaigns because FGM discourse marginalises and stigmatises parents as mutilators and child abusers. Interview participants appeared to display a cohesive and supportive ethos towards each other and their community. The underlying premise is that communities close ranks when they feel under threat.

---

[23] For arguments about a child's right to practice their culture, tradition, and other associated beliefs, see, L Amede Obiora, 'Bridges and Barricades: Rethinking Polemics and Intransigence in the Campaign Against Female Circumcision' (1997) 47 Case Western Reserve Law Review 275 (hereafter Obiora, 'Bridges and Barricades'); Fuambai Ahmadu, 'Rites and Wrongs: An Insider/Outsider Reflects on Power and Excision' in Bettina Shell-Duncan and Ylva Hernlund (eds), *Female 'Circumcision' in Africa: Dimensions of the Practice and Debates* (Lynne Rienner Publishers, Inc 2000).
[24] See, Shweder, 'Female Genital Mutilation' (n 16) and Boulware-Miller, 'Female Circumcision' (n 16).

Communities' resistance to anti-FGM discourse is likely to be partly responsible for limited prosecutions and only one conviction since 1985. Anti-FGM
campaigner, Otoo-Oyortey, argued that the first conviction for FGM could
have been at the expense of further engagement with communities who are
likely to feel targeted and stigmatised by anti-FGM discourse.[25] Another challenge in identifying FGM cases is that the practice appears to continue underground, making it difficult, if not impossible, for law enforcement officers to
detect cases.

FGM, Race, and Racism

The experience and attitudes of women from FGM-performing communities
towards anti-FGM laws are often compounded by structural inequalities such
as gender, race, and class. Women of colour usually experience intersecting pat-
terns of institutional racism and sexism, which could deter them from relying
upon the criminal justice system.[26] Interview participants rarely discussed or
gave examples of discrimination through the law or of racism that they had
personally encountered in the context of FGM.[27] However, many interview
participants linked their hostility towards anti-FGM laws, which directly target
ethnic minority groups, to wider racism in mainstream society. The hyperbole
discourse about FGM has meant ethnic minority communities feel under further threat from law enforcement agents. The relationship between ethnic minority communities and the police is strained due to high levels of community
surveillance, especially communities who are already on the outside of society
due to language barriers and social and economic deprivation. Women and
girls from communities that are perceived to perform FGM are singled out and
targeted as potential perpetrators of child abuse. Scholars contend that women
are often left unprotected from the police because they fear an over-zealous,
discriminatory police response if they report FGM.[28] An interview participant

[25] Naana Otoo-Oyortey, 'Challenges to Ending Female Genital Mutilation in the UK' (2020) 4(1)
Nature Human Behaviour 2 (hereafter Otoo-Oyortey, 'Challenges').
[26] For a discussion about intersectional inequalities from the academic who defined 'intersectionality',
see, Kimberle Crenshaw, 'Mapping the Margins: Intersectionality, Identity Politics, and Violence against
Women of Color' (1991) 43(6) Stanford Law Review 1241 (hereafter Crenshaw, 'Mapping the Margins').
[27] A report by BBC News in January 2019 stated that families of Somali heritage were being racially
profiled over FGM: Rachel Stonehouse, 'UK Somalis "Racially Profiled" over FGM' BBC News (12
January 2020). Families complained that they were being arrested and having their children taken into
care due to the stigma about FGM.
[28] Mary Maynard and Jan Winn, 'Women, Violence and Male Power' in Victoria Robinson and
Diane Richardson (eds), Introducing Women's Studies (Macmillan 1997) (hereafter Maynard and
Winn, 'Women, Violence and Male Power'); Norman and others 'FGM is Always with Us' (n 7); Eiman

of Somali heritage gave an example of direct racism stemming from FGM. Pupils at a school tried to pull another girl's trousers down to see if she had undergone FGM.

> My cousins who are in secondary school already get teased about it [FGM] anyways. Everyone wants to know if they've been cut and how it looks and they haven't [had FGM] they were born in England. I know one girl at secondary school and at PE [sports class at school] she was held down by two girls and they tried to take down her trousers. It's like they are a freak show. [P5, FGM-PCM, *Somalia*]

The traumatic experience the young girl encountered at school stems from racism. However, the interview participants did not draw a direct nexus between FGM and racism or Islamophobia. It would not be an overstatement to say there is a wide-scale perception in the West that Islam and FGM are synonymous.[29] According to Rogers, the conflation of Islam and FGM reinforces an image of barbaric Muslims mutilating women and girls. Visceral images of mutilated clitorises in the public consciousness could arouse racist stereotypes of Muslims as child abusers. These could give rise to the hatred of Islam, which is perceived as a religion that brutalises women. The hatred of Muslims is referred to as Islamophobia. Islamophobia involves misrepresenting the Muslim world to accentuate its difference to the West, for example, reproducing sensationalist images of Muslims as violent terrorists.[30] Popular discourse about the revolting sight of cut vulvas can result in racist and abusive responses to FGM. The interview participant's story relates to an example of Islamophobia featured in a UK report, *Measuring Anti-Muslim Attacks*, where 'a Muslim schoolgirl had her hijab forcibly pulled from her head by the parents of another child at the same school while a crowd of onlookers were looking on and laughing.'[31] From wearing the Islamic veil to being cut, these practices are visible markers of girls' and women's difference to mainstream society and the violence inflicted on Muslim women and girls. The link between Muslim and

Hussein, 'Women's Experiences, Perceptions and Attitudes of Female Genital Mutilation: The Bristol PEER Study' FORWARD (2010) (Hussein, 'Women's Experiences').

[29] Rogers, *Law's Cut* (n 15).

[30] See, Gabriele Marranci, 'Multiculturalism, Islam and the Clash of Civilisations Theory: Rethinking Islamophobia;' (2004) 5(1) Culture and Religion 105.

[31] Chris Allen, Arshad Isakjee, and Özlem Ögtem Young, '"Maybe we are Hated": The Experience and Impact of Anti-Muslim Hate on British Muslim Women' University of Birmingham: Institute of Applied Social Studies, School of Social Policy (2013) <https://www.tellmamauk.org/wp-content/uploads/2013/11/maybewearehated.pdf> accessed 7 March 2021.

mutilated underpins a historical need to rescue Other women from oppressive religion.[32] The hostility that girls and women encounter as a result of preconceived notions about FGM could make them less inclined to seek support from service providers. Salmon, Olander and others 2020 examined the success of public health campaigns centred on FGM within the UK Somali community. Fathers in particular felt unfairly targeted, with many members of the community concerned that FGM was being associated with religion, especially Islam, more than culture.[33] An NGO worker states that the media focus on FGM has caused more harm than good and could have encouraged a backlash.

> The publicity has done more damage than any good for the victims, because now the communities don't want to talk to us, they don't want us to go to work to do anything with them. Because we are calling them barbaric, we are calling them inhumane, and we forget that older women are victims of this practice, we forget that they also suffer, by saying they are barbaric and abusing their children, they get really angry. It hasn't been any help at all. First of all it's coming from activists most of them are based in London who don't work directly with grassroot communities and they can say what they want. Also, some of these activists are young Somali women who are free [names of activists removed], they can do and say what they want. But they have nothing in common with other Somali girls who are living with their parents who are afraid of speaking out or challenging their families. [P64, NGO worker, F]

The NGO worker's experience of working with Somali girls and women at a grassroots level shows the disconnect between them and anti-FGM activists who have courageously gained status through speaking about their stories of FGM. Anti-FGM activists often speak about the practice at governmental level and on other high-profile platforms. They are valuable in sharing their experiences, which legitimates the need for government intervention in communities. However, government intervention can be responsible for stigmatising communities as barbaric. Anti-FGM laws have further legitimated police surveillance of migrant communities, and in turn the fraught relationship

---

[32] See, Rogers, *Law's Cut* (n 15). Muslim women are represented as in need of liberation: 'The veil becomes what must be removed and her flesh revealed—in the same vein as her flesh must be restored in anti-FGM discourse. In both these representations it is the body of the Muslim woman that requires liberation' (39).

[33] A study in Oxford concerning Kenyan, Nigerian, Somalian, and Sudanese communities locally found that participants believed that UK legislation alone was not sufficient and was alienating communities. The article concludes that community-led solutions are desirable and that further research is needed to examine the impact of the UK legislation. See, E Plugge and others, 'The Prevention of Female Genital Mutilation in England: What Can Be Done?' (2019) 41(3) Journal of Public Health e261.

between the police and migrant communities has been exacerbated. As legal scholar Crenshaw identified, women's race, gender, and cultural identity affects the likelihood of women seeking support from the police.[34] FGM is a unique offence, as it is a crime implemented by the dominant class against marginalised communities. During the interviews, women from FGM-performing communities linked anti-FGM laws to broader structures of racism and structural oppression stemming from law and policy that is enforced upon them despite community objection.[35] An FGM-performing community member highlights the hostility and mistrust that FGM-performing community members feel towards the police.

> I think because the police are always received with a lot of suspicion. I don't know how much work the police can accomplish. I don't think the police is a good kind of candidate to get involved [with cases of FGM]. [P7, FGM-PGM, *Somalia*]

Rather than anti-FGM laws encouraging cooperation between law enforcement agents and community members, the law could have inadvertently resulted in communities distancing themselves from the police. Many women described feeling fearful of state intrusion into the lives of disenfranchised communities. State involvement in migrant communities can exacerbate the disempowerment of those already subordinated by the structures of domination; for example, women might fear that the police could become aware of their insecure immigration status.[36] The interview participant's comment that 'the police is not a good kind of candidate to get involved' with communities exemplifies many women's feelings of ambivalence towards the police addressing FGM. A report published by an anti-FGM NGO stated that current FGM safeguarding measures have left families feeling racially profiled, criminalised, and stigmatised.[37] In addition, health and social care practitioners, teachers, and the police are concerned about the growing mistrust and disconnect between them and their communities. These findings suggest that some

---

[34] Crenshaw, 'Mapping the Margins' (n 26) 1250.
[35] For a wider discussion about community objections to anti-FGM laws and other legislation that targets ethnic minority groups, see, Cecilia Menjívar and Oivia Salcido, 'Immigrant Women and Domestic Violence: Common Experiences in Different Countries' (2002) 16(6) Gender & Society 898; Rogers, *Law's Cut* (n 15).
[36] Crenshaw, 'Mapping the Margins' (n 26).
[37] Amy Abdelshahid, Kate Smith, and Khadra Habane, ' "Do No Harm": Lived Experiences and Impacts of FGM Safeguarding Policies and Procedures, Bristol study' FORWARD UK (2021) <https://www.forwarduk.org.uk/wp-content/uploads/2021/02/FORWARD-UKs-FGM-Safeguarding-Resea rch-Report-Bristol-Study-2021.pdf> accessed 6 March 2021.

African diaspora communities in the UK feel alienated. An interview participant of Somali heritage argues that the policing of FGM translates into the surveillance of migrant communities, which creates further disharmony rather
than deterring the practice.

> When people say police working closely [with communities], black people
> are so heavily policed already I don't understand how much closer they can
> get. Once people in our community know that the police are watching them,
> they keep away from them and keep themselves to themselves. [P5, FGM-
> PCM, *Somalia*]

Similar to interview participants' attitudes towards the increased involvement
of the police, critical race theorists argue that the overreliance on law enforcement to deal with social problems in ethnic minority communities has unintended consequences, including increased surveillance, use of force, mass
incarceration, police brutality, and the removal of children into state care.[38]
FGM-performing communities might refuse to engage with law enforcement
agents for fear of racist reprisals. A Peer in the House of Lords appeared to
understand the impact of criminalising FGM, as she stated that FGM laws
could alienate communities and result in the further segregation of migrant
communities from mainstream society.

> If they [law enforcement officers] are against families it will simply make
> families turn in and become more cut off from wider society. I think it's po-
> tentially damaging. We want integration in this country ... Not if these com-
> munities are alienated anyway and pretty cut off from society. They will
> simply feel more alienated and cut off and it could really be quite damaging.
> [P23, Member of the House of Lords, F]

Rather than deterring and eliminating FGM, the House of Lords Peer cautions
that communities could feel stigmatised by anti-FGM laws and sensationalist
discourse and thus retreat within their community. Indeed, during parliamentary debates in respect of the 1985 Act, Parliament was acutely aware of the
racist overtones of the legislation, which made the implementation of the law

---

[38] For a discussion on the unintended consequences of law enforcement surveillance of ethnic mi-
nority communities see, Natalie J Sokoloff and Ida Dupont, 'Domestic Violence at the Intersections of
Race, Class and Gender Challenges and Contributions to Understanding Violence against Marginalized
Women in Diverse Communities' (2005) 11(1) Violence Against Women 38 (hereafter Sokoloff and
Dupont, 'Domestic Violence').

even more challenging. Despite being cognisant of such issues, parliamentarians appear to have done little about this. Lord Hatch of Lusby is recorded in *UK Hansard* as saying in a House of Lords debate in 1985:[39]

So far as the racial overtones of the Bill are concerned—and I would ask noble Lords to note it very carefully because this is from those women on whom we are depending to put this Bill into practice in such a way that there is no social disturbance, no social anguish, as a result of the Bill—they say: 'If the Bill is seen as unjust and racist then groups like ours which are trying to initiate debate and to educate people about the dangers of the practice will be seen as attacking the communities involved and it will make our task harder.'

African-American legal scholar, Gunning, cautions against invoking the criminal law to eliminate FGM, which she warns could have the unintended consequence of reinforcing the practice.[40] Instead she argues for a grassroots approach focusing on education and health initiatives led by FGM-performing communities. A Bristol PEER study that interviewed four women of Somali heritage and four women of Sudanese heritage found that passing legislation as a 'quick fix' does not necessarily address the needs of African women in the diaspora who need self-empowerment to protect themselves and their own children.[41] Whilst the research was conducted in 2008, over a decade ago, the lessons learned remain relevant today.[42] Professionals cautioned that the criminalisation of FGM could lead to communities resisting the law and performing FGM underground. According to a criminal lawyer, anti-FGM laws could have had an adverse effect with communities resisting the law and continuing to perform FGM.

The law can harden attitudes. If the UK law says a particular thing, one could imagine a community, which practices FGM to have allegiance to FGM strengthened to what it perceived as a dismissive or unsympathetic community. [P48, Lawyer, F]

---

[39] Prohibition of Female Circumcision Bill, HL Deb 18 June 1985, vol 465, cols 207–24 <https://api.parliament.uk/historic-hansard/lords/1985/jun/18/prohibition-of-female-circumcision-bill> accessed 4 March 2021 (hereafter Prohibition of Female Circumcision Bill, HL Deb).

[40] Isabelle Gunning, 'Arrogant Perception, World-Travelling and Multicultural Feminism: The Case of Female Genital Surgeries' (1991) 23 Columbia Human Rights Law Review 189.

[41] Hussein, 'Women's Experiences' (n 28).

[42] For PEER research in London also see, Norman and others 'FGM is Always with Us' (n 7)

Indeed, during the passage of the 1985 Act through Parliament concerns were raised by NGO groups working with FGM-performing communities that introducing a new law could result in the practice continuing underground, thus there were calls for support within communities rather than simply criminalising FGM. Baroness Masham of Ilton is recorded in *UK Hansard* as stating in a House of Lords debate in 1985:[43]

> There are two main bodies from the immigrant communities concerned who are involved in the campaign to educate those communities on the undesirability of female circumcision. They are the London Black Women's Health Action Project and FOWARD. Both are strongly in favour of the possibility of a delay in the coming into effect of the Bill. I shall quote the words of the former group: 'Outlawing female circumcision in other countries has been partially successful but the practice continues underground where proper work has not been done to re-educate and support families, particularly women, in opposing the practice. Legislation which does not allow a period of time in which educational work can be done will not succeed in stamping out the practice of female circumcision in the UK.'

Parallels can be drawn between present day resistance efforts and resistance towards colonial attempts to ban FGM in parts of Africa. During the British Empire, FGM became a symbol of anti-colonial solidarity and resistance in parts of Africa, including in Sudan when the British Empire imposed a ban on FGM in the 1940s yet it continued to be performed.[44] Colonial efforts to ban FGM were abandoned in the 1940s and 1950s. Academics cautioned against criminalising cultural practices because such practices can gain power through becoming acts of resistance to quasi-imperialism.[45] France is a notorious

---

[43] Prohibition of Female Circumcision Bill, HL Deb (n 39).

[44] African-American academic Wairimũ Ngarũiya Njambi contends that the banning of FGM in Kenya mobilised women to engage in anti-colonial struggles from the 1920s to the 1960s: Wairimũ Ngarũiya Njambi, 'Irua Ria Atumia and Anticolonial Struggles among the Gĩkũyũ of Kenya: A Counternarrative on "Female Genital Mutilation"' in Oyèrónké Oyĕwùmí (ed), *Gender Epistemologies in Africa* (Palgrave Macmillan 2011) 180. Initiation rituals were central to everyday life and thus the ban of FGM sparked women's involvement in the anti-colonial resistance. Women's resistance to anti-FGM laws symbolised their resistance to colonialism. Women engaged in militant activity in ways that signified their strength and bravery and in turn they were perceived to be coequal with men. Njambi contends that the Western story of FGM is hegemonic and fails to reflect the complexities of women's experiences of FGM in different contexts (180). She further argues that there is a persistent colonial legacy, which is still present today, one that presumes the right of the civilised West to intervene in the cultural practices of the barbaric other.

[45] Comparisons between anti-FGM laws can be drawn with laws prohibiting the wearing of the Islamic veil. According to scholars Joan W Scott and Yvonne Y Haddad, rather than unveiling women, Muslim women resisted anti-veiling laws law by adopting the veil as a public show of anti-colonial solidarity and resistance to efforts to eliminate Islam. The refusal of Western society to acknowledge the

example of a secular country that has criminalised the veil and prosecuted more cases of FGM than most other countries. In public debates on veiling in France, many view veiling as a public violation of secularism and a sign of contempt for French identity by those who practice Islam.[46] Rather than unveiling women, anti-veil laws have had the opposite effect of Muslim women resisting the law by adopting the veil. It is important to acknowledge how cultural practices including veiling and FGM could gain further power in part through being conceptualised as cultural practices of resistance to colonialism and imperialism. Indeed, the UK has had limited success in reducing the prevalence rate of FGM through criminalisation, arguably because of the perception of a liberal state reflecting homogenous values of the white majority and imposing its values on immigrants who need to be civilised to our level.[47] The laws arguably generate a new form of vulnerability for ethnic minority communities who are targeted by legal initiatives designed by the dominant class against them. Rather than including them as part of anti-FGM initiatives, dissenting voices are excluded from the hegemonic discourse that drives anti-FGM laws. Instead, it is proposed that a more nuanced articulation of gender at the intersection of migration status, ethnicity, and neo-colonial relations would deter and prevent FGM.

oppression of women by colonialism and by racism today has resulted in resistance of Muslim women to racist representations of indigenous customs through publicly wearing the veil, a symbol of solidarity to their Muslim sisters and brothers: Joan W Scott, *The Politics of the Veil* (Princeton University Press 2009) (hereafter Scott, *Politics of the Veil*); Yvonne Y Haddad, 'The Post-9/11 Hijab as Icon' (2007) 68(3) Sociology of Religion 253; Meyda Yegenoglu, *Colonial Fantasies: Towards a Feminist Reading of Orientalism* (Cambridge University Press 1998); Sirma Bilge, 'Beyond Subordination vs. Resistance: An Intersectional Approach to the Agency of Veiled Muslim Women' (2010) 31(1) Journal of Intercultural Studies 9 (hereafter Bilge, 'Beyond Subordination'). These scholars show that as Muslim women have resisted the subordination thesis put on them by wearing the Islamic veil to show their agency and reject Western norms, the veil is now associated with a threat to Western modernity. The veil has come to represent the 'clash of civilization' and the peril of multiculturalism that should be curbed by coercive action against Islam through dominant national laws: Bilge, 'Beyond Subordination'. Similarly, narratives depicting FGM interchange from girls and women being portrayed as victims and those that seek to undergo FGM being defined as cultural dupes, to the practice being defined as a threat to Western civilisation and hegemony. Women who adopt practices associated with Islam are now seen as dangerous: Gholam Khiabany and Milly Williamson, 'Veiled Bodies—Naked Racism: Culture, Politics and Race in the *Sun*' (2008) 50(2) Race & Class 69.

[46] See, Scott, *Politics of the Veil* (n 45).
[47] Moira Dustin and Anne Phillips, 'Whose Agenda Is It? Abuses of Women and Abuses of 'Culture' In Britain' (2008) 8(3) Ethnicities 405. Dustin and Philips contend that government policies designed to curb FGM could have provoked resentment and hostility amongst FGM-performing communities, eg,

> In July 2002 ... the Sheffield Area Child Protection Committee wrote an open letter to all Somali parents warning them to reconsider if they were planning to take their children on holiday to be circumcised ... By July 2007, there had still been no prosecutions under the 2003 Act and the London Metropolitan Police had taken the remarkable course of offering a maximum £20,000 reward for information leading to a prosecution (416).

There is concern amongst frontline professionals that policies designed by the dominant and powerful in society to target and change the practices of marginalised minority groups could result in reinforcing the very practices that society seeks to eradicate. A local authority employee who works closely with FGM-performing communities explained that communities are concerned about the punitive nature of policing FGM, which involves targeting migrant communities.

> I mean I've heard some communities who say they want to go to their country of origin, in this case Somalia and they are nervous about going to the airport with two daughters because they think social services will take them off them because of the airport checks that were being done last year. [P20, local authority employee, F]

The professional explained the punitive forms of policing that FGM-performing communities encounter from law enforcement agents to deter and prosecute cases of FGM. Many FGM-performing community members report feeling targeted by professionals when they seek to travel to high-prevalence FGM countries often to visit relatives. Policing can be regarded as a structural form of oppression enforced upon migrant communities, as concerns about FGM legitimise the surveillance of ethnic minorities. Women may fear calling the police as it could subject them and their families to racist treatment by the criminal justice system, as well as reinforcing racist stereotypes of ethnic minority families as violent child abusers, which could result in the state removing children from their care. Communities might distance themselves from law enforcement agents rather than engaging and cooperating in anti-FGM initiatives. An NGO worker described an evocative case in which the police had wrongly accused a family of intending to perform FGM on their daughters.

> Local police depends, it's kind of a lottery, they either overreact or not react at all ... There's still no trust between the police and community organisations because they get it wrong quite a lot. We've had cases where people are just travelling to a country where FGM is performed and the father went to get the jabs for the girls and the doctor was alarmed because three girls were travelling to Somalia. The doctor reported it to social services, that's fair enough. The police went in without an interpreter, mum couldn't speak English, dad was away. Procedure to take everyone's passports that was even before the current change in legislation. They took everyone's passports, the woman was in complete shock because there was no interpreter and no one was there

to assess them. They [the family] were completely against FGM, I mean the woman had the infibulation and she was actually accessing one of our projects and she was very vocally against FGM. And they missed the flight and they had been saving the flight for years to visit the grandparents, so yeah there's instances like that all the time. [P59, NGO worker, F]

The information conveyed by the interview participant indicates that the police do not have a standard approach to addressing cases of FGM; instead the approach of the police is haphazard and can hinder rather than help anti-FGM efforts. The punitive approach experienced by one family is likely to have been shared with other community members, which may result in women's reluctance to cooperate with the police due to fears of arrest or prosecution. Government policies designed to curb FGM in migrant communities could have provoked resentment and hostility in communities. A Crown Prosecution Service (CPS) worker explained the difficulties of the police working closely with migrant communities, particularly individuals who have insecure immigration status and fear removal from the UK.

INTERVIEWER: Would it help if the police worked closely with communities?
PARTICIPANT: Of course, yes. But it's difficult because a lot of the affected communities are asylum seekers, or they have tenuous immigration status or they are hidden in some other way from authorities and they tend to be communities that are marginalised and the police don't have particularly good established links with those communities as they do with the diaspora communities. [P69, CPS employee, M]

There are practical difficulties of the police forging relationships with migrant communities when they are marginalised and disenfranchised due to language barriers, economic and social deprivation, and tenuous immigration status. Many women's experiences of discrimination through the law deterred them from coming forward and seeking support from the criminal justice system. Police have attempted to forge relationships with self-appointed male community leaders in order to engage and have dialogue with FGM-performing communities. An NGO worker criticises the police for focusing resourses on building relationships with patriarchal community leaders who often render women's experiences invisible.[48]

---

[48] See, Tamsin Bradley, *Women, Violence and Tradition: Taking FGM and other Practices to a Secular State* (Zed Books Ltd 2011) (hereafter Bradley, *Women Violence and Tradition*).

We think the police don't work closely enough with the right people in communities, in particular women. We think the police all too quickly engage with self-appointed leaders or perhaps the Imam and so on and neglect to really engage with women in the community, mothers and so on. We need to get to that silent majority. [P63, NGO worker, F]

There has been much discussion in the literature about service providers working with male self-appointed community leaders to build relationships and prevent any offence to the community.[49] Academics have criticised service providers, including the police, for privileging race over gender as they work with male community leaders who are often responsible for reinforcing patriarchal power relations within minority communities.[50] Minority ethnic women often find themselves excluded from support services because gender-based violence is excused for 'cultural reasons' because of assumptions of 'cultural privacy', which renders the violence less visible and justifiable on cultural grounds.[51] Many professionals described experiencing race anxiety, which means that they were reluctant to involve themselves in suspected cases of FGM due to fears that they could be branded racist. Psychologist Burman argues that professionals such as teachers, police, social workers, and medical practitioners are particularly conscious of being labelled racist if they address so-called culturally specific practices.[52] Ethnic minority girls are then left unprotected by mainstream society because of professionals' race anxiety.[53] Burman argues that through efforts to avoid being racist the opposite occurs, as ethnic minority girls are marginalised by white frontline workers that were supposed to protect them. The failure to challenge assumptions about culture and traditions of minority groups being violent towards women feed racist stereotypes that other communities condone violence and are oppressive to women.[54] Dustin argues that an obstacle for professionals supporting women is that violence against ethnic minority women is viewed as intrinsic

---

[49] See, Erica Burman, Sophie L Smailes, and Khatidja Chantler, ' "Culture" as a Barrier to Service Provision and Delivery: Domestic Violence Services for Minoritized Women' (2004) 24(3) Critical Social Policy 332 (hereafter Burman, Smailes, and Chantler, "Culture' as a Barrier); Bradley, *Women Violence and Tradition* (n 48).

[50] See, ibid.

[51] See, ibid.

[52] Erica Burman, 'From Difference to Intersectionality: Challenges and Resources' (2003) 6(4) European Journal of Psychotherapy & Counselling 293, 298 (hereafter Burman, 'From Difference to Intersectionality').

[53] Maynard and Winn, 'Women, Violence and Male Power' (n 28).

[54] See, Burman, 'From Difference to Intersectionality'.

to their culture.[55] Women might be reluctant to seek support due to fears of stigma and fuelling racism from service providers.[56] In contrast, violence performed against Western women is seen as an aberration of the individual man. Violence defined as perpetrated by cultural traditions should be reframed as gender-based violence rather than linked to culture, race, or religion (9),[57] which might encourage professionals to be proactive in cases of FGM. A social worker explained that professionals are paralysed into inaction in cases of FGM because of race anxiety.

> Sometimes professionals don't want to talk about abuse that's related to certain cultures or race. Some of them don't even want to get involved because they are not sure how to handle the case and they are scared of being called racist. [P75, social worker, F]

It is not uncommon for frontline professionals to present as insufficiently equipped to work with ethnic minority women due to sensitivities about culturally inappropriate questions. All of the professionals interviewed believed that concerns about being labelled racist impaired professionals from complying with child protection duties, which could have resulted in vulnerable children being left unprotected. An NGO worker who was involved in the FGM legislative process stated that politicians and law enforcement agents failed to ensure that the law was enforced because there was no interest in protecting ethnic minority girls from violence.

> There was an unwillingness to take the issue seriously. For me the why, why goes, because of who it is happening to, these are mainly black refugees, asylum seekers and most of the cases that are found are people in that category and it's not in the interests of the British public to actually do something. [P34, NGO worker, F]

Ethnic minority girls from migrant communities who are at risk of FGM are sometimes poor and disenfranchised and lacking the resources to seek support. The failure of professionals to protect young, often Black girls from FGM

---

[55] Moira Dustin, 'Female Genital Mutilation/Cutting in the UK: Challenging the Inconsistencies' (2010) 17(1) European Journal of Women's Studies 7, 9.

[56] See, Crenshaw, 'Mapping the Margins' (n 26); Burman, Smailes, and Chantler, ' "Culture" as a Barrier' (n 49); Sokoloff and Dupont, 'Domestic Violence' (n 38).

[57] Re-framing violence as an aberration of the individual could be criticised for essentialising women and failing to recognise their unique experiences of violence based on their identity and intersectional inequalities.

is an example of discrimination on racial grounds. Academics have also argued that leaving vulnerable girls without protection is racist, as white professionals prioritise their own concerns above the needs of vulnerable girls.[58] The government introduced a series of legislative changes to the Serious Crime Act 2015 including a provision that makes it mandatory for teachers, social workers, and medical practitioners to report cases of FGM to the police.[59] An NGO worker explains that some professionals are not trained about FGM, thus they continue to lack knowledge and understanding about the practice and the law.

> There hadn't been much effort in enforcing the law. Enforcing the law requires training, people being informed. But they hadn't been. It also requires making sure people have clarity in terms of the protocol and guidelines, in terms of how you follow. [P34, NGO worker, F]

The lack of training about FGM for professionals is a barrier to the implementation of the law. The failure to enforce the law sends out a message that the government is inadvertently legitimising the oppression of ethnic minority women, which leaves them without adequate legal protection and redress.

Pushing FGM Underground

As pressure continues to mount on the police and the CPS to prosecute and convict cases of FGM, there are concerns that the dynamics of FGM have changed to enable FGM-performing communities to evade detection and prosecution. Interviews and focus groups with women suggest that the practice continues to be performed but underground.[60] Findings from the interviews with professionals suggested that the practice has become increasingly more difficult to detect due to the practice being hidden from public view. The changes to the dynamics of FGM that were identified by women and professionals include changing the type of FGM to Types I and IV FGM, which are considered the least physically invasive types of FGM,[61] medical practitioners performing FGM on the black market, cutting girls at a younger age to avoid detection,

---

[58] See, Maynard and Winn, 'Women Violence and Male Power' (n 28).

[59] Female Genital Mutilation Act 2003, s 5B (hereafter FGM Act 2003).

[60] Whilst there is not sufficient evidence to draw a firm conclusion that FGM is being performed underground due to the limited interviews and focus groups, the evidence presented indicates that it is highly likely that FGM continues to be performed outside of the purview of law enforcement agents.

[61] It is highly contested whether Type I and IV are less physically invasive than Type II and III. It often depends on women's experiences of FGM and the long-lasting damage caused to a woman's genitalia.

and cutting girls abroad which makes it difficult for law enforcement agents to gather evidence to prosecute and convict perpetrators. Potential changes to the nature of the practice will limit the detection of FGM making prosecution less likely. Changes to the dynamics of the practice could serve as further barriers to the criminal justice system deterring and prosecuting FGM cases.

The Changing 'Types' of FGM

The types of FGM performed by communities appear to have changed. The reason for the change in the type of FGM is unclear. However, historically Type III was considered to be the most prevalent type of FGM and the most physically invasive form of FGM.[62] Types I and IV FGM are now more likely to be performed. Interviews with women and professionals suggest that Types I and IV are the preferred types of FGM because they are difficult to detect on a girl's genitalia, making it less likely that parents or perpetrators will be prosecuted for performing the practice. A woman from an FGM-performing community who is also an NGO worker explained that Type I and Type IV FGM are performed because they are difficult to detect on girl's genitalia, which in turn reduces the likelihood of prosecution and conviction.

> So now with legislation and everything that is happening they said ok at least if we just do sunna or just prick it's difficult when I go for a physical examination to find out but this is wrong you can still find out when you've been through type I. So, there might be shifts but they don't talk about it in the communities, it's taboo. Nobody will tell you I have changed my mind I don't want to do type III I will just be doing sunna. [P11, FGM-PCM and NGO worker, F]

The interview participant refers to Type I FGM as 'sunna' and to Type IV FGM as 'just a prick', which reflects the language often used by women interviewees. Despite the participant suggesting that there has been a shift in the types of FGM performed on women, the issue is 'taboo' and therefore rarely discussed, which highlights the secret nature of FGM. A research study found that Type IV FGM had become more widely accepted in the UK than other forms of FGM, even Type IV FGM was referred to by FGM-performing community

---

[62] See former medical practitioner's work about FGM: Harry Gordon, 'Female Genital Mutilation: A Clinician's Experience' in Comfort Momoh (ed), *Female Genital Mutilation* (Radcliffe Publishing 2005).

members as 'sunna' meaning a 'little cut' or prick.[63] If communities have changed the type of FGM performed to avoid prosecution, one could conclude that FGM-performing communities are well informed about the criminalisation of FGM. The consequent changes to the practice allow it to be maintained whilst preventing detection and criminalisation. The next interview participant states that Type I is the preferred type of FGM because it is perceived as less physically harmful than Type III, which has, according to the participant, been abandoned. Some scholars have advocated a harm reduction approach as a means of slowly eradicating FGM and reducing the harmful consequences as a result.[64] However, medicalised FGM is a human rights abuse with lifelong consequences.

> The kind of practice has changed, so from being Type III it is Type I . . . it's seen that Type I as not being FGM, that's another issue with the generation where type III is bad, oh no that doesn't happen, that shouldn't happen, as soon as you mention type I it is all of a sudden it's not FGM, it's just a little bit being removed. It's not a big deal it's not a crime. [P8, FGM-PCM, *Somalia*]

Furthermore, the interview participant highlighted that communities are under the misapprehension that Type I FGM is not a criminal offence and only Type III FGM is a criminal offence. This suggests that women lack knowledge about the criminal status of all types of FGM. It also suggests that FGM communities have changed the type of FGM in order to comply with the law. Communities appear to have negotiated their commitment to performing FGM within the boundaries of the law. It remains unknown whether communities might abandon the practice entirely if they were properly informed that *all* types of FGM are a criminal offence or whether the practice would continue but pushed further underground. Professionals also stated that in their experience FGM-performing communities are unaware that Type I FGM is a

---

[63] Brown and Porter, 'The Tackling FGM Initiative' (n 4). The research had the backing of a number of anti-FGM organisations including Trust for London, Esmee Fairbairn Foundation, Rosa, and Options UK. The qualitative research involved 70 peer researchers interviewing one to three friends each, resulting in 130 respondents in total.

[64] See, 'An Agonising Choice. After 30 Years of Attempts to Eradicate a Barbaric Practice, It Continues. Time to Try a New Approach' *The Economist* (18 June 2016) (hereafter *Economist* 'An Agonising Choice'). The Economist article resulted in a backlash from anti-FGM survivors and activists; Kavita S Arora and Allan J Jacobs, 'Female Genital Alteration: A Compromise Solution' (2016) 42(3) Journal of Medical Ethics 148 (hereafter Arora and Jacobs, 'Female Genital Alteration'); Andrew J Pearce and Susan Bewley, 'Medicalization of Female Genital Mutilation. Harm Reduction or Unethical?' (2014) 24(1) Obstetrics, Gynaecology & Reproductive Medicine 29; Bettina Shell-Duncan, 'The Medicalization of Female "Circumcision": Harm Reduction or Promotion of a Dangerous Practice?' (2001) 52(7) Social Science & Medicine 1013.

criminal offence. An employee of a Police and Crime Commissioner explained during an interview that communities differed in their understanding of the criminal status of different types of FGM, particularly Type I.

> A mixture of responses in relation to Type I as well. In one of the groups that I attended where there was the 35 women. The one group that was saying yes, it is illegal and you shouldn't do it. The other group were saying it's absolutely fine. The middle group, 10 women, they were the ones saying well it's alright if it's only Type I because it's just a pin prick so that's ok. [P67, employee of a Police and Crime Commissioner, F]

It appears that a key obstacle to eliminating FGM is that communities continue to practice some types of FGM, particularly Type I FGM, because they are not aware that it is a criminal offence. Some individuals are aware that Type I FGM is a criminal offence but continue to perform it because it is difficult for medical practitioners to detect that a girl has undergone FGM. As a result, FGM continues to be performed but steps are taken to reduce the likelihood of detection of FGM. A consultant gynaecologist and obstetrician who specialises in FGM explains that there are key obstacles in identifying Type I through physical examination:

> I have been working with people with FGM for 30 years and even I sometimes look at a vulva and think has this undergone FGM or has she just got a small labia I don't know. It might be Type I or Type IV [FGM], or it might be a variant because vulvas are enormously variable. [P40, consultant obstetrician and gynaecologist, F]

The interview participant highlights the difficulties in identifying whether Type I or IV FGM has been performed. Without medical evidence that FGM has been performed, it is highly unlikely that there would be a conviction for FGM. In fact, medical evidence in 'the Bristol case' was unable to establish that FGM had been performed, which contributed to the case collapsing. As highlighted in the interviews with women from FGM-performing communities, it is likely that individuals have changed the type of FGM, which is performed to Type I or IV FGM, to evade detection and prosecution. Given the challenges of encouraging FGM-performing communities to abandon FGM, an NGO worker explained that some NGOs and FGM-performing communities are arguing for a harm reduction approach where the least physically invasive types of FGM are performed.

There have been people who have criticised me for saying it should be stamped out immediately. What they do say is that the mildest form of FGM should continue to happen because it would take too long for them to part ways with it altogether. [P65, NGO worker, F]

There have been numerous calls for a 'harm reduction' approach, which calls for the least physically severe Types of FGM to be performed on girls, such as a nick or a prick of the clitoris, until the practice is eventually eliminated.[65] Some scholars have argued that a blanket ban on FGM has not eliminated FGM, therefore a new approach is required. Harm reduction strategies have been a source of contested debate amongst scholars since the anti-FGM movement gained traction in the 1970s and 1980s. American medical practitioners, Arora and Jacobs, argue that to protect women and girls from the long-term harms of some types of FGM, a more nuanced position is required that acknowledges the wide spectrum of procedures on the female genitalia, particularly those that do not carry long-term medical risks yet are culturally sensitive.[66] They contend that Type IV FGM is less physically harmful than male circumcision and therefore should not be prohibited on medical grounds. Indeed, symbolic circumcision, otherwise known as Type IV FGM, is still highly controversial but it has been proposed as an alternative to more severe forms of cutting in both African and other countries where FGM is performed.[67] The World Health Organization takes a strong line, stating that allowing the mildest form of FGM legitimises the mutilation of a female's genitalia for non-medical purposes and could serve to push back efforts to eliminate FGM altogether.[68]

The media reported on an alleged case of Type IV FGM, which involved a British baby of Malaysian descent who had allegedly been taken abroad when only a few months old to have the girl's clitoris pricked.[69] The CPS decided not to prosecute the parents because 'there is insufficient evidence to prove FGM . . . due to a lack of medical evidence of anything that could fall within the

---

[65] *Economist* 'An Agonising Choice' (n 64); Arora and Jacobs, 'Female Genital Alteration' (n 64).

[66] Arora and Jacobs, 'Female Genital Alteration' (n 64).

[67] See more on the arguments for the harm reduction approach: Obiora, 'Bridges and Barricades' (n 23); Doriane L Coleman, 'The Seattle Compromise: Multicultural Sensitivity and Americanization' (1998) 47 Duke Law Journal 717; American Association of Pediatrics, 'Policy Statement: Ritual Genital Cutting of Female Minors, American Academy of Pediatrics' (2010) 125(5) Pediatrics 1088; UNICEF, 'Female Genital Mutilation/Cutting: A Statistical Overview and Exploration of the Dynamics of Change' UNICEF (2013).

[68] World Health Organization, 'Eliminating Female Genital Mutilation: An Interagency Statement OHCR, UNAIDS, UNDO, UNECA, UNESCO, UNFPA, UNHCR, UNICEF, UNIFEM, WHO' (2008).

[69] See, Martin Bentham, '"Baby FGM" Court Case Thrown out Due to Lack of Proof' *Evening Standard* (London, 18 January 2016) <https://www.standard.co.uk/news/crime/baby-fgm-court-case-thrown-out-due-to-lack-of-proof-a3159056.html> accessed 7 March 2021.

definition of FGM'.[70] Cases of Type IV FGM could have become more prevalent because this type of FGM reduces the likelihood of detection and prosecution. There have been a number of alleged Type IV FGM cases in other parts of the world, which highlight the complexities in prosecuting cases where the medical evidence regarding FGM is contested and even when Type IV FGM has been established, it is difficult to prove that the girl or woman has suffered 'harm'.

In 2016 there was a landmark FGM case in the Supreme Court New South Wales in Australia[71] that resulted in the conviction of a girl's mother, a former nurse and community leader of the Dawoodi Bohra sect of Islam, for performing 'khatna' otherwise defined as Type IV or Type I FGM.[72] Two sisters between the age of six or seven had allegedly undergone the procedure at their homes during two separate ceremonies between 2009 and 2012. The jury rejected the defence case that Type IV was 'purely symbolic and inflicted no injury' and no mutilation and they were found guilty and sentenced to fifteen months in jail. The defendants appealed the convictions and the charges were quashed in 2018 by the New South Wales Court of Appeal.[73] At that stage, new evidence showed that there was no visible physical damage to either girl as the tip of the clitoral head was visible in both girls. Type IV FGM performed by the Dawoodi Bohra community was said to involve the nicking or minor cutting of the girl's clitoris during the ceremony. It could not be said therefore that the legal term 'otherwise mutilates' has occurred when the girl has suffered no visible damage to her genitalia and it was arguable whether the word 'clitoris' extended to clitoral hood or prepuce. The prosecution appealed to the High Court which ruled in 2019 that the New South Wales Court of Criminal Appeal erred in quashing their convictions. A majority of the High Court held that the phrase 'mutilates' extends to the cutting of the clitoral hood which is considered a part of the clitoris. Chief Justice Susan Kiefel and Justice Patrick Keane held in a joint judgment that they were upholding a 'broader construction' of the definition of mutilation that 'would best promote the purpose or object of prohibiting such procedures generally'. As such, the judgment reinforced that all

---

[70] ibid.

[71] See, judgment of Mr Justice Johnson in *R v A2; R v Magennis; R v Vaziri (No 23)* [2016] NSWSC 282; Juliet B Rogers, 'The First Case Addressing Female Genital Mutilation in Australia: Where Is the Harm?' (2016) 41(4) Alternative Law Journal 235.

[72] Anti-FGM organisation, We Speak Out, states that the community performs Khatna which is equivalent to Type I or IV FGM; We Speak Out, 'Khatna: What Is Khatna in the Bohra Community?' <http://www.wespeakout.org/fgm/what-is-khatna/> accessed 7 March 2021 (hereafter We Speak Out, 'Khatna').

[73] See Court of Appeal Judgment in *R v A2; R v Magennis; R v Vaziri* [2018] NSWCCA 174 <http://www.austlii.edu.au/cgi-bin/viewdoc/au/cases/nsw/NSWCCA/2018/174.html> accessed 7 March 2021.

types of FGM are a criminal offence. Two dissenting judges, Justices Virginia Bell and Stephen Gageler, took a narrower view of the offence and argued that the Court of Criminal Appeal made the correct decision, stating, 'The Court of Appeal was right to hold that superficial tissue damage, which leaves not physical scarring and which on medical examination is not shown to have caused any damage to the skin or nerve tissue, is not in law capable of amounting to mutilation.' The case was not remitted for a new trial due to the psychological harm that might be caused to the complainants. However, the case was again before the New South Wales Court of Appeal in 2020,[74] which ruled to quash the convictions and it confirmed that the defendants should stand a re-trial in the Supreme Court.

In Detroit, Michigan, eight members of the Dawoodi Bohra sect of Islam were indicted on charges of FGM relating to Type IV.[75] Similarly to the case before the court in Australia, the court was concerned with the Dawoodi Bohra community who allegedly performed 'khafz', which is regarded as Type I or IV FGM.[76] This case was the first time the US government has prosecuted an FGM case since the federal law was introduced by Congress and passed in 1996. The court found that the federal law is unconstitutional as the law should have been introduced at state level and thus dismissed the indictments in November 2018.[77] The Attorney General decided not to appeal the case. Titled, 'Dawoodi Bohra women of Detroit speak up', five women from the Dawoodi Bohra community wrote a letter published in the Detroit News, stating that the practice of 'khafz' is 'a harmless form of female circumcision that in no way can be defined as female genital mutilation'.[78] They added that it is less invasive than male circumcision and more akin to body piercing. They accused the media's presentation of the case as being politicised and showing 'religious intolerance and gender bigotry'.

Another case concerning the Dawoodi Bohra community in India rose to prominence in 2017. A lawyer referred a public interest litigation case to India's Supreme Court to seek a prohibition on FGM in India, where it is understood

[74] Tiffanie Turnbull, 'Retrials for Genital Mutilation Accused' *Goulburn Post* (Australia, 7 February 2020) <https://www.goulburnpost.com.au/story/6620104/retrials-for-genital-mutilation-accused/> accessed 7 March 2021.
[75] Brian D Earp, 'Does Female Genital Mutilation Have Health Benefits? The Problem with Medicalizing Morality' *Quillette* (15 August 2017) <https://quillette.com/2017/08/15/female-genital-mutilation-health-benefits-problem-medicalizing-morality/> accessed 7 March 2021.
[76] See definition of the types of FGM performed in the community, We Speak Out, 'Khatna' (n 72).
[77] See court judgment <https://content-static.detroitnews.com/pdf/2018/US-v-Nagarwala-dismissal-order-11-20-18.pdf> accessed 7 March 2021.
[78] Letter: Dawoodi Bohra Women of Detroit Speak Up, *Detroit News* <https://eu.detroitnews.com/story/opinion/2018/12/12/letter-dawoodi-bohra-women-detroit-speak-up/2278119002/> accessed 7 March 2021.

that there are one million members. The Supreme Court of India is due to decide the issue of FGM in the context of women's rights and freedom of religion. A research study by Lakshmi and others in 2018 found that 75% of their respondents from the Dawoodi Bohra community had subjected their daughters to FGM in India.[79] There is limited evidence available on the prevalence of Type IV FGM across the world and particularly in the UK. The evidence deficit is perhaps due to the secretive nature of the practice and the difficulties of gaining access to communities that continue to perform FGM.

FGM Performed on Younger Girls

As highlighted in this chapter, FGM-performing communities are negotiating their commitment to continuing the practice in a context of criminalisation by changing the dynamics of the practice. A further change to the dynamic of the practice, which makes it increasingly more difficult to detect is the age when the girl is cut.[80] Determined to preserve the cultural practice in a context in which FGM is a criminal offence, girls are likely to be cut at a younger age to avoid detection from professionals who work with children. Anecdotally it is thought that girls are cut at a younger age before they enter education to prevent questions being asked about their health or wellbeing. A woman of Somali heritage explained that girls are cut just a few days after birth to prevent suspicion arising.

> Age has changed as well because children are going to schools and schools are being trained so what communities are doing is taking the girls as babies and they are cutting them as babies because when they come back they can't talk, they don't really know what's happened, the age has changed … the main change is the age, they are getting younger and younger. [P13, FGM-PCM and nurse, *Somalia*]

---

[79] Lakshmi Anantnarayan, Shabana Diler, Natasha Menon, WeSpeakOut, and Nari Samata Manch, *The Clitoral Hood A Contested Site Khafd or Female Genital Mutilation/Cutting (FGM/C) in India* (2018) http://www.wespeakout.org/site/assets/files/1439/fgmc_study_results_jan_2018.pdf accessed 17 May 2021.

[80] The likely cutting of girls at younger ages was published in the mainstream press in the *Evening Standard* in March 2014 following concerns reported by the NSPCC children's charity, see, Martin Bentham, 'FGM Parents "Are Having Girls Cut at Younger Age"' *Evening Standard* (London, 27 March 2014). This followed a further news report by the BBC in February 2019: Anna Collinson and Jessica Furst, 'FGM "Increasingly Performed on UK Babies"' *BBC News* (London, 4 February 2020).

Changing the age at which children are cut has a significant impact on the meaning ascribed to FGM. In some communities FGM symbolised a rite of passage from childhood to adulthood.[81] However, that appears to have changed, as girls are cut when they are only a few days old to prevent FGM from being detected. Professionals working closely with FGM-performing communities were acutely aware that girls are likely being cut at an early age. An NGO worker who works with FGM-performing communities explained that children are cut when they are babies to avoid detection when they commence school.

> Anecdotally, we are told that the children affected by FGM are becoming younger, so the hypothesis has been since criminalising FGM … Families have been performing FGM at a younger age to avoid the scrutiny that they come under in school. [P57, NSPCC, F]

Professionals are aware that the practice has been driven further underground to avoid detection. The difficulty is that professionals are unable to detect FGM when performed on young girls. A police officer highlights the barriers implicit in enforcing anti-FGM laws when children are cut at a younger age.

> If you put yourself in the position of the child most children get this done when they are very young. Most children won't know they've got it done. They will regard it as natural. They won't compare their anatomy with others. If they aware they might think this is how it is. They will have heard from parents that it was done with the best of intentions really and in their long-term interests. So, the chances of a child coming forward and testifying in the first instance, which means giving evidence to the police against the parents is never going to happen. [P66, police officer, M]

As stated by the interview participant, children who are cut as babies will be unaware FGM has been performed unless their parents inform them that they have undergone FGM. When children are informed that they have undergone FGM, parents are likely to state that the cultural rationale for FGM is legitimate. Prosecuting cases of FGM raises nuanced problems that do not exist for other crimes, namely that the offender is likely to be a parent or relative of a

---

[81] See, Janice Boddy, *Wombs and Alien Spirits. Women, Men, and the Zar Cult in Northern Sudan* (The University Of Wisconsin Press 1989).

victim whom they implicitly trust. Cutting girls at a much younger age is likely to result in the law being unable to detect and prosecute cases of FGM.

Medical Practitioners Perform FGM

A surprising finding from the empirical research is that medical practitioners are potentially performing FGM on women and girls. It was suggested by interview participants that medical practitioners in Britain are performing the practice underground or that they are performing FGM under the guise of female genital cosmetic surgery (FGCS), which is tolerated by law enforcement agents. It is likely to be difficult to identify cases of FGM when medical practitioners are responsible for performing it. After all, medical practitioners will be armed with the knowledge of the law and the means of performing FGM in such a way that detecting the practice on a female's genitalia will probably be difficult.

INTERVIEWER: Who performs female circumcision in the UK?
PARTICIPANT: The black market ... Or private. Some black market in some communities they do, privately [private medical practitioners] they do, privately not statutory. Practicing communities may do it like Sudan. There may be doctors who have been doing this after that [when she has given birth] because the woman needs to [be re-infibulated after she has given birth]. [FG2]

In one of the focus groups, women participants openly stated that private medical practitioners from FGM-performing communities, particularly Sudanese communities, are performing FGM or re-infibulation after they have given birth. Other interview participants from FGM-performing communities confirmed that medical practitioners perform FGM on the black market or in private hospitals under the guise of female genital cosmetic surgery.[82] Medical practitioners are often outside of the purview of legal surveillance and thus are

---

[82] News reports confirm that professionals have been struck off for offering to perform FGM. On 30 August 2013, a dentist was struck off by the General Dental Council for offering to perform FGM on two children following a meeting with a woman who was subsequently identified as an undercover journalist: <https://www.thetimes.co.uk/article/dentist-struck-off-for-offering-female-mutilat ion-63sw5f3gdfq> accessed 17 May 2021. Similarly, a doctor was struck off the medical register on 30 May 2014 after a Medical Practitioners Tribunal Service panel found he offered advice on arranging FGM: ' "Genital Mutilation" Doctor Struck off after Undercover Press Sting' *BBC News* (30 May 2014) <http://www.bbc.co.uk/news/uk-england-birmingham-27641431> accessed 17 May 2021.

probably one of the most able groups of professionals to perform FGM without detection. However, medical practitioners have a mandatory duty to report cases of FGM, which they discover during the course of their work, to the police.[83] When one of the focus group participants was probed about the identity of medical practitioners who perform FGM, she explained that she did not know the identity of the medical practitioner (or perhaps she was not willing to disclose it) because their identity is kept in the strictest confidence due to fears of prosecution:

> They are not necessarily things that people will tell you. Now everyone knows the law, they won't tell you, 'Oh I am going to cut my daughter and so and so is going to do it.' It is just kept silent. To find out who does it is really difficult. [P8, FGM-PCM, *Somalia*]

Rather than eliminating FGM, increased legal surveillance following the criminalisation of the practice appears to have resulted in FGM being performed further underground. Far from reducing the incidence of FGM, fears of punitive sanctions could have resulted in the dynamics of the practice changing to avoid detection. Findings from the interviews with professionals who work closely with FGM-performing communities, such as NGO workers, highlighted that they are aware that medical practitioners are performing FGM. A local authority employee who works with women at a grassroots level explained that communities pay medical practitioners to perform FGM in Britain, which makes it increasingly difficult to detect.

> You've got communities paying medical practitioners. Paying them off, making a quick buck on the side, it's disgusting … You've got two key figures that are in a position of trust, you've got your parents who you implicitly trust anyway and then you've got a doctor who you'd always trust as they are a doctor, wouldn't you … A child would think, mum and dad aren't going to hurt me, the doctor isn't going to hurt me. [P20, local authority employee, F]

The interview participant notes that girls who undergo FGM are unlikely to understand that the practice is illegal because they will probably implicitly trust their parents and medical practitioners. The different layers of secrecy of family and professionals makes the practice further concealed from public attention. Whilst some interview participants alleged that medical practitioners

---

[83] The focus group participants did not disclose the identity of the medical practitioners.

perform FGM, they also alleged that medical practitioners conceal information about FGM cases rather than referring cases to the police for safeguarding
purposes. According to an NGO worker specialising in FGM, medical practitioners are the most likely group of professionals to come into contact with
girls who have been cut and are at risk of FGM. However, medical practitioners
have been accused of not referring such cases to the police, which is in breach
of their professional obligations pursuant to section 5B of the FGM Act 2003
and could result in disciplinary sanctions.

> They [medical practitioners] have totally failed to report it. You can talk to
> the police and they will tell you that, exactly that ... They [police] were simply
> not getting any cases through. And then the NSPCC did that massive study
> in London finding out how many women with FGM had been diagnosed in
> clinic services and it was massive, huge amounts, 2000 women, one of whom
> was 12, there was a 12-year-old who had been diagnosed with FGM no follow
> up, no reporting, nothing. So, they have totally failed to report. [P58, NGO
> consultant, F]

Medical practitioners who were interviewed for this research explained that
there are a number of reasons why they do not report cases of FGM, namely
patient confidentiality, lack of training about FGM, a belief that punitive sanctions will not eliminate the practice, and a desire to work with communities to
change attitudes and beliefs. Medical practitioners appeared confused about
when and how to report cases of FGM even though mandatory reporting of
FGM makes it clear that when FGM has been discovered on a girl the case must
be reported to the police. Medical practitioners stated that they needed training
and clear guidance about when and how to act in cases of FGM. Without safeguards in place, this could leave girls at increased risk of FGM. However, it is
clear from a Home Affairs Select Committee report about FGM in 2015 that
medical practitioners continue to examine a number of patients with FGM, yet
these cases have not been referred to the police or the CPS, which suggests a
lack of coordination with law enforcement agents.[84]

---

[84] 'In Heartlands Hospital in Birmingham alone, 1,500 cases of FGM were recorded over the last five
years, with doctors seeing six patients who have undergone the procedure each week. There seems to
be a chasm between the amount of reported cases and the lack of prosecutions. Someone, somewhere,
is not doing their job effectively': House of Commons Home Affairs Committee, 'Abuse Unchecked' (n
14) 26. It goes on to state that Royal Colleges are not doing enough to encourage their members to report cases of FGM (27)..

FGM Performed abroad

Interview and focus group participants confirmed that girls are usually cut in Britain or are returned to their country of heritage to undergo FGM. One participant in the focus group explained that FGM is usually performed in the families' country of heritage during school holidays. Choosing to perform FGM in a family's country of heritage perhaps reinforces the cultural motivations for the practice and establishes a belonging to a sacred kinship group.

> I have heard of parents taking their girls back to the country, for the home country, like for a holiday and something happens during the holiday and then they come back and they are not the same again [laughs]. [FG1]

The quotation from the interview participant shows the difficulties of enforcing anti-FGM laws when FGM is performed outside of the jurisdiction. If FGM is performed abroad, it is difficult to gather evidence to prosecute for FGM in the UK, which is a further barrier to enforcing anti-FGM laws. A police office explains the challenges in gathering evidence against perpetrators when the practice is performed outside of the jurisdiction.

> It's a lot to do with gathering the evidence and actually getting people prepared to give evidence and to actually go to court is the main reason. And also, FGM is being performed abroad and places like that. It is probably a difficulty. It is really just evidential difficulties in knowing who to charge and it's just the families really refusing to give details. [P66, police officer, M]

The police officer interviewed appears to suggest that FGM-performing communities work together to ensure the practice is maintained without scrutiny from professionals, therefore gaining evidence from witnesses within the community is challenging. An NGO worker who works closely with women from FGM-performing communities explained that some families choose for FGM to be performed in a country where the practice is legal and medicalised, for example, in Dubai:

> We have certainly heard in Dubai that UK customers are their top customers for FGM. I'm sure there's other markets. In Dubai it's not illegal, it's a big holiday destination for Muslim people ... I was at the airport operations a couple of times. Airport Operation Limelight, Project Azure runs them with a couple of survivors who campaign, so they target countries with high

prevalence of FGM ... There's loads of police officers and survivors together talking to people on their way out [of England] and asking people about FGM. We identified at least one case, when I was there, one case of a trafficked girl and then there was another woman from Sierra Leone and she had with her the traditional stuff they use for the cutting celebrations, so she was stopped. I don't think they could prove anything. It would have been impossible to prove. [P59, NGO worker, F]

The NGO worker describes an initiative known as Operation Limelight[85] run by Project Azure, which is part of the Metropolitan Police. It is a safeguarding operation at the UK border to prevent and detect cases of FGM. The police and survivors speak with FGM-performing community members at the airport who are intending to travel abroad about FGM and the legal consequences of performing the practice. Whilst this initiative could raise awareness and even deter the practice, the efficacy of the initiative is less understood due to the lack of research. Otoo-Oyortey cautions against criminalising or stigmatising members of communities where FGM is present.[86] One example given is when 'Border Force' target flights destined for countries where FGM is present (especially during the Summer holidays). Instead, trained community champions are considered by NGOs to be best placed to conduct community outreach. A further challenge for professionals is proving that a girl has been cut on their return from abroad. Medical examinations are not permitted without the girl's parent's consent, as explained by a medical practitioner who specialises in FGM:

If children are taken home to be cut and returned to the UK that's a criminal offence ... the difficulty is that you can't examine them when they come back in again without the parents' consent otherwise it's an assault. [P43, doctor, F]

The ever-changing dynamics of the practice of FGM represent barriers to preventing FGM and prosecuting perpetrators. The changes to the

---

[85] See more information about the operation: Home Office and Border Force, 'Operation Limelight: Instructions to Police and Border Force Staff' (Guidance) (24 January 2020) <https://www.gov.uk/government/publications/operation-limelight-instructions-to-police-and-border-force-staff> accessed 7 March 2021. The operation has been adopted in the US by the US Immigration and Customs Enforcement, see, US Immigration and Customs Enforcement, 'ICE Leads Effort to Prevent Female Genital Mutilation at Newark Airport' (Newark NJ, 25 June 2018) <https://www.ice.gov/news/releases/ice-leads-effort-prevent-female-genital-mutilation-newark-airport> accessed 7 March 2021.

[86] Otoo-Oyortey, 'Challenges' (n 25).

practice identified by women from FGM-performing communities were well known amongst professionals. Despite awareness about the changes to the practice, FGM is able to continue underground without detection by professionals. If the law is unable to adapt to the changing nature of FGM, the law will become an ineffective tool in preventing FGM and prosecuting perpetrators.

Conclusion

The barriers to criminalising FGM through introducing laws that effectively deter and prevent FGM are complex and multifaceted. This chapter was only able to address a limited number of barriers that were identified by women from FGM-performing communities and professionals during interviews.[87] Despite heightened focus on anti-FGM initiatives, many women reported being unaware that FGM is a criminal offence, which reflects the marginalisation of FGM-performing communities from a political and democratic system that is responsible for designing and implementing laws. Indeed, women expressed reluctance to use the criminal justice system to provide legal redress in cases of FGM because of their experiences of structural racism and sexism through the law. When women experience discrimination through the law, they are less likely to seek protection through the law for FGM. One of the fundamental barriers to anti-FGM laws is public and political anti-FGM narratives, which have been described by interview participants as alienating communities because they cannot identify with labels of barbarism and child abuse. Instead, hyperbole rhetoric could further a racist and anti-immigration agenda whilst undermining anti-FGM initiatives. In fact, there was a strong suggestion that bold anti-FGM narratives that stir racist sentiments could have a counterproductive impact as communities resist efforts to encourage them to abandon the practice and instead continue it. Women and professionals highlighted the fluidity of the practice, as communities have changed the dynamics of FGM to ensure the practice continues underground without detection. The continuation of FGM but in an alternative way shows the entrenched nature of the practice and the need to encourage community collaboration in the end-FGM movement. To change community attitudes and beliefs towards FGM, a

---

[87] Chapter Four addresses the impact of female genital cosmetic surgery on the end-FGM campaign, as there are suggestions that the permissibility of female genital cosmetic surgery is perceived as hypocritical when FGM is prohibited and as a result is undermining attempts to abandon FGM.

narrative supported within the community is needed rather than a discourse which alienates and angers community members. Instead of singling out so-called cultural violence, FGM amongst other forms of violence against women and girls ought to be seen as an aberration of the individual man rather than framing it as stemming from patriarchal cultures, race, or religion.

4

Legal Hypocrisy: Female Genital Mutilation v Female Genital Cosmetic Surgery

Introduction

Female genital cosmetic surgery (FGCS) is widely performed by medical practitioners in Britain. There are many overlaps between FGCS and FGM, both practices involve unnecessary body modification for cultural or aesthetic reasons. However, there any many distinctions between the practices. FGCS is often sought by adult women for personal reasons attributed to individual decision-making,[1] whereas FGM is mainly performed on children for the purpose of continuing a cultural norm on the next generation. The arbitrary differentiation of FGM and FGCS is subject to extensive scholarly criticism.[2] Without imposing a value judgment on either practice, the practices are often compared and contrasted by academics and women from FGM-performing communities for different political aims. On the one hand, they are compared to further the objective of eliminating all forms of body modifications upon girls and women, whether FGM or FGCS. On the other hand, they are compared to support the proposition that FGM, like FGCS, should be permissible for adult women who exercise agency and choose to undergo the practice. Regardless of the political objectives for comparing and contrasting the practices, there are inevitable overlaps between the practices.[3] The perceived

---

[1] Surgeries on women's genitalia has a chequered history with reports that FGCS was carried out in the 1800s onwards to control women's sexuality under the guise of curing masturbation, hysteria, and lesbianism in the US and the UK. See, Isaac Baker Brown, 'On the Curability of Certain Forms of Insanity, Epilepsy, Catalepsy, And Hysteria' (1866) 1(278) The British Medical Journal 438; Ben Barker-Benfield, 'Sexual Surgery in Late-Nineteenth-Century America' (1975) 5(2) International Journal of Health Services 279; GJ Barker-Benfield, *The Horrors of the Half-Known Life: Male Attitudes toward Women and Sexuality in 19th. Century America* (Routledge 2004).

[2] For an analysis of the contradictory policy and legislative framework for FGM and FGCS see, Lisa R Avalos 'Female Genital Mutilation and Designer Vaginas in Britain: Crafting an Effective Legal and Policy Framework' (2015) 48(3) Vanderbilt Journal of Transnational Law 621 (hereafter Avalos, 'Designer Vaginas').

[3] There is extensive literature exploring the contradictions in law and practice in criminalising FGM whilst permitting FGCS. For a review of the inherent contradictions see, Marge Berer, 'Labia Reduction for Non-Therapeutic Reasons vs. Female Genital Mutilation: Contradictions in Law and Practice in Britain' (2010) 18(35) Reproductive Health Matters 106.

Female Genital Mutilation. Charlotte Proudman, Oxford University Press. © Charlotte Proudman 2022.
DOI: 10.1093/oso/9780198864608.003.0005

double standard in law which permits FGCS whilst criminalising FGM could act as a barrier to ending FGM. The legal hypocrisy inherent in the FGM and FGCS debate has roused anger amongst FGM-performing communities who perceive the law as discriminating against ethnic minority women. The double standard in law is used as an advocacy tool to defend the right to practice FGM. Professionals who were interviewed mainly rejected the perception that there is a legal double standard and thus did not regard the acceptability of FGCS as a barrier to ending FGM. The toleration of FGCS may result in unintended consequences for the anti-FGM movement because it could provide an avenue for the continuation of FGM under the guise of cosmetic surgery. It is likely that the debates about the criminalisation of FGM and acceptability of FGCS will become increasingly more significant as FGCS becomes more commonplace for adolescent girls and adult women. The permissibility of FGM is a barrier to the end-FGM movement and the criminalisation of FGM.

A Double Legal Standard?

The Prohibition of Female Circumcision 1985 Act and later the FGM Act 2003 permitted a legal double standard that has been the subject of extensive scholarly debate.[4] There are exceptions to the offence of female genital mutilation under the Prohibition of Female Circumcision 1985 Act and the FGM Act 2003, which has resulted in a legal loophole allowing FGCS to be performed by medical practitioners. A House of Lords Peer who was involved in the criminalisation of FGM in the early to mid-1980s explains that there was discussion with medical practitioners about ensuring an exception to the 1985 Act to allow FGCS to be performed.

> But apparently there are those women who feel somehow their genitalia don't match up to what they should be, rather like my nose or something like

---

[4] For an overview of the double standard see, Isabelle R Gunning, 'Arrogant Perception, World-Travelling and Multicultural Feminism: The Case of Female Genital Surgeries.' (1991) 23 Columbia Human Rights Law Review 189; Sally Sheldon and Stephen Wilkinson 'Female Genital Mutilation and Cosmetic Surgery: Regulating Non-Therapeutic Body Modification' (1998) 12(4) Bioethics 263 (hereafter Sheldon and Wilkinson, 'Non-Therapeutic Body Modification'); Clare Chambers, *Sex, Culture, and Justice: The Limits of Choice* (Penn State Press 2008); Moira Dustin, 'Female Genital Mutilation/Cutting in the UK: Challenging the Inconsistencies' (2010) 17(1) European Journal of Women's Studies 7 (hereafter Dustin, 'Inconsistencies'); Avalos, 'Designer Vaginas' (n 2); Ronan M Conroy, 'Female Genital Mutilation: Whose Problem, Whose Solution?: Tackle "Cosmetic" Genital Surgery in Rich Countries before Criticising Traditional Practices Elsewhere' (2006) 333(7559) British Medical Journal 106.

that, I find it very odd but I'm an old fashioned person and they seek ways of doing it, and having it fixed, and they get into a massive depression if it cannot be done. It's not for me to judge. You would have to talk to a doctor. Clinicians say if you were to ban all this, you would ban a legitimate operation to make a person happier, cosmetic surgery, I find it slightly odd but I am a man. I wouldn't have said it was a lobbying [medical] group, I would say that everyone deplored what Somalis and others do and all the historic stuff which is beyond belief but if you are enacting a piece of legislation you have to en-sure that it doesn't prevent legitimate forms of surgery.

[P21, House of Lords Peer, M]

The FGM Act 2003 did not amend the exemption in the 1985 Act and thus it allows operations to be performed by a registered medical practitioner when the operation is *necessary* for a girl or woman's *physical and mental health*.[5] For the purpose of determining whether an operation is neces-sary for the mental health of a girl or woman it is immaterial whether she or any other person believes that the operation is required as a *matter of custom or ritual*.[6] The crux of academics' criticism as highlighted by Dustin and Phillips is that the law allows a girl or woman to conform to Western norms of how her genitalia should physically look, but is prevented from conforming to minority cultural norms.[7] Concerns emerged during polit-ical debates about the Prohibition of Female Circumcision 1985 Act that the wording would criminalise cases where girls or women have anxieties about the shape or size of their healthy genitalia and their distress can only be al-leviated through surgery.[8] Medical colleges mobilised to block legislation that would criminalise FGCS and, as a result, the government introduced an amendment to the proposed legislation to allow for surgery which is ne-cessary for physical or mental health.[9] In a parliamentary debate about the 1985 Act, Baroness Masham of Ilton noted that she had received a letter from the Royal College of Obstetricians and Gynaecologists making clear that the initial draft of the legislation needed to be amended to permit sur-gery on medical grounds.

---

[5] Female Genital Mutilation Act 2003, s 1(2)(a) (hereafter FGM Act 2003).
[6] ibid s 1(5).
[7] Moira Dustin and Anne Phillips, 'Whose Agenda Is It? Abuses of Women and Abuses of "Culture" in Britain' (2008) 8(3) Ethnicities 405 (hereafter Dustin and Phillips, 'Whose Agenda Is It').
[8] ibid.
[9] ibid.

The amendment, if it prohibits female circumcision, might prohibit legitimate surgery. I should like to read a letter I received only last night from the president of the Royal College of Obstetricians and Gynaecologists, after I had written to him and sent a copy of Hansard containing the proceedings of the Committee stage. The letter says: It is in the view of this college very important to have 'mental' and 'physical' included, as mental conditions may require surgical treatment to get rid of the mental problems. The idea that mental problems are all treated by psychiatric means is just not true. I note that Lord Hatch is keen to substitute 'non-medical factors'. This would not be acceptable as it is very unclear what 'non-medical factors' are. If, for example, a girl had a mental illness as a result of not having circumcision, would she then have a medical reason for doing it? It is very unclear. In my view, this could make female circumcision legal. After long reflection it seems to me that it is necessary to ban female circumcision on the grounds of custom and ritual. One has to balance the benefits of offending a few who object to the wording on racist grounds against obtaining a Bill which bans what is barbaric practice. I think a few who are offended would need to accept a wording in the interests of banning this practice. I am myself no longer worried about the word 'ritual'. I have discussed this with my own bishop and he said it was a useful word in this context and he felt the Bill was clearer for it.[10]

It is clear that parliamentarians at the time intended to permit surgery when it is necessary for mental or physical health but there is no mention of surgery on aesthetic grounds. Furthermore, Baroness Masham of Ilton noted that ritual justifications must not be used to justify surgery on mental health grounds. Interestingly, Baroness Masham appears acutely aware of objections on grounds of racism but these arguments are not developed further in the debates, which reflects the fact that those participating in parliamentary debates lack experience and knowledge of FGM. The intention of the exemptions was to ensure neutrality, thus the exemptions are supposed to relate to anyone. However, in practice the laws are targeted towards girls and women from FGM-performing communities as they are refused FGCS. Lord McNair commented:[11]

---

[10] Prohibition of Female Circumcision Bill, HL Deb 18 June 1985, vol 465, cols 207–24 <https://api.parliament.uk/historic-hansard/lords/1985/jun/18/prohibition-of-female-circumcision-bill> accessed 4 March 2021.

[11] ibid.

The purpose of the amendment is to find, as the noble Lord put it, a neutral formula which not even the most hypersensitive, race-conscious person could possibly find offensive.

Lord Kennett noted in a straightforward fashion that the intention is to prohibit surgeries on Black people's genitalia:[12]

> My Lords, I shall be very brief. Lord McNair asked: what do we mean by female circumcision? It was a rhetorical question. The answer he expected to leap into our minds was, 'Operations carried out on the female genitalia by black people'. That, in his view, would be the honest and straightforward and frank answer.

A strict interpretation of section 1 of the FGM Act 2003 makes it plain that surgery on a girl or woman's genitalia for aesthetic purposes is a criminal offence when the person does not have mental health issues and there is no physical health justification for the surgery. Consider a situation which often arises in contexts where women and girls seek FGCS. A person is experiencing mental health concerns because her genitalia does not conform to beauty ideals because her labia majora should be small and thin.[13] However, the person's mental health issues arise from mainstream culture or customs that depicts ideal female genitalia, which is often unattainable without surgery. According to section 1 of the FGM Act 2003, a person's beliefs about matters of custom are immaterial when assessing their mental health, thus any surgical operation is likely to constitute a criminal offence. A Peer in the House of Lords who was involved in the amendments to the FGM Act 2003, which were adopted in the Serious Crime Act 2015, discussed her concerns that FGM could be performed under the guise of FGM. However, she noted that this did not appear to be a significant concern at present.

Is FGCS criminalised by the FGM Act 2003?

> My understanding was, it wasn't. We did have some discussions about it. The worry was always someone would be taken to a clinic and under the guise of cosmetic surgery they would be mutilated. If you got as far as getting to a prosecution you would be able to identify medically whether it was genuinely

---

[12] ibid.
[13] As highlighted by medical professionals, there is wide variation in female genital appearance and as such there is no 'normal' appearance, see, Jillian Lloyd and others, 'Female Genital Appearance: "Normality" Unfolds' (2005) 112(5) British Journal of Obstetrics and Gynaecology 643.

cosmetic surgery or a child had been mutilated. It may turn out to be an issue but I am not convinced it's the biggest issue we are dealing with. It may be further down the line when we have made progress on some other stuff that we look at whether mutilation is being done by pretending it is cosmetic surgery but the two are very different.

[P22, House of Lords Peer, F]

The House of Lords Peer appears to remember some discussions about FGCS and as can be seen from the *UK Hansard* debates, there were debates about FGM and FGCS when the 1985 Act was debated. An ethical opinion paper published by the Royal College of Obstetricians and Gynaecologists in 2013 notes that there is a perceived overlap between FGCS and procedures under the FGM Act 2003 which leads to complications, but the case for an outright ban on FGCS is weak because there is no evidence that FGCS is 'generally harmful'.[14] Unfortunately, the paper offers limited guidance on the legal status of FGCS. The Home Affairs Committee published a report about FGM: 'Abuse Unchecked' in 2016, noting that evidence from the police, midwives, and campaigners confirms that greater clarity is required in respect of the law on FGCS. The ambiguity about the legal position of FGCS under the FGM Act 2003 continues.

Under the FGM Act 2003, FGM is a criminal offence and consent is no defence. It is harder to justify the ban on FGM for adult women when FGCS is permitted without any meaningful opposition. The law tolerates a girl or woman undergoing FGCS in order to conform to Western cultural norms in having the 'ideal' feminine genitalia, while conformity to minority cultural norms in the form of FGM is criminalised. The permissibility of FGCS whilst FGM is criminalised for adult women is attributed to unattractive presumptions about the capacity of women of colour to consent to surgery on their genitalia. The Western woman is constructed as superseding the influence of culture, making an autonomous, empowered, and authentic choice to undergo FGCS.[15] The question of choice to undergo FGM for a women of colour is seen as overdetermined by culture and therefore impossible.[16] If FGM was banned

---

[14] Royal College of Obstetricians & Gynecologists, 'Ethical Opinion Paper, Ethical considerations in relation to female genital cosmetic surgery (FGCS)' (October 2013) <https://www.rcog.org.uk/globa lassets/documents/guidelines/ethics-issues-and-resources/rcog-fgcs-ethical-opinion-paper.pdf> accessed 17 May 2021.

[15] Rosemary Gillespie, 'Women, the Body and Brand Extension in Medicine: Cosmetic Surgery and the Paradox of Choice' (1997) 24(4) Women & Health 69 (hereafter Gillespie, 'Women, the Body and Brand Extension').

[16] See Deborah A Sullivan, *Cosmetic Surgery: The Cutting Edge of Commercial Medicine in America* (Rutgers University Press 2001) (hereafter Sullivan, *Commercial Medicine in America*); Virginia Braun, "THE WOMEN ARE DOING IT FOR THEMSELVES." The Rhetoric of Choice and Agency Around

because of the harm to women, scholars[17] contend that we might expect the law to ban FGCS for adult women—or—permit less invasive forms of FGM for adults which are akin to FGCS.[18] The key distinction according to the law is that cosmetic surgery reflects 'choice' defined by sexual freedom outside of cultural pressures, while FGM reflects cultural coercion and the absence of agency.[19] The law could be guilty of infantilising women of colour who are deemed incapable of consenting to surgery on their genitalia.

A case of FGCS performed for purely aesthetic purposes, where the patient had no mental or physical health concerns, was reported in the academic literature and referred to the police. In a highly unusual case, Veale and Daniels performed a cosmetic clitoridectomy on a thirty-three-year-old woman and wrote about the operation in a journal article.[20] The woman had already had cosmetic labiaplasty and sought a clitoridectomy for aesthetic reasons. The patient was assessed by a psychiatrist, Dr Veale, and it was confirmed that there were no mental health concerns. The operation was performed by Dr Daniels who noted that the procedure improved her genital appearance, sexual satisfaction, and quality of life. The woman had reportedly shaven her pubic hair for the past fourteen years and was in the process of permanent hair removal, feeling it was more hygienic and preferred by her husband.[21] The authors note that there were 'no cultural or religious reasons for having a clitoridectomy' because she did not identify with FGM cultures.[22] The authors took the view that if labiaplasty is undertaken for cosmetic reasons then there is 'no reason that a clitoridectomy should not be done on the same grounds'.[23] Consultant obstetrician, Professor Susan Bewley, referred the case to the police as she believed

Female Genital 'Cosmetic Surgery' (2009) 24(60) Australian Feminist Studies 233 (hereafter Braun, 'DOING IT FOR THEMSELVES').

[17] See Dustin and Phillips, 'Whose Agenda Is It' (n 7); Sheldon and Wilkinson, 'Non-Therapeutic Body Modification' (n 4).
[18] Dr B Kelly and C Foster explore three case studies to show the overlap between the two practices. They note that many forms of FGCS are anatomically covered by the FGM Act 2003 and would thus constitute FGM. Moreover, the pressures that women experience to undergo FGCS are pressures which society should disapprove and that legislation may have a place in resisting. In contrast, genital piercing is perceived as entirely separate to FGM and FGCS and therefore should not be regulated by the law: C Foster and B Kelly, 'Should Female Genital Cosmetic Surgery and Genital Piercing be Regarded Ethically and Legally as Female Genital Mutilation?' (2012) 119(4) British Journal of Obstetrics and Gynaecology 389.
[19] Juliet Rogers, Law's Cut on the Body of Human Rights: Female Circumcision, Torture, and Scared Flesh (Routledge 2013).
[20] David Veale and Joe Daniels, 'Cosmetic Clitoridectomy in a 33-Year-Old Woman' (2012) 41(3) Archives of Sexual Behavior 725 (hereafter Veale and Daniels, 'Cosmetic Clitoridectomy').
[21] ibid 726.
[22] ibid 727.
[23] ibid 728.

it constituted FGM.[24] After a three-year police investigation, the Crown Prosecution Service dropped the case[25] concluding that there was no realistic prospect of conviction.

Typically, the domains of FGM and FGCS have been constructed as polar opposites.[26] However, increasing numbers of academic studies explore the fluidity and parallels between the practices.[27] There are obvious differences between FGM and FGCS, such as the demographic of women and girls undergoing the practices, the context in which the practices are performed, and the purpose and the meanings ascribed to the practices. There are also similarities between FGM and FGCS in that the practices involve excision of women's and girls' genitalia for the purpose of conforming to an 'ideal' standard defined by cultural and social norms of their kinship groups. A key argument for undergoing FGM or FGCS is that women's bodies in their natural state are unattractive and in need of surgical modification.[28] FGM is performed due to cultural beliefs about the need for clean, attractive, and feminine genitalia, which is similar to the justification for FGCS, where women seek prepubescent genitalia featured in mainstream advertisements.[29] Both FGM and FGCS are performed to ensure that women comply with cultural and societal norms about how women's bodies should look and function.[30]

Scholars including African-American women and cultural relativists connect FGM and FGCS as a means of arguing for the decriminalisation and medicalisation of FGM, like FGCS. Scholar, Korieh, compared the practices and argued that one might conclude that neither practice is oppressive because the resulting appearance is considered by Western and African women as an

---

[24] Bewley has written extensively about the hypocrisy in criminalising FGM whilst turning a blind eye to FGCS, see, Susan Bewley, 'Disingenuous Lack of Interests in Labiaplasty Debate' (2015) 122(3) British Journal of Obstetrics and Gynaecology 444.

[25] Martin Bentham, 'Doctor Cleared Over FGM Says Women Should Be Free to Have Intimate Surgery' Evening Standard (London, 28 February 2017) <https://www.standard.co.uk/news/health/doctor-cleared-over-fgm-says-women-should-be-free-to-have-intimate-surgery-a3477941.html> accessed 4 March 2021.

[26] This is not only the case in the UK but also in Switzerland with FGM depicted as the product of 'primitive society' and FGCS as the product of a science-orientated one, see, Dina Bader, 'Picturing Female Circumcision and Female Genital Cosmetic Surgery: A Visual Framing Analysis of Swiss Newspapers, 1983–2015' (2019) 19(8) Feminist Media Studies 1159.

[27] While the focus of this study is on Britain, the global beauty market is impacting upon the prevalence of FGM across the world, as the practice continues to be performed but under the guise of FGCS.

[28] Lois Bibbings and Peter Alldridge, 'Sexual Expression, Body Alteration, and the Defence of Consent' (1993) 20(3) Journal of Law and Society 356; LS Bibbings, 'Female Circumcision: Mutilation or Modification' in Jo Bridgeman and Susan Mills (eds), Law and Body Politics: Regulating the Female Body (Dartmouth 1995) 151.

[29] Dustin, 'Inconsistencies' (n 4).

[30] For an analysis on the drivers behind the growing phenomenon of FGCS, the following book has been written by multi-disciplinary experts: Sarah M Creighton and Lih-Mei Liao, Female Genital Cosmetic Surgery: Solution to What Problem? (Cambridge University Press 2019).

improvement of normal genitalia.[31] Intersectional identity vectors of gender, race, class, and culture determine how women from different backgrounds with different experiences choose to express their sexuality. African women may *choose* FGM, while Western women may *choose* FGCS. Women's choices are likely to be linked to their cultural backgrounds and motivated by cultural factors. Some African women do not consider FGM as mutilation just like many Western women do not view cosmetic procedures as mutilation, and yet both procedures involve excision of women's genitalia. Women from FGM-performing communities argue that if Western women have a right to express their sexuality and are pro-*choice*, then women of colour should also have the right to choose how they express their sexuality.[32] Similar language and rhetoric to the cosmetic surgery or beauty industry is adopted by women interview participants who argue that FGM is a choice, liberating and empowering for the individual woman rather than using language of cultural norms and expectations.

Feminist scholars also draw links between FGM and FGCS, but for a different political purpose. While feminist groups did not raise the legal double standard as an issue when the Prohibition of Female Circumcision Act 1985 was introduced, since the late 1980s feminists have begun to address the cultural arrogance that has seeped through the international campaign against FGM, while FGCS is tolerated.[33] There has been a growth in feminist literature linking FGM and FGCS due to concerns that FGCS is another form of FGM performed in cosmetic surgery clinics. Some Western feminists have begun to draw analogies between FGM and FGCS to show that the issue is not just about barbaric Africa and the control of African women's sexuality, but it is about the abuse of women's bodies on a global scale, suggesting that *both* practices are oppressive to women.[34] Indeed, defining both practices as partly emanating from culture could have the effect of preventing the racial stereotyping of FGM as a backwards cultural practice that needs to be challenged.

---

[31] Chima Korieh, '"Other" Bodies: Western Feminism, Race, and Representation in Female Circumcision Discourse' in Obioma Nnaemeka (ed), *Female Circumcision and the Politics of Knowledge: African Women in Imperialist Discourses* (Praegar 2005) 111 (hereafter Korieh, '"Other" Bodies"').

[32] See, ibid and Obioma Nnaemeka 'African Women, Colonial Discourses, and Imperialist Interventions' in Obioma Nnaemeka (ed), *Female Circumcision and the Politics of Knowledge: African Women in Imperialist Discourses* (Praegar 2005) 27.

[33] Dustin and Phillips, 'Whose Agenda Is It' (n 7).

[34] Germaine Greer, *The Whole Woman* (Doubleday 1999) (hereafter Greer, *Whole Woman*); Simone Weil Davis, 'Loose Lips Sink Ships' (2002) 28(1) Feminist Studies 7 (hereafter Weil Davis, 'Loose Lips'); Kathy Davis, 'Responses to W. Njambi's "Dualisms and Female Bodies in Representations of African Female Circumcision: A Feminist Critique": Between Moral Outrage and Cultural Relativism' (2004) 5(3) Feminist Theory 305 (hereafter Davis, 'Responses').

Making connections between non-Western cultural practices and Western beauty practices has allowed scholars to deconstruct the binary of 'liberated uncovered Western woman' and 'oppressed veiled Muslim woman'.[35] Feminist scholars, Jeffreys, Weil Davis, and Duits and Van Zoonen argue that girls wearing the headscarf or undergoing FGM and girls engaging in beauty practices or undergoing FGCS are denied agency and autonomy by cultures that compel them to conform to patriarchal and oppressive norms.[36] FGCS is a cultural practice, which has emerged because of deep-rooted discourses and beliefs about beauty that emanate from societal norms. FGM and FGCS are both constructed as patriarchal practices imposed on women to ensure that they conform to ideal body types within their communities.

The political agenda of the Western feminist comparative thesis is to reconceptualise FGCS as a harmful cultural practice in the West, thus inviting the legal prohibition of FGCS as commensurate to FGM. Western feminists, Davis and Weil Davis, contend that the practices are linked to ideas about gendered body performance and gendered body norms that dominate their communities.[37] Body norms are enforced through feelings of bodily shame when women are unable to conform, for example, uncut girls might worry that their genitalia are unclean. When there is no reasonable alternative to undergoing FGM or FGCS, consent to either practice is highly suspect. According to Dustin, one way of facilitating a decline in harmful practices 'would be to argue for the application of consistent principles of choice and the recognition of all non-therapeutic bodily modifications as "cultural"'.[38] There are variations in how this would work in practice. For instance, both practices might be criminalised for children but permitted for adult women or there would be a blanket ban on all practices regardless of the age of the subject person.

Comparing and making links between the practices, also known as the 'analogue approach' as coined by academic Carolyn Pedwell, has become a way of countering cultural essentialism.[39] The purpose of making links serves different

---

[35] Carolyn Pedwell, 'Sometimes What's Not Said Is Just as Important as What Is: Transnational Feminist Encounters' in K Davis and M Evans (eds), *Transatlantic Conversations: Feminism as Travelling Theory. The Feminist Imagination—Europe and Beyond* (Ashgate Publishing Limited 2011) 188 (hereafter Pedwell, 'What's Not Said').

[36] Sheila Jeffreys, *Beauty and Misogyny* (Routledge 2005) (hereafter Jeffreys, *Beauty and Misogyny*); Weil Davis, 'Loose Lips' (n 34); Linda Duits and Liesbet Van Zoonen, 'Headscarves and Porno-Chic: Disciplining Girls' Bodies in the European Multicultural Society' (2006) 13(2) European Journal of Women's Studies 103 (hereafter Duits and Van Zoonen, 'Headscarves and Porno Chic').

[37] Davis, 'Responses' (n 34); Weil Davis, 'Loose Lips' (n 34).

[38] Dustin, 'Inconsistencies' (n 4) 20.

[39] Carolyn Pedwell, 'Theorizing "African" Female Genital Cutting and "Western" Body Modifications: A Critique of the Continuum and Analogue Approaches' (2007) 86(1) Feminist Review 45.

political agendas. Feminists have compared the practices to bolster their argument that FGM and FGCS are oppressive to women and both practices should be criminalised. Defenders of FGM, on the other hand, have used FGCS to further their argument that if FGCS is tolerated on the basis of 'individual choice', FGM should also be permitted for adult women who choose to undergo the practice. Making links between FGM and FGCS has become increasingly common amongst scholars, but it is not without criticism. Pedwell criticises scholars who seek to mobilise a narrative of gendered similarity across cultures and practices.[40] In doing so, scholars slip back into a form of essentialist cultural difference. Western feminists essentialise women by lumping them into one group based on their gender rather than recognising how intersections of race, class, and culture impact upon women's unique experiences of FGM and FGCS. As a result, scholars are criticised for failing to provide an intersectional analysis of power based on race, class, nationality, and religion, which have varying implications for women's agency to consent to surgical interventions.[41] Whilst feminists are criticised for comparing the practices, defenders of FGM are rarely criticised for making analogies between the practices to serve their political goals, perhaps due to fears that already marginalised groups of women of colour would be further criticised.

What Women Really Think to FGCS

There is a growing volume of literature debating the double standard in law that permits FGCS while criminalising FGM. Interview participants from FGM-performing communities and professionals were well informed of the legal double standard. Women and professionals who opposed FGM were vocal in highlighting the perceived double legal standard, which they argued is undermining anti-FGM initiatives because the law tolerates FGM under the guise of FGCS. Interviews with women from FGM-performing communities who supported FGM strategically linked FGM and FGCS as comparable practices, which reaffirmed their arguments that FGM should *also* be permitted in law. Findings from two focus groups showed that women of Somali heritage connected the practices and advocated for the decriminalisation and the medicalisation of FGM.

---

[40] Pedwell, 'What's Not Said' (n 35).
[41] ibid.

- If a woman volunteers that she wants female circumcision, I think that's her choice the same way cosmetic surgery is her choice. If it's on a child either of them [FGM or FGCS] it's wrong. But if it's a woman who [is] over the age of 18 [and] wants to get this done for her own reasons I don't see the problem with it.
- I agree. If they want to put silicon pads in the foreheads or in their arms that's up to them because it's choice.
- I think you should implement the same laws as plastic surgery, so it's your choice. If you want it. Obviously give her a few pamphlets and an introduction on the side effects.
- I don't think it's [FGM] different to any plastic surgery as long as you are the age of consent you should be able to do everything and anything.
- These women do it [FGCS] cosmetically when they have grown up and they do it to make it look nice and tidy what is the problem if they are doing it from a young age because FGM sometimes is similar to that except it's from the clitoris and stitching up. So why is there any difference between that and FGM? If someone is getting it done at a young age. So for example someone is getting it done at 7 or 8 years of age back home they do that but without touching the clitoris and stitching it up, would that be seen here as wrong because people are doing that here where they have grown up for cosmetic reasons. What's the difference? [FG1]

Similarly to the women in the focus groups, scholar Korieh connected FGM and FGCS as a means of arguing for the equal treatment of the practices.[42] One of the key arguments in the focus groups for linking the practices is women's *consent* to FGM or FGCS. If women in the West have a right to express their sexuality and undergo FGCS then African women should have the same right to choose FGM regardless of the reasons for the practice. Women in the focus group adopted the language of individual choice to support FGM, arguing that it is performed for 'her own reasons'. FGM is justified for individual reasons which reflects Western discourse of individual rights and freedoms. Rather than arguing that FGM is imperative for group identity or cultural reasons, Western narratives of individuality and liberty have been co-opted by women to support the legalisation of FGM. Anger and hostility towards the legal double standard could justify the continuation of FGM and encourage communities to resist anti-FGM initiatives, resulting in the criminal law having

---

[42] Korieh, ' "Other" Bodies" ' (n 31).

limited impact. There was evidence to suggest during the interviews that FGCS could offer a legitimate avenue for individuals to continue FGM under the guise of FGCS. In a focus group, an eighteen-year-old Somali-born woman explained that two friends also of Somali heritage were subjected to FGM but under the guise of FGCS in the UK before they married.

PARTICIPANT: My generation because they can't practise female circumcision, female cutting, they consider other avenues like cosmetic surgery of the vagina. The younger generation are not happy with the shape of it, that's the thing. I don't really talk to them in that explicit language. I have friends of mine who were going to get married and they said they were not happy with how it looks so they were trying to find other ways they could enhance it. They just want it to look better because we, they are from Somalia and they are worried they have a large clitoris or something like that. So they have to get it done because they [their husbands] will see and if they go down the FGM avenues they can get negative conditions [they could be prosecuted]. I have two friends who have done it.

INTERVIEWER: Was it done privately or on the NHS?

I don't know. They didn't do it outside [the UK].

INTERVIEWER: Was it the labia or the clitoris [that was cut]?

I am not sure they just told me they got it done. I wasn't aware. They are in their 30s, they don't live with their mum and they are getting married.

INTERVIEWER: Why don't they have FGM instead?

PARTICIPANT: Because it's not the same I think. Anaesthetic. They will have anaesthetic. I think it's different than the FGM but it's not good. They weren't happy with how it looks for cosmetic reasons. But that's also abuse if it would be done to a young person. [FG2]

The interview participant describes two friends of Somali heritage who exercised their agency and chose to undergo FGCS. The participant adopted the Western discourse of choice, arguing that the surgery was performed to make the genitalia 'look better' or 'enhance it' and she was not happy with the appearance 'for cosmetic reasons'. The language of the beauty industry has been co-opted by communities that support FGM as a means of legitimising the practice. There was no mention of culture as a reason for undergoing the surgery, but she did mention the impending life-changing event of marriage. The cultural expectation for women to undergo FGM and to ensure that their genitalia looks similar to other Somalian women could have resulted in pressure to have the surgery. In reality, both practices emanate from cultural pressures in the West[43] or in Somalia to have genitalia that conform to norms and values within a cultural context. However, the permissibility of FGCS, allowed two women to surgically alter their genitalia and evade anti-FGM laws. Women who undergo FGCS, such as in this quotation, exercise agency to navigate the legal system to continue the practice of FGM. Rather than deterring and preventing FGM, the law has given women a legal avenue to continue FGM. The legal double standard also roused anger and frustration amongst FGM-community members. An interview participant in a focus group argued that it is disproportionate for a parent to arrange for her child to undergo FGM and they could be imprisoned for up to fourteen years but if a cosmetic surgeon performed FGCS on their child, they would not be criminalised.

> If these parents take the child to a clinic and say I want this [FGCS] done to my child they will not get 14 years imprisonment. However, if [it was] some-body from Somalia, they would [be criminalised]. So I think it's totally unfair. This gets 14 years, I think they should get 14 years as well. [FG1]

FGCS is legitimised by the law because it is performed by cosmetic surgeons upon women who are presumed to be capable of consenting.[44] In contrast, FGM is a crime which specifically targets and criminalises migrant communities who continue to perform the practice. The specific criminal offence of FGM raises issues of cultural diversity, race, and respect for cultural customs, particularly in a context where FGCS is permitted.[45] The legal double standard incites anger and resentment among FGM-performing communities who describe feeling discriminated against by the law.

> Yes, I do think there is a double standard in law. I think there should be one law for all whether for women over a certain age or not because there are double standards. We are trying to bring change in practicing communities about cutting and removing parts of the female genitalia and I think it should be the same for all. [P13, FGM-PCM and nurse, *Somalia*]

---

[43] Research undertaken by Bramwell shows that women's external genitals as depicted in women's magazines are usually obscured in some way or represented as forming a smooth curve between the thighs which can result in unrealistic expectations about how women's genitalia look. Ros Bramwell, 'Invisible Labia: The Representation of Female External Genitals in Women's Magazines' (2002) 17(2) Sexual and Relationship Therapy 187.

[44] Sullivan, *Commercial Medicine in America* (n 16); Braun, 'DOING IT FOR THEMSELVES' (n 16).

[45] Bronwyn Winter, 'Women, the Law, and Cultural Relativism in France: The Case of Excision' (1994) 19(4) Signs: Journal of Women in Culture and Society 939.

FGM for me is against the law. It should be against the law irrespective of who you are and where you come from. [P11, FGM-PCM and NGO worker, *Unknown*, F]

The participants argue that the law should apply to all women rather than targeting ethnic minority communities. Furthermore, the interview participant of Somali heritage highlights that the legal double standard impacts upon attempts to eliminate FGM within communities. There is a profound difference in the legal treatment of the two practices, which is likely to increase concerns that women are being discriminated against. The criminalisation of FGM legitimises state interference into the lives of marginalised ethnic minority women, which increases the risk of their children being moved into state care and the arrest and prosecution of women who are themselves victims of FGM.[46] Women are likely to experience structural barriers through the criminal justice system that might deter them from accessing the law. Targeting migrant communities with anti-FGM legislation could inhibit change in eliminating FGM rather than encouraging it.

One way of eliminating the legal double standard is to criminalise FGCS, thus both practices would be prohibited in law. A minority of women interview participants linked FGM and FGCS and argued for the prohibition of both practices for children whilst allowing the practices for adult women. Interview participants used a rhetoric that mirrored feminist scholars' analysis of genitalia modification. Interviewees argued that FGM and FGCS stem from cultural pressures that seek to regulate girls' and women's bodies and sexuality.[47] Women are undergoing surgery to conform to the ideal genitalia defined by cultural expectations in mainstream Western society and in other cultures.

- I think the problem really lies with, why does a 13-year-old or adult really think that her private part is not beautiful. It's this whole sexualized society that they've been exposed to.
- In a way it's down to socialisation. She would probably see it from other girls and think that hers is not pretty enough. In the same way in Somalia they will probably see other girls with it done and think why is not mine looking that way. So, it's the same reason but with different cultures.

---

[46] For an overview on the layers of discrimination that ethnic minority women experience through the criminal justice system see, Nathalie J Sokoloff and Ida Dupont, 'Domestic Violence at the Intersections of Race, Class, and Gender Challenges and Contributions to Understanding Violence against Marginalized Women in Diverse Communities' (2005) 11(1) Violence Against Women 38.

[47] Duits and Van Zoonen, 'Headscarves and Porno Chic' (n 36).

I think in a way they are both wrong and they should both be illegal if they are under 18. [FG1]

INTERVIEWER: Have you come across FGCS?
PARTICIPANT: It's like the same thing [as FGM] ... you are not doing it for you, you are doing it for men. It's exactly the same. They made the name [FGCS] sound nicer than infibulation. [P12, FGM-PCM and teacher, *Somalia*]

The arguments advocated by a minority of participants evoke the same thesis as feminist scholars who have drawn links between FGM and FGCS for different political ends. Feminists argue that the issue of FGM is not *just* about African communities but about the abuse of women's bodies on a global scale. The political purpose of comparing both practices is to advocate for reconceptualising FGCS as a harmful cultural practice in the West that should be criminalised. Similarly, women interview participants argued that both practices stem from cultural socialisation about the accepted physical appearance of one's body and underlying pressures to conform to one's kinship group.[48] Women experience cultural pressure to conform to body modification surgeries for fear of rejection and social stigma in Western societies and in FGM-performing communities.[49] If women are socialised or pressurised to undergo FGM or FGCS, it raises questions about the validity of women's consent to the embodied practices. Academic Carolyn Pedwell cautioned feminists against mobilising a narrative of gendered similarity across cultures, due to fears of essentialising women rather than recognising differences on the basis of race, class, age, and culture.[50] Quotations from the interviews show that women from FGM-performing communities mobilised a narrative of gendered similarity when arguing for the equal treatment of FGM and FGCS. Pedwell does not consider the likelihood that women from across the globe, not solely Western feminists, draw comparisons between divergent cultural practices for different political ends.[51] Furthermore, Pedwell's approach lacks nuance in the conceptualisation of culture, as she overlooks the comparable cultural drivers that underpin FGM and FGCS, such as the cultural pressures emerging from beliefs about beauty and women's roles in society.[52]

---

[48] Greer, *Whole Woman* (n 34); Weil Davis, 'Loose Lips' (n 34); Davis, 'Responses' (n 34).
[49] Dustin, 'Inconsistencies' (n 4).
[50] Pedwell, 'What's Not Said' (n 35).
[51] ibid.
[52] ibid.

FGCS: Divergent Opinions amongst Professionals

Women interview participants from FGM-performing communities linked the practices for the purpose of opposing anti-FGM laws and supporting the decriminalisation and medicalisation of FGM in line with FGCS for adult women. In contrast, the majority of professionals believed that the practices are manifestly different. Many professionals failed to consider whether women might believe that there is a double legal standard and whether such attitudes might present as a barrier to ending FGM. A lawyer resisted any attempt to suggest that FGCS and FGM are comparable practices:

> Is there anything wrong with a woman who has the capacity to make a choice and is not under any duress, cultural pressure and goes into Harley Street and says this [FGCS] is what I want, is this wrong? [P46, lawyer, M]

There was a general perception amongst professionals that women who are not from FGM-performing communities are able to supersede cultural influences and make empowered choices to undergo FGCS while women from FGM-performing communities are influenced by culture and unable to make autonomous decisions.[53] The lawyer did not believe that defining the practices as different in law constitutes a barrier to the law being implemented; instead the participant defined the practices as divergent. A cosmetic surgeon also distinguished between the practices on the grounds of culture and religion, which often underpin the motivations for FGM but these motivations are irrelevant when a woman is considering undergoing FGCS.

> Surgery on the labia [FGCS] I think is a distinctly different procedure from FGM. In the sense that it is clearly on cultural and religious grounds. [P73, cosmetic surgeon, M]

The cosmetic surgeon believed that cultural and religious reasons for undergoing genital surgery only exist within FGM-performing communities. The participant did not acknowledge that women undergo FGCS because of cultural norms in Western society about how a woman's genitalia should look and function. Similarly, a consultant gynaecologist and obstetrician disassociated FGM and FGCS on the grounds of divergent motivations.

---

[53] Gillespie, 'Women, the Body and Brand Extension' (n 15); Sullivan, *Commercial Medicine in America* (n 16); Braun, 'DOING IT FOR THEMSELVES' (n 16).

FGM is more obviously about removing sexual pleasure and access and the other [FGCS] is about enhancing or about improving sexuality and have enhancements, or you remove the clitoral hood so the clitoris sticks out more, in the sense of it is a cultural determination of what is normal for a woman's behaviour. So, no I don't think they are the same thing. [P42, consultant gynaecologist and obstetrician, F]

The interview participant describes FGCS as enhancing and empowering in liberating a woman's sexuality to make her more sexually enticing, while FGM is described as curtailing a woman's sexuality and 'removing sexual pleasure and access'. The interview participant does not consider that women in different cultural contexts *choose* to express their sexuality in a variety of ways.[54] African women who undergo FGM also use the language of liberation and individualistic choice to justify *choosing* FGM. Furthermore, the two interview participants fail to consider whether both practices stem from cultural beliefs about women's bodies. Feminists Davis and Weil Davis argue that FGM and FGCS are linked to ideas about gendered body norms within different cultural contexts.[55] Cultural norms are the drivers for the persistence of FGM and FGCS. Women conform to ideals of 'normal' genitalia due to fear of shame and rejection within their respective communities.[56]

A small number of professionals argued that there is a double standard in law in prohibiting FGM while permitting FGCS, which reflected the attitudes of women from FGM-performing communities. Many of the professionals who believed that there is a legal double standard work closely with women from FGM-performing communities who use the law as an advocacy tool to undermine the end-FGM movement. A lawyer who also works closely with women from FGM-performing communities explained that both practices stem from patriarchal and oppressive norms that dictate how a woman's genitalia should look and function.

When women are starting to mutilate themselves, whether FGM or female genital surgery, that's a very different animal because it is a legacy of male cultural dominance and oppression ... It seems to me that the genesis of that cultural practice is also steeped in patriarchy, conforming to some idealized, stereotyped view of an acceptable sexually enticing woman, which derived

---

54 Korieh, ' "Other" Bodies" ' (n 31).
55 Davis, 'Responses' (n 34); Weil Davis, 'Loose Lips' (n 34).
56 Dustin, 'Inconsistencies' (n 4).

from male dominance it seems to me ... I have got no problem whatsoever in a radical critique in saying what it [FGM and FGCS] is doing is reinforcing not only the social control of women but also demeaning and objectifying women more generally, for me those considerations prevail over, I want to opt into it. [P47, lawyer, M]

The interview participant's quotation reinforced the work of Western feminists who compared FGM and FGCS.[57] Whether performed in the West or in minority communities, genital surgeries reflect dominant norms and values about the physical appearance of a girl's and woman's genitalia. Girls and women who undergo genital surgery are denied agency and autonomy by cultures that coerce them to conform to patriarchal body norms, thus their consent to the surgeries is undermined by duress. The harm caused to women who undergo genital modification for the purpose of conforming to cultural norms is harmful to the individual woman and to women as a social class because such surgeries reinforce their objectification and subservience to men. An NGO worker who works with women from FGM-performing communities believed that the cultural pressures to undergo FGM and FGCS are comparable.

The pressure for that white girl to undergo any form of labia reduction is the same pressure as girls undergoing FGM. But for me the issue should be if you are able to empower women this is why we need to talk about FGM, at the continuum of women inequality, because why should a woman do this to her body. And because there is pressure by society and social norms either through the media, or through the community or through traditional leaders it is a continuum of dictation. [P34, NGO worker, F]

The interview participant describes a 'continuum of women's inequality', which relates to the concept of 'continuum of violence against women' coined by feminist academic, Liz Kelly,[58] which shows the connections between various forms of abuse and violence towards women and girls. The pressures women experience to undergo FGM or FGCS might also exist on a continuum of different forms of duress, which are interconnected. For example, a woman might

---

[57] Weil Davis, 'Loose Lips' (n 34); Jeffreys, *Beauty and Misogyny* (n 36); Duits and Van Zoonen, 'Headscarves and Porno Chic' (n 36). There is a compelling argument to be made that children should be protected from any form of genital alteration, see, F Finlay, A Baverstock, and H Marcer, 'G134 A Debate on Female Genital Mutilation, Cosmetic Genital Surgery and Genital Piercings' (2016) 101(1)British Medical Journal.

[58] Liz Kelly, *Surviving Sexual Violence* (John Wiley & Sons 2013).

be influenced to undergo FGM to ensure that she is able to marry within her community, whilst a woman might be pressured to undergo FGCS because she feels that her labia is excessive in size in contrast to airbrushed images of women's genitalia featured in pornography. A midwife who specialises in FGM outlined concerns that the legal double standard is discriminatory because it reinforces racial stereotypes, as white women are depicted as making an empowered decision by undergoing FGCS, while women of colour who undergo FGM are defined as victims of torture and cultural dupes.

> On the one hand we are campaigning to stop FGM and it is horrid and FGM is child abuse and awful and these women are treated like nothing and in our own culture when white women do it then that's fine, it's normal. I think there is a big sort of racist element in that. White women are allowed that autonomy and this labiaplasty culture is white and it is part of the body beautiful, slim, blonde hair, big breasts, I don't think of it in terms of ordinary women. I associate it with women who would try and perfect other areas of their bodies and lifestyles. [P36, midwife, F]

The racial stereotypes that dominate the practices of FGM and FGCS could serve as a barrier to the end-FGM movement. Women from FGM-performing communities described their anger and hostility towards the toleration of FGCS whilst FGM is prohibited. The interview participant uses sensationalist language to highlight the contradictions inherent in defining women of colour as 'treated like nothing' whilst white women who undergo FGCS are seen as autonomous in choosing to conform to Western beauty norms, which operate outside of cultural norms and instead emanate from individual choice. An NGO worker of Somali heritage notes the similarity in the cultural norms to undergo FGM and FGCS, for example, to make their genitalia prettier and cleaner.

> If it's anything to do with the private part, I find it [FGCS] similar because some of the people who have done FGM they find it's pretty, they say it's cleaner, I am not sure about that. The cosmetic people they say that it's much prettier than it is then there's the freedom again. I do think it's similar there's not that much difference in my opinion. [P1, FGM-PCM and NGO worker, *Somalia*]

The participant strategically linked the practice of FGM to FGCS in order to argue that the aesthetic motivation for FGCS is similar to FGM. Women are undergoing genital surgery for similar reasons that women undergo FGCS, for example, pressures from societal norms about the physical appearance of the ideal genitalia. A consultant obstetrician who works with women who have undergone FGM and FGCS highlights the pressures on girls and women to have genital modification.

> We know that the images that most young people are seeing whether through the internet or the before and after pictures or pornography has got an unnatural ideal which is prepubescent and hairless and practices are changing, very few women have pubic hair nowadays ... I heard about a case where a mother turned up pulled her daughter in and said look doctor isn't it abnormal down there, you know, a 13-year-old going through puberty ... It is mothers, isn't it, in FGM, it's mothers, it's got to look right for society, for marriageability, [P61, obstetrician, F]

Unattainable images of girls' and women's genitalia are rife in the media, whether through pornography or women's magazines, which pressurise women to conform to unhealthy body expectations. The cultural pressures to conform to FGCS are as significant as cultural pressures to have FGM, particularly when mothers are encouraging their daughters to have surgery.

Campaigns designed to eliminate FGM often start from the standpoint that FGM causes long-term health consequences. However, there are long-term health risks that can follow FGCS.[59] The interview participant describes cosmetic surgeons as performing 'bad operations' that involve the 'amputation of the inner labia', which resembles narratives of FGM involving excision of a girl's or woman's genitalia.

> The risks are exactly the same [for FGCS] as any other cosmetic surgical procedure, and they include infection, loss of nerve ends, complications etc. etc. I must however point out that what I do is not an amputation of the inner labia, I reconstruct. A lot of colleagues of mine will just chop it off amputate the labia. It's a very bad operation. In cosmetic surgery there's no room for amputation that doesn't make sense to me, it never has, I condemn the operation. What I do is design a little flap which is basically the ridge of the labia which is reserved and stitched down onto the base of the labia, it's a beautiful

---

[59] For a discussion about the risks of FGCS see, Sarah M Creighton and Lih-Mei Liao, 'Requests for Cosmetic Genitoplasty: How Should Healthcare Providers Respond?' (2007) 334(7603) British Medical Journal 1090.

operation because the scar is in a hidden part, you can't see the scar, the labia is still sensitive and it looks very, very natural. [P72, cosmetic surgeon, M]

The harm caused by FGCS could also be significant according to the cosmetic surgeon, yet the two practices were described as polar opposites by the interview participants because they are performed for manifestly different reasons—FGM is performed for restrictive cultural or religious reasons and FGCS is performed to enhance a woman's sexuality. The interview participant described a woman's vulva after undergoing FGCS as 'beautiful', which is similar language to that used by women from FGM-performing communities to describe a woman's vulva after undergoing FGM.

A strict interpretation of the FGM Act 2003 is likely to mean that FGCS performed solely for cosmetic, aesthetic purposes is a criminal offence. FGCS can only be performed if it is necessary for the woman's mental or physical health. Cosmetic surgeons, who are not qualified psychologists or psychiatrists and often have no experience in mental health, are deciding whether FGCS is necessary for a person's mental health.

How to you decide whether FGCS is necessary for a girl or woman's mental health?

I always see my patients twice for half an hour to discuss everything to send them home and think about it after they've heard from me what it entails. I am not a psychologist, I am not a counsellor, I am just a technician who can change their vulva and also they ask me how I want it changed. Whereas a lot of cases surgeons will just go and amputate. That's terrible. [P72, cosmetic surgeon, M]

How to you decide whether FGCS is necessary for a girl or woman's mental health?

I am not an expert in mental health issues, and actually that is one problem that I am always having to be mindful of or aware of ... Well they haven't been defined [the exceptions]. That's why I had to do it [FGCS] on the hoof because nobody has. This is what is dangerous at the moment because the home office and the director of public prosecutions is a peasant and is trying to test out the boundaries of what exceptions are ... Mental health grounds doesn't mean problems it means psychological benefit so mental health grounds. This is what people want to test out you see. I think it's a load of nonsense. I think it's a complete distraction of the major problem of FGM and trying to stop it. [P59, cosmetic surgeon, M]

How to you decide whether FGCS is necessary for a girl or woman's mental health?

I am not trained in mental health, I couldn't assess if someone was depressed or anxious. Most [cosmetic] surgeons are not skilled in their understanding of mental health. [P61, obstetrician, F]

Cosmetic surgeons who were interviewed had no experience in mental health and yet determined whether FGCS is necessary for a woman's mental health according to the FGM Act 2003. One cosmetic surgeon stated that patients defer to him to decide how their genitalia should be modified, which shows the power differential between cosmetic surgeons and patients. Similarly, in cases of FGM, the cut is often determined by the cutter who performs FGM. The growth of FGCS has worried many medical practitioners, particularly when readily performed on girls. A consultant obstetrician explained that she referred a case of labiaplasty performed on girls under the age of sixteen or eighteen to the police. In this particular case, the cosmetic surgeon who performed the surgeries on young girls wrote about the procedures for an academic publication, which suggests that they were attempting to legitimise the procedures.

I have reported it to the police ... There was a case, this was really bizarre, in the academic literature someone has written up a case about an adolescent's [labia]plasty, 4 [girls] under the age of 16 or 18 ... the police went and talked to the people involved and they wrote back to me and said oh the clinic is going. And the doctor involved came back to me through a social route, and said it was terrible the police were investigating what I was doing, and I was trying to be a nice doctor and help patients and obviously people come distressed, now they didn't come distressed twenty years ago but they come distressed now ... The police went to the clinic they talked to the local safeguarding team, they talked to the doctors, and they looked at the notes and they decided there wasn't enough for a prosecution because they documented something about why the girls were unhappy ... they didn't tell me the details, but what they did say is there wasn't enough for a case under the FGM Act.

[P61, consultant obstetrician, F]

Similar to the case of Veale and Daniels, which involved a surgical clitoridectomy that resulted in the doctors being reported to the police for FGM, another medical practitioner was reported for performing FGM on girls where there did not appear to be any underlying mental or physical health reasons.[60] There is an overlap between the practices which, according to a strict interpretation of the FGM Act 2003, prohibits both FGM and FGCS. However, the police and the CPS have thus far ruled out prosecuting at least two cases involving FGCS. One of the police officers investigating a medical practitioner for performing FGCS, which allegedly amounted to FGM, explained further.

> Have you come across labiaplasty?
> That's a surgical changing of the vagina, isn't it? I have come across it be-
> cause the case that was being dealt with which was in effect a complaint by a
> doctor about other surgeons and this doctor complained that various surgical
> procedures were performed on young girls to alter their labia majora and the
> doctor felt that amounted to FGM. Of course, the FGM Act gives a defence
> which says anything that is done for medical reasons in effect [it] is ok. So,
> I do know about it, and that particular case was dealt with by the police, and
> I had an oversight over it, and it was concluded by ourselves that surgical pro-
> cedures were justified medically because they were carried out by surgeons
> within a clinic and for medical reasons and if there were misgivings about
> it then that's something the BMA needed to deal with rather than it being a
> criminal offence. [P60, police officer, M]

Even in a case which appeared to constitute FGM according to the legal definition in the FGM Act 2003, the cosmetic surgeon was not prosecuted. Some
of the women interview participants from FGM-performing communities
resisted anti-FGM laws because of the legal double standard. A minority of
professionals explained that the legal double standard could act as a barrier to
anti-FGM laws deterring and preventing FGM, as communities resist the law.
An NGO worker working in the end-FGM movement explained that the legal
double standard is a further obstacle to using the law as an advocacy tool to encourage communities to abandon the practice.

> Community groups who were doing community awareness, it was quite hard
> for them, because people would say well what if I had a designer vagina, what
> if I trimmed my labia, does that count as FGM, why is that FGM, why is this
> not FGM. So, it was raised as an issue and that's when there were lots of voices
> coming back from the community groups themselves [who] were often quite

---

[60] Veale and Daniels, 'Cosmetic Clitoridectomy' (n 20).

nervous about talking about FGM. They really sort of progressed in terms of their arguments. [P58, NGO consultant, F]

Findings from interviews with professionals who work closely with FGM-performing communities shows the challenges they confront when encouraging women to abandon FGM in a context where FGCS is permitted. The legal double standard appears to have cemented women's resistance to abandoning FGM and it could have resulted in women reinforcing the practice. In fact, the double legal standard could have resulted in FGM continuing under the guise of FGCS. A woman interview participant of Somali heritage suggested that two of her friends chose to undergo FGCS, which is permitted, instead of FGM, which is prohibited, shortly before marriage. Professionals working directly with FGM-performing communities highlighted concerns that communities are circumventing the law by continuing genital surgery through FGCS.

I think we fear that it [FGCS] may become more and more a kind of a presence in these communities as a way of avoiding the illegality of FGM. And then their parents may be, those who know well enough will take a young child, a 16-year-old through cosmetic surgery they can do it especially because the NHS according to some research, 140 cases of cosmetic surgery has been funded by the NHS [on girls under the age of 16]. [P11, FGM-PCM and NGO worker, *Unknown*, F]

The practice of FGM could continue under the guise of FGCS. The interview participant who described FGM being performed under the guise of FGCS is in the privileged position of speaking as a member of the FGM-community and as an NGO worker. As the participant mentions, FGCS is performed by the NHS on girls under the age of sixteen due to perceptions that their healthy genitalia is abnormal because it does not conform to an ideal physical appearance. Two interview participants who work for the Crown Prosecution Service confirmed that they are aware that there is a risk that FGM is performed under the guise of FGCS.

I can see the risk if people were allowed to describe what would be seen as FGM in other circumstances as a labiaplasty instead that may offer a way for them to continue to carry out the practice unless there was an equality of the treatment of the two [in law]. [P69, Crown Prosecution worker, M]

The interview participant explains that unless the law treats both practices equally there will always be a possibility that community members may try to subvert the law by undergoing FGCS. A cosmetic surgeon described a situation where a woman from an FGM-performing community was seeking FGM, or re-infibulation because of her husband's wishes.

> I have only ever seen one patient who had undergone FGM in Africa and I decided not to operate on her or do anything surgical on her, but I referred her to a clinical psychologist. She wanted to be closed even further, further FGM. I said I cannot do that, I'm unwilling to do that … She wanted it done because her husband wanted it. [P72, cosmetic surgeon, M]

The case study described by the cosmetic surgeon shows an overlap between FGM and cosmetic surgery. It also highlights that FGM-performing communities are aware of how to continue the practice in legitimate contexts without fear of prosecution. The cosmetic surgeon could have justified FGCS on the basis of altering the physical, aesthetic appearance of the genitalia to make it more appealing for the woman and her husband, as probably occurs in cases of cosmetic surgery on women's bodies. However, the cosmetic surgeon instead referred the woman to a psychologist which suggests that a Black woman seeking to modify her body is pathologised as having a mental health problem. It is highly unlikely that the cosmetic surgeon would have preferred a white woman to a psychologist if she sought FGCS, which reinforces perceptions that the legal loophole is discriminatory. An NGO worker said that she worked with a Sudanese woman who attempted to undergo FGM under the guise of FGCS but she was prevented from undergoing FGCS.

> I know of women who have tried to do that [FGCS] but couldn't so there's some sort of discrimination going on in a way. I think she was Sudanese. She wanted to go to the clinic to make her genitals look more like they used to because that was what she was accustomed to … She wanted to make her genitals look smaller, make the opening look smaller. She had been opened up to give birth and she felt she wasn't normal anymore because that wasn't what she was accustomed to. She wanted to go to have cosmetic surgery on what was being offered, but they turned her down effectively because she was from an affected community, there is no other reason because if she was a white woman she would have had the procedure. It's a weird one. [P59, NGO worker, F]

According to the interview participant, there is a double standard in law and practice, as women from FGM-performing communities are denied FGCS while such surgery is permitted for women who are not from FGM-performing communities. The double standard is a form of racial discrimination that women of colour experience on the basis of a preconceived stereotype that culture overrides their capacity to consent to surgery. In the case study described above, one can empathise with women who feel hostile and angry towards the legal hypocrisy that directly discriminates against them by preventing them from undergoing the same genital surgery that another woman is permitted because of their race. This was acknowledged by the Home Affairs Select Committee in its report about FGM in 2014 and a later report in 2016, which states, 'We cannot tell communities in Sierra Leone and Somalia to stop a practice which is freely permitted in Harley Street. We recommend that the Government amend the Female Genital Mutilation Act 2003 in order to make it very clear that female genital cosmetic surgery would be a criminal offence.'[61]

Conclusion

There is a legal double standard at present, which prohibits FGM while permitting FGCS. The legal hypocrisy is undermining attempts to use the law as an advocacy tool to change attitudes, beliefs, and behaviours towards FGM. Whilst there are differences between the practices in terms of the excision performed, the demographic background of the women and girls, and the pressure exerted from societal norms, there is a perception amongst FGM-performing communities that the practices are similar and this is undermining attempts to eliminate FGM. Whilst there are merits in acknowledging that there are similarities between the practices from a theoretical perspective, the reality is that permitting FGCS is preventing FGM from being abandoned. The legal double standard incited anger and hostility amongst community members who argued that FGM should also be permitted. In contrast, professionals argued that the law is justified in permitting FGCS because it is an entirely different practice to FGM. This shows professionals' lack of understanding about the impact of cultural pressures within different contexts, which creates pressure upon women to undergo genital surgeries. Culture is nuanced and exists

---

[61] House of Commons Home Affairs Committee, 'House of Commons Home Affairs Committee: Female Genital Mutilation: Abuse Unchecked' (Ninth Report of Session 2016–17) (2016) 26.

in Western societies as well as in other societies. Professionals' lack of understanding about the similarities between FGM and FGCS impacts upon their insight into how communities perceive the legal double standard and the hostility that it arouses amongst communities towards anti-FGM laws. There is a practical consequence to the legal double standard. The law provides women with a means to continue the practice of FGM under the guise of FGCS. One way of preventing the current lacuna in the law is to criminalise FGM and FGCS, thereby ensuring equal treatment of the practices. Criminalising both practices also sends out a symbolic message that any form of cultural pressure to change a woman's body through surgery is prohibited.

5

A Novel Legal Remedy: Female Genital Mutilation Protection Orders

Introduction

As the criminalisation of FGM has failed to prevent FGM, family law remedies have been used to protect children from the practice.[1] The development of jurisprudence in family law remains at a slow pace due to few FGM cases reaching the family court arena. The first family law case involving an allegation of FGM was in 2015.[2] The case involved care proceedings brought by the local authority due to concerns that a girl aged three had been cut. There is a high legal test to initiate care proceedings; the state must prove that there are reasonable grounds to believe that the child has or is likely to suffer significant harm.[3] Care proceedings are often considered a draconian step because they involve the interference of the state in a family's private and family life.[4] Rather than initiating care proceedings, there is now a novel legal remedy that is designed to protect women and girls from the risk of FGM in England and Wales and abroad.

In 2015, a ground-breaking legal remedy was introduced into law, FGM protection orders[5] (FGMPOs).[6] FGMPOs do not involve state-sanctioned removal of a child from the care of their parents unlike care proceedings, instead the focus is on proactive measures to prevent FGM, for example injunctive measures to remove a child's passport from their parent's possession and to compel a child to undergo a medical examination. Since the introduction of

---

[1] Ruth Gaffney-Rhys argues that the civil remedies introduced to combat FGM, FGMPOs, have been more successful than criminal legislation: Ruth Gaffney-Rhys, 'Female Genital Mutilation: The Law in England and Wales Viewed from a Human Rights Perspective' (2020) 24(4) The International Journal of Human Rights 457 (hereafter Gaffney-Rhys, 'Female Genital Mutilation: The Law').

[2] B and G (Children) (No 2) [2015] EWFC 3.

[3] The Children Act 1989, s 38 (hereafter CA 1989).

[4] Care proceedings interfere with a right to private and family life in accordance with Article 8 of the European Convention on Human Rights (hereafter ECHR).

[5] Female Genital Mutilation Act 2003, sch 2 (hereafter FGM Act 2003).

[6] The Female Genital Mutilation (Protection and Guidance) (Scotland) Bill passed into law on 24 April 2020, amending the Prohibition of Female Genital Mutilation (Scotland) Act 2005 such that FGMPOs can be granted in Scotland, putting it on par with the rest of the UK.

Female Genital Mutilation. Charlotte Proudman, Oxford University Press. © Charlotte Proudman 2022.
DOI: 10.1093/oso/9780198864608.003.0006

FGMPOs, there has been an increase in the number of court cases involving FGM. Having analysed FGMPO cases since 2015, there are overlapping issues prevalent within several FGM cases which require further exploration. There is limited academic scrutiny of the effectiveness of FGMPOs. The publication of FGMPO cases is left to the discretion of the presiding judge; as a result not all FGMPO cases are published.

The FGMPO cases that have been published show key themes: assessing the risk of harm caused by FGM, travel restrictions imposed upon women and girls at risk of FGM abroad, and the need for medical examinations to prove a woman's or girl's cut or uncut status. However, the family courts have failed to protect non-British children who do not have secure immigration status from the risk of FGM. The family courts' powers under FGMPOs are limited when the subject child does not have secure immigration status. The family courts cannot curtail the immigration powers of the Home Secretary. Even if the family court considers that the child is at high risk of FGM on return to her home country, the family court cannot stop the Home Secretary from re-moving the child to a country where FGM is prevalent. A number of cases are drawn upon to highlight the inconsistent protection afforded to girls at risk of FGM who have and do have secure immigration status. The consequence is stark, girls without secure immigration status are afforded less or second-rate protection from FGM than British children, which is arguably discriminatory.[7]

Background to FGMPOs

FGMPOs were introduced by the government as a response to increased pol-itical concern that the current legal remedies were insufficient to protect girls and women from FGM. The government appeared receptive to introducing na-tional laws designed to protect against and eliminate FGM. The Home Affairs Select Committee's inquiry into FGM in 2013 reviewed what needs to be done to protect girls at risk of FGM and why there has not yet been a successful prosecution in the UK.[8] The Bar Human Rights Committee's working group on FGM[9] submitted evidence to the inquiry[10] in which it made a number of

---

[7] This could constitute a breach of Art 14 ECHR.

[8] Home Affairs Committee 'Female Genital Mutilation: The Case for a National Action Plan (second report)' <https://publications.parliament.uk/pa/cm201415/cmselect/cmhaff/201/20102.htm> ac-cessed 6 March 2021.

[9] The author of this book was a member of the Bar Human Rights Committee's working group into FGM.

[10] Bar Human Rights Committee, 'Report of the Bar Human Rights Committee of England and Wales to the Parliamentary Inquiry into Female Genital Mutilation' <https://www.barhumanrights.org.uk/

proposals,[11] one of which was to introduce FGMPOs, as the report stated, 'the BHRC has grave concerns about the efficacy of the UK's response to FGM, and has concluded that the UK has been in breach of its international law obligations[12] to protect young women and girls from mutilation'.[13] FGMPOs were supported by the Muslim Women's Network and the National Police Chiefs Council. The Home Affairs Select Committee recommended to the government in its report that FGMPOs are introduced. The government introduced FGMPOs pursuant to section 73 of the Serious Crime Act 2015, which led to FGMPOs being incorporated under schedule 2 of the FGM Act 2003. FGMPOs are modelled on forced marriage protection orders, which were introduced in 2007.[14]

Prior to the introduction of FGMPOs, the court could still grant similar orders to protect and prevent FGM by invoking the inherent jurisdiction of the High Court. The court had a wide range of powers under the inherent jurisdiction which can include making injunctions to prohibit a child from being removed from the jurisdiction or mandating that a child undergo a medical examination. Furthermore, a non-molestation order could be made by the family courts to protect victims from risk of FGM. However, the numbers of orders (other than FGMPOs) to prevent FGM is unknown. FGMPOs assisted in raising awareness of the legal remedies available to protect girls from FGM and provided a clear avenue to gain a legal order through the courts.

Since the introduction of FGMPOs, in July 2015 to September 2019 a total of 408 applications were made for FGMPOs in England and Wales and 489 orders were made.[15] Sometimes multiple orders are granted stemming from a single application or orders could be granted without a formal application having

---

wp-content/uploads/2015/07/FGM-report.pdf> accessed 6 March 2021 (hereafter Bar Human Rights Committee, 'Report to the Parliamentary Inquiry into FGM').

[11] The Bar Human Rights Committee's working group on FGM also supported the opening of an FGM Unit specifically to address FGM. The FGM Unit was launched on 5 December 2014 and it operates in the Home Office to coordinate efforts across government and offer outreach support to local areas: Home Office, 'Female Genital Mutilation' (Collection) <https://www.gov.uk/government/collections/female-genital-mutilation> accessed 6 March 2021. The National FGM Centre was established in 2015 as a partnership between Barnardo's and the Local Government Association and provides services for children and their families affected by FGM <http://nationalfgmcentre.org.uk> accessed 6 March 2021.

[12] For example, the UK is in breach of the Convention on the Elimination of All Forms of Discrimination Against Women 1979, the UN Convention on the Rights of the Child 1989, and the UN Convention Against Torture 1984 in not taking all legislative steps available to prevent and prosecute cases of FGM.

[13] Bar Human Rights Committee, 'Report to the Parliamentary Inquiry into FGM' (n 10) 1.

[14] Pursuant to the Forced Marriage (Civil Protection) Act 2007 (hereafter FM(CP)A 2007).

[15] Minister of Justice, 'Family Court Statistics Quarterly, England and Wales, July to September 2019' (UK Ministry of Justice, 13 December 2019).

been made. Family and criminal courts have the power to make FGMPOs to protect a girl or woman from FGM having 'regard to all the circumstances, including the need to secure the health, safety and well-being of the girl to be protected'.[16] The test for applying for an order is low and is not comparable to the threshold required to be met for care proceedings.[17] As well as considering the specific legal test within schedule 2 of the FGM Act 2003, the court must always consider the welfare of the child and the child's welfare is of paramount consideration.[18] An application can be made by the girl who is to be protected or by a relevant third party. The only 'relevant third party' that can apply for an FGMPO is local authorities.[19] Any other third party, such as a family member, would need to seek an application for leave to apply for an FGMPO from the court.[20] The evidential burden is on the party bringing the application and the standard of proof is the ordinary civil standard: on the balance of probabilities it was more likely than not that the event occurred.[21]

The terms of court orders can be broad and flexible in nature, for example, they can prohibit foreign travel, order mandatory medical examinations, and confiscate passports. Orders can be made in relation to conduct overseas.[22] However, it is unclear whether FGMPOs would be effective abroad. For example, it is perhaps unlikely that an FGMPO ordered in the High Court of the Family Division would be effective in Lagos, Nigeria. It may depend upon the country in question and this might only be discernible with the assistance of a country legal expert report.

The gravity of the harm alleged or committed is assessed on an individual case-by-case basis. FGMPOs are intended to be protective in preventing FGM from occurring. The advantage of FGMPOs is that they are not criminal in nature unless the orders are breached which could result in a prison term of up to five years.[23] Furthermore, FGMPOs do not automatically result in children being removed from families into state care[24] unlike care proceedings. As

---

[16] FGM Act 2003 (n 5) sch 2 s 1(2).

[17] CA 1989 (n 3) s 31 or 38.

[18] On 15 March 2019, the Children Act 1989 (Amendment) (Female Genital Mutilation) Act 2019 came into force, which included family proceedings for an FGMPO within the definition of 'family proceedings' in the Children Act, s 8(4). It also now enables care proceedings to be brought within the same application as an application for an FGMPO.

[19] See the Female Genital Mutilation Protection Order (Relevant Third Party) Regulations 2015 and FGM Act 2003 (n 5) sch 2 s 2(s).

[20] FGM Act 2003 (n 5) sch 2 s 2(3).

[21] The standard of proof is the civil standard: the balance of probabilities as set out in *Re B (Care Proceedings: Standard of Proof)* [2008] UKHL 35, [2008] 2 FLR 14, as set out by the House of Lords and confirmed by the Supreme Court in *Re S-B (Children)* [2009] UKSC 17.

[22] FGM Act 2003 (n 5) sch 2 s 1(4)(a).

[23] ibid sch 2 s 4(1).

[24] The child's relevant local authority would need to initiate care proceedings before the court would consider the removal of a child into state care pursuant to CA 1989, ss 31 and 38.

noted by legal scholar, Ruth Gaffney-Rhys, social workers are often reluctant to pursue care proceedings in cases where FGM is the only concern; instead, they prefer to apply for FGMPOs because such orders do not impact upon the parental responsibility of parents or lead to the removal of children from the family.[25] Gaffney-Rhys contends that the impact of FGMPOs upon individuals' and families' private and family life has been to a lesser degree than other civil law alternatives.[26]

In some family law cases concerning injunctive remedies,[27] respondents may invite the court to accept undertakings, which are promises made to the court, rather than make a court order against them. Undertakings are usually drafted in similar terms to court orders. Unlike court orders, there is no power of arrest automatically attached to undertakings. If an undertaking is breached, the case would need to be returned to the family court and the court would decide whether to fine or imprison the perpetrator. It is less clear whether undertakings can be given in FGM cases. There is no specific provision under schedule 2 of the FGM Act 2003 which allows for undertakings to be given to the court.[28] In contrast, there is a specific provision for undertakings to be given to the court instead of court orders in forced marriage protection order cases.[29] However, legislation states that the court must not accept undertakings instead of making an order if a power of arrest would otherwise have been attached to the order or if there has been used or threatened violence against the person to be protected.[30] Zimran Samuel notes that schedule 2 of the FGM Act 2003 is silent on the issue of undertakings; however, in his opinion, undertakings can be given to the court in FGM cases.[31] In my opinion, if Parliament had intended for undertakings to be given in FGM cases, schedule 2 of the FGM Act would have made this clear. Given the gravity of harm that could potentially occur in FGM cases, it is unlikely that the court would accept undertakings to be given as they are woefully inadequate in such grave cases. In non-molestation

---

[25] Ruth Gaffney-Rhys, 'From the Offences Against the Person Act 1861 to the Serious Crime Act 2015—The Development of the Law Relating to Female Genital Mutilation in England and Wales' (2017) 39(4) Journal of Social Welfare and Family Law 417 (hereafter Gaffney-Rhys, 'Development of the Law Relating to FGM').

[26] Gaffney-Rhys, 'Female Genital Mutilation: The Law' (n 1).

[27] For example, non-molestation orders or forced marriage protection orders.

[28] The author acted for a mother in a case where the father gave an undertaking not to subject the child to FGM rather than there being an FGMPO in force.

[29] FM(CP)A (n 14) s 63E.

[30] ibid s 63E(3).

[31] Zimran Samuel states that 'Where an application is made for an FGM protection order, the court may accept an undertaking if the parties are in agreement and if the court is satisfied that a full hearing and findings of fact are not necessary to protect an individual': Zimran Samuel, *Female Genital Mutilation (FGM): Law and Practice* (Jordan Publishing 2017) 76, para 7.6 (hereafter Samuel, *(FGM): Law and Practice*).

order cases which concern domestic abuse, the law also stated that undertakings cannot be accepted where the respondent has used or threatened violence
because it may be necessary to protect the applicant or child with a non-molestation order where breach is punishable.[32]

There were long-standing concerns that the police were not aware when
FGMPOs were made by the court and subsequently breached by respondents.
To ensure that the police are aware of FGMPOs, Pilot Practice Direction 36H
of the Family Procedure Rules 2010 came into effect on 23 July 2018.[33] The
Practice Direction was implemented as a means of ensuring that all FGMPOs
and forced marriage protection orders are served on the police through a centralised email address either by the applicant or the court.[34] This ensures that
the police are able to keep a record of the numbers of FGMPOs made by the
court and are able to ensure compliance with such orders. The PD36H remains
in force to date and is continually reviewed by the president of the Family
Division and the Ministry of Justice.

Gaffney-Rhys concludes that the criminal law has proved ineffective in
addressing FGM[35] and the introduction of FGMPOs is a more appropriate
and effective means of ending FGM, but that legal measures need to be reinforced with non-legal interventions, such as education initiatives.[36] Dustin
criticises the emphasis on criminal justice solutions for FGM, which can stigmatise minorities and drive those problems underground; instead, Dustin
favours education and prevention.[37] Unlike criminal sanctions, FGMPOs are
usually preventative rather than punitive in nature and therefore can appear
less threatening to individuals and families who are subject to them.[38] A research study conducted in Bristol 2021 suggests that FGMPOs 'might be issued without enough grounds for suspicion' and families subjected to such
orders live in constant fear that their children could be taken away.[39] The bold

---

[32] Family Law Act 1996 s 46(3A) (hereafter FLA 1996).
[33] The author assisted in the drafting of Practice Direction 36H of the Family Procedure Rules 2010
with the National Police Chiefs' Council.
[34] Service must be by email to the centralised email address.
[35] There has only been one conviction for FGM and a number of failed prosecutions for FGM despite
the practice being a specific criminal offence since 1985.
[36] Gaffney-Rhys, 'Development of the Law Relating to FGM' (n 25).
[37] Moira Dustin, 'Culture or Masculinity? Understanding Gender-Based Violence in the UK' (2016)
24(1) Journal of Poverty and Social Justice 51.
[38] For a practical step-by-step approach to applying for FGMPOs see, Samuel, *(FGM): Law and
Practice* (n 31).
[39] Amy Abdelshahid, Dr Kate Smith, and Khadra Habane, '"Do No Harm": Lived Experiences and
Impacts of FGM Safeguarding Policies and Procedures, Bristol Study' FORWARD UK (2021) 28
<https://www.forwarduk.org.uk/wp-content/uploads/2021/02/FORWARD-UKs-FGM-Safeguarding-
Research-Report-Bristol-Study-2021.pdf> accessed 6 March 2021.

concerns identified in a one-page report are on the basis of a couple of inter-views with individuals and professionals who have never been involved an FGMPO case. The research paper states, 'none of the community members in the research had direct experience of FGM Protection Orders, but some knew of people who had gone through the process'. The concerns outlined appear to have limited evidential value.

The First Reported Family Law Case of FGM

There is usually a balance to be struck between initiating care proceedings and applying for an FGMPO to protect a girl from FGM. To explore the two separate and, at times, overlapping legal remedies, it is important to analyse reported cases that concern FGM. The starting point is the court's acknowledg-ment that FGM constitutes a breach of Article 3 of the European Convention on Human Rights (ECHR). As Baroness Hale observed in *Fornah v Secretary of State for the Home Department* [2006] UKHL 46, [2007] 1 AC 412 at [94]:

> ... the procedure will almost inevitably amount either to torture or to other cruel, inhuman or degrading treatment within the meaning, not only of art-icle 3 of the European Convention on Human Rights, but also of article 1 or 16 of the Convention against Torture and other Cruel, Inhuman or Degrading Treatment or Punishment, article 7 of the International Covenant on Civil and Political Rights, and article 37(a) of the Convention on the Rights of the Child.

And Lord Bingham in the same case said at [8]:

> FGM has been condemned as cruel, discriminatory and degrading by a long series of international instruments, declarations, resolutions, pronounce-ments and recommendations.... Therefore those cultural practices that in-volve 'severe pain and suffering' for the woman or the girl child, those that do not respect the physical integrity of the female body, must receive maximum international scrutiny and agitation. It is imperative that practices such as fe-male genital mutilation, honour killings, Sati or any other form of cultural practice that brutalizes the female body receive international attention, and international leverage should be used to ensure that these practices are cur-tailed and eliminated as quickly as possible.

The first reported case of FGM within care proceedings assists in defining the court's approach to suspected cases of FGM, *Re B and G (Children) (No 2)* [2015] EWFC 3.[40] The issue in the case was whether a girl at the age of three had been subjected to Type IV FGM. The former president of the Family Division, Sir James Munby, found that all types of FGM including Type IV constitute 'significant harm' within the meaning of section 31 of the Children Act 1989 and thus the threshold criteria required to invoke care proceedings would be satisfied. The former president of the Family Division held:

> ... FGM is a criminal offence under the Female Genital Mutilation Act 2003. It is an abuse of human rights. It has no basis in any religion ... it is a 'barbarous' practice.[41]

The president distinguished FGM from male circumcision for the purposes of section 31 of the Children Act 1989. The president found that FGM and male circumcision both involve 'significant harm' pursuant to section 31(2) (a).[42] However, the clear distinction between the two practices is with respect to 'reasonable parenting' in accordance with the second limb of the test pursuant to section 31(2)(b)(i) of the Children Act 1989. FGM can never be a feature of reasonable parenting, whereas society and the law treat male circumcision as a form of reasonable parenting thus male circumcision will not satisfy the threshold criteria.[43] Type IV FGM is as physically harmful as male circumcision but male circumcision escapes care proceedings because it is seen as a legitimate practice. The same arguments could be used to justify Type IV FGM.

Three medical experts were instructed in the case to give evidence as to whether the girl had been cut.[44] On balance, the experts were unable to establish whether the girl had been subjected to FGM.[45] The president preferred the evidence of one of the experts who could not confirm whether FGM had been performed because of her experience in FGM. The case shows the acute difficulties of finding medical practitioners who are trained in FGM.[46] Although

---

[40] For a summary of the case, see, Charlotte Proudman, 'In the Matter of B and G (Children) (No 2) [2015] EWFC 3' (*Family Law Week*, 2015) <https://www.familylawweek.co.uk/site.aspx?i=ed142 550> accessed 5 March 2021.
[41] *Re B and G (Children)* (No 2) [2015] EWFC 3 [55] (hereafter *Re B and G*).
[42] ibid [67], [70]–[71], [73].
[43] ibid [72].
[44] ibid [13]–[36].
[45] ibid [52].
[46] ibid [79].

FGM was not found to have been performed in this case, the president added, 'local authorities and judges are probably well advised not to jump too readily to the conclusion that proven FGM should lead to adoption'.[47] Where FGM has already been performed, the damage has been done and a girl is unlikely to be subject to FGM again thus decreasing the potential for future harm.[48] In single issue cases where FGM is the only issue, cases require careful consideration. For example, a girl at risk of FGM might have a male sibling who does not require protection, which could result in the girl only being placed in state care and the siblings being separated from each other. FGMPOs are more likely to be suitable in cases where FGM is the single issue and FGM has not been performed.[49]

A further published case concerning FGM in the context of care proceedings is, *A London Borough v B and others (Female genital mutilation: FGM)* [2016] EWFC B111. The local authority issued care proceedings due to concerns that two girls would be taken to Guinea by their parents where they would be cut.[50] They were placed into foster care. The local authority's final care plan was for the girls to return to their parents' care following the evidence of two experts.[51] All parties agreed that future medical examinations would act as a deterrent to the parents performing FGM and safeguard the girls from FGM. The local authority sought an order for regular medical examinations.[52] The guardian who represented the children, supported by the parents, argued that such a court order would breach the girls' right to private and family life under Article 8 ECHR and should instead only be undertaken if the local authority have evidence of a cogent risk of FGM.[53] The judge made a specific issue order permitting the local authority to request and arrange a medical examination for not more than once per year.[54] The case highlights the interrelationship between the risk of FGM and medical examinations, which are used as a deterrent to prevent FGM. However, the case of *Re B and G* shows that there are significant concerns about the reliability of medical examinations on a girl's anatomy to either prove or disprove FGM.

---

[47] ibid [77].
[48] ibid [76].
[49] ibid.
[50] *A London Borough v B and others (Female genital mutilation: FGM)* [2016] EWFC B111 [6] (hereafter *London Borough v B*).
[51] ibid [2].
[52] ibid [4].
[53] ibid [4], [9].
[54] ibid [3].

Female Genital Mutilation Orders

Travel Bans

Since FGMPOs were introduced in 2015 there have been a number of published cases. These cases provide important guidance on the court's approach to assessing the risk of FGM and ordering FGMPOs. The majority of published FGM cases concern travel bans for women and girls who are British citizens and are at risk of being removed from the jurisdiction to a high prevalence FGM country. Where the risk of FGM is abroad, the court readily orders FGMPOs to prevent the protected person from traveling. However, travel bans are only usually ordered in respect of British citizens. Courts rarely grant travel bans when women and girls do not have immigration status. The family courts provide a lower level of protection to women and girls who do not have immigration status. The conflict in the protection given to different groups of women and girls is discussed further below. There is often an overlap between cases that concern travel bans and medical examinations for girls at risk of FGM. Medical examinations are sometimes ordered by the courts as a deterrent against FGM. Regardless of whether the court assesses the risk of FGM as low, medium, or high, the family court will often make FGMPOs. The key guiding principles from the published FGM cases is that even a low risk of FGM is sufficient to make an FGMPO. Travel to FGM-prevalent countries is either prohibited by the family courts or subject to rigid restrictions including medical examinations of a girl at risk of FGM on return to England and Wales.

Worldwide Travel Ban Is Unlawful

In *Re X (FGMPO No 2)* [2019] EWHC 1990 (Fam) the High Court outlined the key factors that the court must consider when assessing the risk of FGM and deciding whether to impose a travel ban upon a woman or girl at risk of FGM.[55] The case has been cited by later FGMPO cases that assess the risk of FGM.[56] The long-running 'travel ban' case is *Re X (A Child) (Female Genital Mutilation Protection Order) (Restrictions on Travel)* [2017] EWHC 2898

---

[55] For a legal analysis of the case see, Charlotte Proudman and Nkumbe Ekaney, 'Reviewing the Law on Travels Bans in FGM Cases' (2019) 49(11) Family Law Journal 1305.

[56] See, *Re A (A child) (Female Genital Mutilation Protection Order Application)* [2020] EWHC 323 (Fam) in which the court addressed a number of key questions in order to determine whether there is a risk of FGM.

(Fam). The family court was concerned with a young girl who was fourteen months old at the time of the first judgment. The child was born in England to a white English mother while her father was Egyptian and lived in Egypt. The mother met the father during a trip to Egypt where they were both working in the tourism industry and the mother later converted to Islam.[57] The father was not able to travel to the UK to stay with the mother because he could not secure immigration status.[58] The mother wanted to visit Egypt for a short holiday but to reside in England. The mother allegedly raised concern with the health visitor that the paternal family support FGM and as a consequence, the health visitor alerted the local authority.[59] Section 5B of the FGM Act 2003 imposes a duty on professionals including health and social workers to inform the police if, during the course of their work, they discover that an offence of FGM appears to have been carried out.[60] The mother had planned a trip to Egypt with her daughter so that she could meet her father. The local authority was concerned that the child could be cut and thus applied for an FGMPO.

The father and his parents gave evidence by video-link from Egypt. The judgment highlighted a number of concerning aspects of the case, particularly the evidence given by the parties. The father claimed that FGM had not been carried out in his family and neither of his sisters were cut as children. The paternal grandmother had been cut. The father had allegedly told the mother that his sisters had undergone FGM, later the paternal family tried to deny this.[61] The paternal grandfather's professed belief is that 'it is neither necessary or desirable to tell women within the family the decisions that have been taken'.[62] He took his daughters to be medically examined without speaking with his wife who was unaware of this; the judge did not find the medical evidence credible.[63] He claimed that his two daughters had not been cut.[64] During the parents' relationship, the father queried whether the mother had undergone FGM due to the appearance of her genitalia.[65] The father denied the conversation in evidence, which concerned the mother and the court.[66] The mother reported that the father allegedly said that FGM should be legalised and performed in

---

[57] *Re X (A Child) (Female Genital Mutilation Protection Order) (Restrictions on Travel)* [2017] EWHC 2898 (Fam) [6] (hereafter *X (A Child FGMPO)*).
[58] ibid [10].
[59] ibid [2].
[60] ibid [11].
[61] ibid [7].
[62] ibid [9].
[63] ibid [9], [47].
[64] ibid [16].
[65] ibid [7].
[66] ibid.

hospitals.[67] The mother denied that the father had ever suggested that their daughter should be cut.[68]

The court gave permission to instruct an expert in Egyptian law to provide advice on the enforceability of a British FGMPO, the punishment equivalent in Egypt if the order was breached, and the existence of any equivalent FGMPO in Egyptian law.[69] The report confirmed that the prevalence rate of FGM in Egypt was 92%; English law is not applicable or enforceable in Egypt; and there is no equivalent of an FGMPO in Egyptian law.[70] CEWLA Foundation in Egypt also completed a report on the attitudes of the paternal family towards FGM after a short visit to meet them.

The mother and the father wanted the travel ban to be lifted to allow her to travel to Egypt.[71] The mother was found to be vulnerable and unable to protect her child from the risk of FGM. The mother could not speak Egyptian Arabic and the paternal grandparents could not speak English, thus it would be diffi-cult for her to protect the child as she would not know that they were discussing FGM.[72] The family court made negative credibility findings about the paternal family. The learned judge found that the father held an 'intrinsic belief that FGM is necessary to exert some social control over women's sexuality' and he was unable to give any examples of the negative impact of FGM on a woman.[73] The learned judge did not accept that the family had decided to eradicate FGM when there was no discussion about how this decision was reached.[74] The court found that the paternal grandfather had lied when he claimed that no female members of his family had been cut because his wife had been cut.[75] The court found that it was not possible to accept that FGM was abandoned in the paternal family because there was no independent evidence, such as verifi-able medical examinations.[76] The implicit suggestion is that the paternal family had to prove a negative, which is wrong in law, for example that the girls in the family had not been cut. However, if the local authority is asserting that the girls in the paternal family had been cut then they must prove this on the evi-dence. Instead, the court found against the father because he failed to adduce

---

[67] ibid [13].
[68] ibid [7].
[69] ibid [24].
[70] ibid [27].
[71] ibid [40].
[72] ibid [9].
[73] ibid [50].
[74] ibid [53].
[75] ibid [46].
[76] ibid [77].

evidence to rebut a presumption that the family had been cut. This approach has been followed in similar FGMPO cases involving travel bans. The court ordered that the child is prohibited from travelling outside of the jurisdiction of England and Wales until 22 August 2032, when she is sixteen years old.[77] It was ordered that contact between the child and her father should take place in England and Wales. However, the father was not able to obtain a visa to travel from Egypt to England and Wales.[78] The parents could be prosecuted if they fail to protect the child from FGM.[79]

The father appealed the prohibition on the parents removing the child from the jurisdiction of England and Wales until she is sixteen years old.[80] The Court of Appeal allowed the appeal and the case was remitted for a full re-hearing.[81] This was the first time the FGM Act 2003 was considered by the Court of Appeal. The Court of Appeal made a number of observations including that the court will need to consider Article 3 and Article 8 ECHR when deciding how to exercise its powers to make an FGMPO.[82] The court will need to consider the degree of risk (which must be a 'real risk'); the quality of protective factors available including the court's assessment of the parents; and the extent of the interference with family life. Each term within an FGMPO needs to be separately justified.[83] The father said that he had been refused a visitor visa to enter the UK and therefore he was unable to have a meaningful relationship with his daughter contrary to his family life in England and Wales. The judge had not made findings or reached any conclusions as to the prospects of the father being able to travel to the UK.[84] The travel ban amounts to a disproportionate

---

[77] ibid [81].

[78] ibid [83].

[79] FGM Act 2003 (n 5) s 3A(3)(a) and (b) and a defence under s 3A(5)(a).

[80] X (A Child FGMPO) (n 57)

[81] ibid [7].

[82] As to the arrangements for assessing and processing risk, Moylan LJ in the appeal hearing in the instant case offered the following observations at [2018] EWCA Civ 1825 at [31]–[32]:

> [31] The court will have to consider the degree of the risk of FGM (which, I would suggest, needs to be at least a real risk); the quality of available protective factors (which could include a broad range of matters including the court's assessment of the parents); and the nature and extent of the interference with family life which any proposed order would cause.
>
> [32] The need for specific analysis balancing these and other relevant factors extends to any additional prohibitions or other terms the judge may be considering including in the FGMPO. This is because each term included within the FGMPO must be separately justified. In this exercise, although the nature of the harm would, self-evidently, be a breach of Article 3, it is the court's assessment of the degree or level of the risk which is central to the issue of proportionality and to the question of whether a less intrusive measure, which nevertheless does not unacceptably compromise the objective of protecting the child, might be the proportionate answer.

[83] ibid [31]–[32].

[84] ibid [16], [47].

interference with the family life of the child and her parents.[85] The court held that there was no evidential basis for the decision to impose the travel ban; the judge failed to give sufficient reasons for imposing the travel ban; and there was no real consideration of the risk of FGM if the child travels to any country except Egypt.[86] The Court of Appeal held that the FGM Act 2003 'is very broad and provides no real guidance as to the approach the court should take when determining whether, and if so, in what manner to exercise its powers.'[87]

The case was remitted to the High Court of the Family Division for a new decision about whether the child could visit her father and paternal family in Egypt.[88] Neither parent contested the making of an FGMPO nor did they oppose the continuation of a worldwide travel ban. However, they sought for the travel ban to be relaxed to allow the child to visit Egypt for one week to meet her father for the first time. The court accepted that a number of safeguards could be put in place to mitigate the risk of FGM to the child, including that the maternal grandfather would accompany the mother to Egypt and would supervise contact between the child and the father. The paternal family were not permitted to meet the child for the first visit. The learned judge noted that the case had gained much traction in the media and thus NGOs and the police would be on alert and ready to assist the mother should the need arise.[89]

The court permitted the instruction of an independent social worker from the National FGM Centre and anthropologists, Professor Bradley in the UK and Dr Fahmy in Egypt. They wrote a joint report on the prevalence of FGM in Egypt and the consciousness-raising work that Dr Fahmy had undertaken with the paternal family. The report concluded that the risk associated with the child making a trip to Egypt during the summer was low and would need to be continually assessed. The learned judge assessed the risk under the branch of two sets of factors.[90] First, the 'macro-factors' (the contextual considerations), for example, the prevalence rate of FGM (92% in Egypt), the culture and societal expectations of FGM in the country proposed, and the state's role in prohibiting FGM. Second, the micro-factors (the case specific considerations), for example, an examination of the attitudes of the child's family towards FGM

---

[85] See, *E v Chief Constable of the Royal Ulster Constabulary and Another* [2009] 1 AC 536 and *A Local Authority v M & N* [2018] EWHC 870 (Fam), [2018] 4 WLR 98.
[86] *X (A Child FGMPO)* (n 57) [47]–[48], [50], [53]. The consequence of the judge's order meant that it was unlikely that the father and paternal family would be able to see the child.
[87] ibid [24].
[88] *Re X (FGMPO No 2)* [2019] EWHC 1990 (Fam) (hereafter *X (FGMPO No 2)*).
[89] *X (A Child FGMPO)* (n 57) [81].
[90] ibid [91]–[107] for a list of the questions that are helpful to ask and answer in order to assess risk of FGM to the child.

and the safeguards that the family can offer. The court (and the experts) confirmed that the risk of FGM is not static, it is continually changing thus the risk of FGM requires regular re-assessment. For example, in the instant case, the girl faced increased risk of FGM as she grew older when FGM is more likely to be performed.[91] The court held that the risks posed to the girl were significant enough to justify a worldwide travel ban. However, the safeguards put in place alleviated some of the risk posed.[92] The court considered the protection of the child's Article 3 rights and Article 8 rights and struck a balance in allowing a trip to Egypt after the risks had been fully evaluated and safeguarded against. The court declined to order that the child is medically examined on her return, instead finding that whilst it may be a deterrent and may offer professionals some reassurance, it is not proportionate to subject her to an examination.[93]

The judge had similar concerns about the father and the paternal family's evidence as the first trial judge.[94] Similarly to the trial judge's findings, the paternal family again denied that they had discussed FGM within the household, which Dr Fahmy opined was unlikely due to the high prevalence of FGM but their statement was probably attributable to the family's concern that if they admitted to their knowledge of the practice locally this would jeopardise their position within the court.[95] Over the two years of litigation, the paternal family had become more enlightened to the issue of FGM and the gravity of the practice.[96] Dr Fahmy considered that the child would be at low risk of FGM if she were to travel to Egypt for a short holiday, particularly given her young age, the attitudes of the paternal family against FGM, the negative personal experience of FGM by the paternal grandmother, and the aspiration of the father to ultimately reside in the UK.[97] The independent social worker felt the mother was susceptible to easy influence from the father and his family due to the marriage and conversion to Islam but Professor Bradley and Dr Fahmy disagreed.[98] The family travelled to Egypt for a short holiday when the child met her father for the first time and they returned to England and Wales safely. The court will likely reassess the risk of FGM to the girl before she travels to Egypt again.

---

[91] ibid [82], [106].
[92] ibid [122]–[124] for the assurances.
[93] ibid [125]. Notably, two medical advisers contacted were opposed to a medical examination.
[94] ibid [59].
[95] ibid [71(vi)].
[96] ibid [79].
[97] ibid [80], [83].
[98] ibid [85].

Girl Prohibited from Travelling to Guinea

In a similar case to *Re X*,[99] the family court was concerned that a child might be cut when visiting her paternal family in Guinea where the prevalence rates of FGM are high.[100] In *Re Z (A Child) (FGMPO: Prevalence of FGM)* [2017] EWHC 3566 (Fam), the court heard expert evidence and accordingly granted a travel ban, prohibiting the child from travelling.

The mother applied for an FGMPO in respect of her child who was at the time six and a half years of age. The mother is white British and the father's heritage is Black African Muslim from the Fulah community in Guinea, West Africa. The father wanted to take the child to Guinea to visit his family. The mother sought a travel ban due to the risk of FGM posed to the child. According to the UN statistics and expert evidence in the case, the prevalence rate in Guinea is 96%.[101] The court heard evidence from expert, Dr Schroven, an academic and researcher, specialising in FGM in Guinea and adjacent countries. Dr Schroven highlighted the publicity campaigns against FGM since 2016 after the Ebola outbreak. However, 'the vast majority of men and women of all age groups in Guinea agree that FGM should continue to be practiced.'[102] Furthermore, there is 'almost total lack of protective measures that could be put in place through the judicial system' particularly when FGM is considered a family matter not a matter for external police intervention.[103]

There was a relevant background history to the case in which the court had previously made findings that the father had perpetrated domestic abuse against the mother, which resulted in a non-molestation order and occupation order (injunctive remedies) to ensure that the mother was safe from the father.[104] The mother also accused the father of having the child's ears pierced without her consent, which added to her fears that the father might override the mother's consent and have the child cut. As a result of the violence that the mother experienced by the father, the court held that the mother would be 'feeling anxious and unable to trust him' and it is the father's 'behaviour that is at the root cause of the conflict between the parties as has been evidenced

---

[99] *X (FGMPO No 2)* (n 88).
[100] *Re Z (A Child) (FGMPO: Prevalence of FGM)* [2017] EWHC 3566 (Fam) (hereafter *Z (A Child: FGMPO)*).
[101] ibid [2].
[102] ibid [49].
[103] ibid [50].
[104] ibid [5], [6], [8]. Para 6 of the judgment confirms that the father refuses to accept the findings made against him, 'showing no remorse or insight into the impact that this has had on his daughter' and the mother.

by the findings made in the family court …'[105] Similarly in the first trial in *Re X*, the judge found that the mother was vulnerable and might succumb to the pressure and duress of the paternal family to have the child cut.

The court highlighted the importance of medical evidence to prove that the paternal family had not been cut. The court's comments reflected the first trial judge's findings in the case of *Re X*.[106] The trial judge stated in *Re X* that without objective and reliable evidence that the paternal family had not been cut, the court would be concerned that they had been cut. The court's comments suggest that the burden of proof has been reversed, as the paternal family have to prove a negative that they have not been cut. In both cases, the credibility of the paternal family abroad was called into question. In this case, the father's sister gave evidence from Guinea. The father's sister claimed the practice has ceased outside of her family, most of her friends had not been cut and she had not been cut.[107] The judgment notes that providing evidence of mutilation or lack thereof is 'intrusive' but without such evidence her assertion is unsupported and on the balance of probabilities the judge was unable to reach the conclusion that she had not been cut and that the family are exceptionally opposed to FGM.[108] The court noted that the father had never discussed the idea of his sister being medically examined with her and yet the father had considerable time to arrange an independent medical examination and he 'was aware that such evidence has been presented in other cases before the courts'.[109] The father had submitted that his sister had not been cut. Proving his sister's uncut status might have been 'proof that FGM had not occurred in his immediate family thus reducing any risk to Z' (the child).[110] This could suggest that unless a girl or woman undergoes a medical examination it will be presumed that she has been cut if she is from a high prevalence country. This could set a concerning precedent in other cases in which the judge notes that medical evidence has been used in similar cases. There does appear to be a trend of women and girls undergoing medical examinations to prove their cut status in family and immigration cases. The judgment could be construed as giving credence to the notion that medical evidence is imperative to prove one's cut status,[111]

---

[105] ibid [23]. Somewhat surprisingly the court allowed the mother to be cross-examined by the father who represented himself notwithstanding the findings of domestic abuse

[106] *X (A Child FGMPO)* (n 57). The trial judge in the Guinea FGM case and in the case of *Re X* was the same, Russell J.

[107] *Z (A Child: FGMPO* (n 100) [51] in respect of the father's sister's evidence.

[108] ibid [52].

[109] ibid [51].

[110] ibid.

[111] The necessity of medical examinations in FGM cases is becoming a central issue in family and immigration cases (particularly in respect of FGM asylum claims).

which is arguably likely to be a disproportionate interference with one's human rights.[112]

The family court found that there is no objective or independent evidence about the paternal family's views towards FGM and therefore it was difficult to assess the father's position within his own family and the extended family.[113] The judge accepted the objective evidence of the expert and concluded that the wider paternal family are likely to pressure FGM upon the child.[114] It was found that the father would likely succumb to the pressure from those with authority over him to make his child undergo FGM to ensure respect within his community.[115] The court was concerned that the father's family would have the child cut. The child's guardian supported a travel ban on visiting Guinea until the child attainted the age of sixteen. The court made an FGMPO to protect the child from the risk of FGM and therefore prohibited the child from leaving the country with her father or third party (except her mother) until the age of seventeen, by which time she could be in a position to protect herself.[116] The judgment notes that the child can spend time with the father and extended paternal family in the UK.[117]The court gave the child permission to apply to vary the order to allow her to travel to Guinea to spend time with her father outside of the UK.[118] The court balanced the loss of the child's relationship with her paternal family in Guinea against the life-long effects of FGM.[119] The child's freedom of movement is restricted but that restriction was deemed proportionate given the risk of FGM.

Child Prohibited from Travelling to Sudan

In the case of *A Local Authority v M & N (Female Genital Mutilation Protection Order—FGMPO)* [2018] EWHC 870 (Fam), the court granted a travel ban prohibiting a child travelling to Sudan with her mother to spend time with her father and brothers due to the risk of FGM. Similarly to the cases of *Re X* and *Re Z*, this case also highlights the father's abuse against the mother in the past,

---

[112] Breach of a right to respect for private and family life under Art 8 and the prohibition of discrimination under Art 14 ECHR.
[113] *Z (A Child: FGMPO* (n 100) [58].
[114] ibid.
[115] ibid [59].
[116] ibid [61].
[117] ibid [56].
[118] ibid [61].
[119] ibid [60].

leaving the mother vulnerable in the family, which meant she might struggle to protect her daughter from FGM.

The local authority applied for an FGMPO to prevent the child from travelling to the Sudan with her mother.[120] The mother is a British citizen born in Sudan. The mother and father are habitually resident in the UK. In July 2017, the father, the mother, and their sons visited the Middle East during the school summer holidays and then travelled to Sudan. The father wished to remain in Sudan whilst the mother opposed this. The father had been violent towards the mother in the past but in the UK, he behaved respectfully towards her and she believed the cultural effects have influenced him.[121] The father initially took the mother's passport from her and eventually allowed her to travel back to the UK without the children.[122] At the time the mother was heavily pregnant with a child and required medical treatment. The mother returned to England and contacted social services to report her fears that her daughter would be cut.[123] The mother had been subjected to FGM. The evidence before the court of risk of FGM in Sudan was high: 90% of girls and women in Sudan have undergone FGM.[124]

The father was unaware of the proceedings due to concerns about how he would respond given he has control of the boys' passports.[125] The court granted an *ex parte* FGMPO and as such the father had no notice of the order. The father appears to have been deprived of notice that an FGMPO was sought because of the mother's concern that their daughter would be cut. As it became increasingly more apparent that the mother and her daughter would live separate lives from the father and her sons who were in Sudan, the mother became more desperate to travel to Sudan. The mother minimised the risk of FGM posed by the paternal family due to an eagerness to return to Sudan to care for her boys.[126] The mother highlighted that the anti-FGM criminal law in the UK is a deterrent and she would prevent her daughter being cut.[127]

The mother sought permission to return to Sudan with her daughter in order to encourage the father to allow her to bring her six sons back to England.[128] However, the court found that the father had already subjugated the mother

---

[120] *A Local Authority v M & N (Female Genital Mutilation Protection Order—FGMPO)* [2018] EWHC 870 (Fam) (hereafter *Local Authority v M & N*).
[121] ibid [3].
[122] ibid [4]–[5].
[123] ibid [6].
[124] ibid [25].
[125] ibid [10].
[126] ibid [15].
[127] ibid [14]. See also, FGM Act 2003 (n 5) s 3A (3)(a) and (b).
[128] *Local Authority v M & N* (n 120) [53].

owing to stronger cultural imperatives, which highlights the mother's vulnerable status.[129] The court held that the state has a responsibility to prevent an individual from being subject to FGM contrary to Article 3 ECHR if removed to another country.[130] Furthermore, the court had to ensure that any interference with the child's Article 8 Convention rights, and those of her siblings and family, was limited to protect her Article 3 rights.[131] The court granted the local authority's application to prohibit the child's removal from the jurisdiction of England and Wales.[132]

Authorities Must Inform Parents in Advance of an FGMPO Application

The majority applications for FGMPOs are made by parents or local authorities to prohibit a girl from leaving the jurisdiction to a country where FGM is prevalent. Local authorities and other public bodies rarely have a standardised approach when handling cases concerning girls at risk of FGM. As a result, local authorities have been criticised for acting overzealously in making urgent *ex parte* applications, which means that the child's parents are not put on notice of applications for FGMPOs, instead they learn that an order has been made by a family court when a police officer or social worker arrives at their home with a copy of a court order. The courts have attempted to encourage local authorities to put parents on notice of their intention to apply for FGMPOs to prohibit travel to ensure cooperation between families rather than hostility.

In the case of *Buckinghamshire County Council v MA and another* [2016] EWHC 1338 (Fam), the family court gave guidance to parents and local authorities about the need to cooperate and discuss travel plans to countries where FGM is prevalent. If legal proceedings are necessary, authorities are invited to ensure parents have sufficient notice before proceedings commence. The local authority was concerned that girls of a particular family might be cut

---

[129] ibid [54].

[130] ibid [28]: accordingly, whenever substantial grounds are shown for believing that an individual would face a real risk of being subjected to treatment, contrary to Art 3, if removed to another country, the state becomes responsible for safeguarding against such treatment: *Cruz Varas v Sweden* [1991] 14 EHRR 1 [69]; *Vilvarajah v United* Kingdom [1991] 14 EHRR 248 [103]; *Chahal v United Kingdom* [1996] 23 EHRR 413 [80]; *Z v United Kingdom* [2002] 34 EHRR 3 [C93].

[131] *Local Authority v M & N* (n 120) [41]: '… whilst there can be no derogation from N's article 3 rights, the interference with her article 8 rights, and those of her siblings and family, must be limited to that which is necessary to protect her article 3 rights. Of course, though this is relatively easy to state, it is difficult to apply on the facts of this case and, I suspect, in FGMPO applications generally.'

[132] ibid [57].

in Somalia during a holiday. The girls' elder sisters had been cut in Somalia.[133] Even though the local authority was involved with the family already, the family had not given the local authority notice about the holiday.[134] When the girls returned from Somalia they were medically examined and they had not been cut.[135] After assessing the family, the local authority concluded there was a low risk of FGM[136] and sought permission to withdraw their application. The parents were aggrieved by a third set of court proceedings due to a perceived risk of FGM and sought for the court to make findings of fact that the girls were not at risk of FGM to prevent future applications.[137] The parents' response shows their likely anger towards the local authority for initiating legal proceedings and for the social worker's continued involvement in their family life. The girls' sisters had been cut and risk is not static but fluid, therefore the court could not find that there was no risk of FGM.

The court stated that where the local authority is involved in a family's life there is an expectation on parents to inform the local authority of a planned trip not later than twelve clear weeks prior to travel to a country of high prevalence.[138] Furthermore, it is expected that the local authority will take prompt legal action if protection of the court is required.[139] Whilst the judgment attempted to encourage cooperation between parents and local authorities to prevent hasty legal action, the reality is that many authorities will not be aware of this judgment and decisions are often made by under-resourced local authorities in a short space of time.

FGMPOs Ensured the Return of Children from Sudan

FGMPOs have also been used successfully to return children from abroad to England and Wales. If the orders are breached, the respondents could face criminal sanctions. Criminal consequences can act as a deterrent to parents who would ordinarily refuse to cooperate with a court order. The case of *Re F and X (Children)* [2015] EWHC 2653 (Fam) highlights the creative way in which FGMPOs can be used to return stranded children from countries

---

[133] *Buckinghamshire County Council v MA and another* [2016] EWHC 1338 (Fam) [3] (hereafter *Buckinghamshire v MA*).
[134] ibid [5], [11].
[135] ibid [6].
[136] ibid [7].
[137] ibid.
[138] ibid [15].
[139] ibid.

where there is a risk that FGM will be performed. In this case, the local authority brought proceedings under the inherent jurisdiction and schedule 2 of the FGM Act 2003 in respect of two children, a girl age thirteen and a boy age eleven. The family resided in England and Wales. The mother had alleged domestic abuse which was denied by the father. The mother took the children to Sudan for the school summer holidays. She returned at the end of the school holidays without the children. The mother was arrested for child abduction. The court accepted that there were real grounds of concern that the girl might undergo FGM is she remained in Sudan. The father remained in England and Wales and also sought the children's return.

The mother was ordered to return the children to England and Wales and to make the children present to the British Embassy in Khatoum.[140] The mother failed to comply with the order and claimed that her son wished to remain in Sudan, which the father denied. As a result, the local authority intended to commence committal proceedings to commit the mother to prison for breaching the order.[141] The mother accepted that she will comply with the order and as a result a detailed court order was drafted to facilitate the children's return.[142] The local authority indicated that their attitude to committal proceedings will be affected if the mother complies with the order.[143] As a result, the FGMPO was made and the children were ordered to return to the jurisdiction.

The Interrelationship between FGMPOs and Immigration Law

When FGMPOs were implemented by the government in 2015, it was largely unforeseen that FGMPOs might be used to protect a girl or woman who does not have immigration status.[144] As a result, there is no explicit consideration about the power of family courts to make FGMPOs to protect girls and women at risk of FGM on return to their home countries where FGM is prevalent. Women and girls can qualify for refugee status under the 1951 Refugee Convention due to a well-founded fear of persecution.[145] However,

---

[140] *Re F and X (Children)* [2015] EWHC 2653 (Fam) [4].
[141] ibid [9].
[142] ibid [8].
[143] ibid [9].
[144] There is no reference in *Hansard* parliamentary to Parliament considering how FGMPOs would apply to girls and women at risk of FGM who do not have immigration status.
[145] For an overview of immigration and asylum issues in the context of FGM in the UK, see, Samuel, *(FGM): Law and Practice* (n 31).

the Home Office previously enforced a hostile environment for immigrants seeking asylum, including those claiming asylum on the basis of FGM, and as such offered them limited or no protection. It is well documented that women's and girls' asylum claims on the basis of FGM are refused.[146] This can leave women and girls at risk of being removed from the UK by the Home Office to a country of high FGM prevalence where they might be cut. As a result, there have been a number of reported cases concerning the protection of women and girls without immigration status from FGM. The family court does not have the power to curtail the immigration powers of the Secretary of State for the Home Department (the Home Secretary) and therefore the family court cannot prevent the Home Secretary from removing a complainant from the jurisdiction, even if the family court considers that there is a risk of FGM on return to their country of heritage. If an FGMPO is granted by the family court it might be possible to argue that the Home Office should reconsider any refusal of a family's asylum claim on the basis that the family court considers that there is a risk of FGM. However, an FGMPO will not necessarily change the Home Office's decision.[147]

Family court decisions are made on a case-by-case basis depending on the factual matrix of the case before the court. A review of the reported cases shows the wide discretion that the family court has when making case management decisions and when deciding whether to order an FGMPO. This

---

[146] Some of the common reasons for refusal include parents being found not to be credible possibly due to a delay in claiming asylum; parents unable to evidence the risk of FGM in their home countries which is an almost impossible task; the Home Office argue that the family can be internally relocated in another part of their country of heritage away from the family who intend to cut the girl; FGM is a criminal offence in the country of heritage and thus the Home Office contend there is state protection. For a discussion of the common reasons for refusal of asylum claims across Europe see, Annemarie Middelburg and Alina Balta, 'Female Genital Mutilation/Cutting as a Ground for Asylum in Europe' (2016) 28(3) International Journal of Refugee Law 416. The UK does not hold data on the number of women and girls that claim asylum on the ground of FGM and the number of claims that are allowed and refused.

[147] Home Office guidance dated 10 April 2018 states, 'In cases where there is a protection order the detail of the individual protection order must be carefully considered, for example you may see cases which involve an FGM Protection Order (FGMPO) or Forced Marriage Protection Order. The fact that a protection order has been made by the Family Court may provide strong evidence of risk of persecution or serious harm. However, the order may not provide evidence about risk on return to their country, so does not in itself mean that refugee status should automatically be granted. The asylum claim must still be considered on its individual merits, taking into account that the Family Court has made an order and the reasons for it doing so. Such orders must be considered in the round and given appropriate weight in reaching your decision on future protection needs. The fact that an order has been granted by the Family Court, which may state that the individual concerned should remain in the UK, does not mean that the person cannot be removed from the UK if after careful consideration the asylum claim is to be refused and you have concluded that the individual is not in need of international protection. GD (Ghana) highlights that whilst the Home Office is not bound by Family Court Orders they must be taken into consideration': see, Home Office 'Gender Issues in the Asylum Claim' (2018) 20 <https://assets.publishing.service.gov.uk/government/uploads/system/uploads/attachment_data/file/699703/gender-issues-in-the-asylum-claim-v3.pdf> accessed 7 March 2021.

has resulted in inconsistent decision-making by the courts. In some cases, the family court has been reluctant to make an FGMPO when there are or have been immigration proceedings for fear of FGMPOs being used as a device to undermine the immigration proceedings.[148] In other cases, the family courts have taken a proactive approach to protect vulnerable girls with no immigration status by ordering experts to carry out risk assessments to ascertain the risk of FGM on return to their home countries and then some courts grant an FGMPO.[149] A family court might find that there is a high risk of FGM, which could conflict with decisions made by the Home Secretary or the immigration tribunal that there is a low risk or no risk of FGM. Tensions have emerged between the competing jurisdictions about what weight should be attached to each jurisdiction's evaluation of risk. For example, the Home Secretary and the immigration courts might find that there is a low or no risk of FGM for a child upon return to their home country but a family court might find that there is a high risk of FGM. The family court's decision might encourage the Home Secretary or immigration courts to change their decision and grant the child immigration status. A direct contrast can be drawn between the family court's approach in cases concerning children with and without immigration status. A family court is often reluctant to order FGMPOs when a child has no immigration status and the threat of FGM is abroad. However, the family court will readily impose FGMPOs to protect British children from being removed from the jurisdiction and cut abroad even if the risk of FGM is low.[150] Whilst there are many reasons for the family court's reluctance to intervene in cases concerning non-British children, the consequence is that they are afforded less protection from the risk of FGM than British children. Children who are habitually resident in England and Wales but do not have secure immigration status are arguably discriminated against, which could breach Articles 8 and 14 ECHR. A review of the key cases involving children at risk of FGM who do not have immigration status shows the different approaches taken by the family court.

---

[148] See *A v A (FGMPOs: Immigration Appeals)* [2018] EWHC 1754 (Fam), [2018] 4 WLR 105 (hereafter *A v A*).

[149] See *Re E (Children) (Female Genital Mutilation Protection Orders)* [2015] 2 FLR 997; *W v BBW (Female Genital Mutilation Protection Order)* [2018] EWHC 3862 (Fam), (hereafter *W v BBW*); *A (A Child: Female Genital Mutilation: Asylum)* [2019] EWHC 2475 (Fam) (hereafter *A (Child: FGM: Asylum)*); *A (A child) (Female Genital Mutilation Protection Order Application)* [2020] EWHC 323 (hereafter *A (A Child) (FGMPO Application)*).

[150] See *X (FGMPO No 2)* (n 88) where a British child was subject to a worldwide travel ban outside of England and Wales despite the fact that the risk of FGM was low and the risk of FGM was in Egypt only.

First FGMPO Case: An 'Immigration Scam'

The first published FGMPO case is *Re E (Children) (Female Genital Mutilation Protection Orders)* [2015] 2 FLR 997. The was one of the first published FGMPO cases. It transpired to be an immigration scam in which the mother claimed that her children were at risk of FGM to assist her asylum claim to remain in the UK. It might be partly as a result of this case that the courts are reluctant to intervene in proceedings concerning children without immigration status.

The mother applied for leave to apply for an FGMPO on behalf of her three daughters age twelve, nine and a half, and six. The court granted the mother leave to apply for an FGMPO and heard the application.[151] The mother was divorced from their father. The family's heritage and citizenship were Nigeria. The father was resident in Nigeria. The mother and children did not have secure immigration status in the UK. The mother alleged physical abuse perpetrated by the father upon her and the children. The mother alleged that the father sent ceremonial robes from Nigeria to prepare for FGM. The judge concluded that if the mother's statement was true there would be 'a very high risk indeed to one of more of these three vulnerable girls'[152] of undergoing FGM. The FGMPO was extended beyond the usual terms to provide for,[153] 'The respondent must not himself, or encourage, permit or cause any other people to (a) use or threaten violence against the applicant or children; (b) intimidate, harass, threaten or pester the applicant or the children.'

The mother invited the judge to make an order prohibiting the father from coming within 100 metres of the home or the children's schools to protect the children.[154] The judge cautioned against extending the powers under schedule 2 of the FGM Act 2003 to the extent that it would 'get stretched to providing protection for somebody such as the mother herself in this case'.[155] The judge declined to make an order prohibiting the father from coming into contact with the mother directly; instead, the mother could have applied for a non-molestation order or invited the court to make such an under of its own motion.[156]

---

[151] The case was first heard by a judge at a telephone hearing on a without notice basis, which means that the respondent father had no notice of the hearing. The FGMPO was granted and listed two days later and the order was continued by the court.

[152] *Re E (Children) (FGMPOs)* (n 149).

[153] ibid [25].

[154] ibid [26].

[155] ibid [27].

[156] FLA 1996 (n 32) s 42(2)(a).

The case highlights the wide discretion that the family court has when determining the nature of FGMPOs.[157] The case took an unusual turn of events when it later transpired that the case was part of an 'immigration scam' to obtain refugee status on the basis of a well-founded fear of persecution of FGM in Nigeria rather than there being a genuine risk of FGM. The judge found that the mother had 'fundamentally and dishonestly misrepresented the true position'.[158] The children's father travelled from Nigeria to England and made clear that he did not support FGM. The court permitted the father to remove the children to Nigeria. If the father had not returned the children to Nigeria, it was likely that the local authority would have commenced care proceedings due to concerns that the children were suffering significant harm attributable to the parenting of the mother.[159] The case shows the overlapping nature of asylum claims and FGMPOs. The risk of FGM is often rooted abroad; therefore it is likely that some cases will concern children without immigration status in the UK. In some cases, the family court refused to make an FGMPO where the risk of FGM is overseas or when the child's asylum claim remains undetermined.[160] In some cases, the Home Secretary is invited to intervene because the case is likely to have some repercussions on the pending asylum claim;[161] in other cases the Home Secretary is not even informed of court proceedings. This shows the wide discretion that family court judges have and the different decisions that are made by judges at interim and final stages of proceedings.

Woman from Sierra Leone at Risk of FGM

In the case of *W v BBW (Female Genital Mutilation Protection Order)* [2018] EWHC 3862 (Fam), a twenty-one-year-old woman from Sierra Leone applied for an FGMPO to protect herself from the risk of FGM.[162] The woman had applied for asylum on the basis of FGM. The Home Secretary had refused her claim and the immigration court had yet to determine her appeal. In this case, a woman applied for an FGMPO to protect herself from the risk of FGM and it was granted on 13 December 2016 but was due to expire when she reached

---

[157] For a critique of the wide nature of the FGMPO introduced rather than imposing a non-molestation order see, Gaffney-Rhys, 'Development of the Law Relating to FGM' (n 25).
[158] See, *CE v NE* [2016] EWHC 1052 (Fam).
[159] ibid [84], [108].
[160] See *A v A* (n 148).
[161] See, *A (Child: FGM: Asylum)* (n 149).
[162] *W v BBW* (n 149).

the age twenty-one. Since the initial FGMPO was ordered by the family court, the woman had been free from pressure by her family to undergo FGM. The woman's stepmother is a 'cutter' in the Bondo Society and the woman was afraid that she would be forced to undergo FGM.[163] The woman's stepmother travels between the UK and Sierra Leone and thus an FGMPO is likely to be a deterrent to performing FGM.[164] However, the family court also noted that she remained a young person who required protection, she had uncertain immigration status, as her asylum claims had been refused by the Home Secretary and the immigration court had not determined her appeal.[165] Interestingly, the woman's insecure immigration status weighed in favour of the court granting an FGMPO to provide her with further security from FGM, yet in other cases, the courts have refused to grant FGMPOs due to the child's or woman's uncertain immigration status.[166] The court also dealt with a new situation where an FGMPO had expired but the woman wanted to extend the order. The court held that the woman could not apply to extend an order that had already lapsed in time because there is no mechanism under schedule 2 of the FGM Act 2002 to extend the order once it had expired.[167] As a result, the court made an order afresh under section 2(2)(a) of schedule 2 of the FGM Act 2003.[168] The order was made without notice to the stepmother due to fears the woman would be put at risk; however a return date was listed.[169]

Girls at Risk of FGM in Nigeria Refused FGMPO

In the case of *A v A (FGMPOs: Immigration Appeals)* [2018] EWHC 1754 (Fam), [2018] 4 WLR 105, the court refused to grant an FGMPO to protect two girls from the risk of FGM in Nigeria because their immigration appeals had not yet been determined by the immigration courts and the risk of FGM

---

[163] ibid [5].
[164] ibid [6].
[165] ibid [4].
[166] *A v A* (n 148).
[167] *W v BBW* (n 149) [7] of the judgment states, '... on the clear wording of Schedule 2 section 6 (1)(4) that although the court has the power to vary or discharge an FGM Protection Order, the words "vary" and "discharge" in section 6(1) only apply to an order which remains in force at the date of the application for an extension (which application would constitute, on my reading of section 6, an application to vary and therefore fall within section 6 of the Act)'.
[168] ibid [8].
[169] ibid [9] of the judgment. The woman was given permission to serve her stepmother by WhatsApp or Facebook.

was abroad.[170] This decision is further explored to highlight the inconsistent decision-making in family courts.

An urgent *ex parte* application was made for an FGMPO to prevent two girls from being subject to FGM in Nigeria. The girl's parents applied for an FGMPO. They are of Nigerian descent and are citizens of Nigeria. They travelled together as a family to England in August 2010 and since then the mother gave birth to a son and two daughters. They are not British citizens and they do not have immigration status. The family contend that they are members of the Yoruba Tribe where FGM is the norm. The mother reported that she was cut and her sisters were cut. The father's two sisters were also cut. The head of the mother's family and the head of the father's family will allegedly bring about FGM in Nigeria. The Home Secretary had already refused the family's asylum claim. The asylum appeal was before the immigration tribunal and a decision had yet to be made.

The family court refused to make the order on the basis that there was 'currently no actual risk of mutilation of either of these daughters unless and until they are actually removed by the Secretary of State to Nigeria'.[171] The learned judge reinforced that the making of orders is 'discretionary' and ought only to be made when there is an appropriate level of current risk against the girls.[172] However, there is no legal threshold that determines what the appropriate level of risk is; as such, another judge might have reached an entirely different decision. The court determined that the risk of FGM should be in the UK or the risk of FGM abroad should be foreseeable for an FGMPO to be granted, which conflicts with other court decisions. The court made an FGMPO and imposed a travel ban in the case of *Re X (FGMPO No 2)* to protect a British girl from a low risk of FGM in Egypt.[173]

The family court was concerned that, 'the making of a genital mutilation order in this case might be seen as impacting upon, or influencing in some way, the discretionary decision which requires to be taken in October by the immigration appeal tribunal'.[174] Due to a reluctance to influence the decision of the immigration tribunal, the judge declined to make any order. However, should the family lose their appeal and the Home Secretary attempts to remove

---

[170] *A v A* (n 148) [10]: the court concluded that it would decline to make any orders for the following reasons, 'first, that there is, in fact, no current or immediate risk of genital mutilation to these two girls; and, second, that it is quite wrong of this court to make any sort of order in these circumstances until the immigration tribunal system has decided upon the underlying asylum claims'.

[171] ibid [6].

[172] ibid.

[173] *X (FGMPO No 2)* (n 88).

[174] *A v A* (n 148) [7].

the two girls from the jurisdiction, the family could make a further application during the removal window notice period, which can be a matter of days.[175] No consideration was given to the short time frame in which removal directions are issued by the Home Secretary and therefore the limited time available to apply for an FGMPO when a family is due to be removed abroad. The purpose of another application would not be to prohibit removal of the girls but rather to ascertain whether an FGMPO could be enforced in Nigeria, thereby protecting the children from FGM. If 'the applicants consider that there is still a purpose or benefit for the children in Nigeria in obtaining a female genital mutilation protection order here in the very last period before the children are actually removed to Nigeria, then, of course, they can make a further application'.[176] The court would have jurisdiction to make such an order because they are habitually resident in England and Wales; however, issues could arise in respect of extraterritoriality.[177] The court's refusal of the initial application for an FGMPO is likely to act against any further application for legal aid to make an FGMPO.

The court will not grant FGMPOs where there are ongoing immigration proceedings because it does not want to impact upon the decision-making of the immigration courts.[178] It is questionable whether the family court made the correct decision in refusing to order an FGMPO. The family court decision in this case conflicts with the divergent decision made in the same year of 2018 in the case of *W v BBW (Female Genital Mutilation Protection Order)* [2018] EWHC 3862 (Fam) where the family court granted an FGMPO to protect a woman at risk of FGM in Sierra Leone and there were subsisting immigration proceedings. As a result of this decision it is likely to be increasingly difficult for women and girls to obtain FGMPOs when their immigration case has yet to conclude and the risk of FGM is abroad. However, there is no jurisprudence that the family courts *must* decline to make orders concerning a child's welfare when there are subsisting immigration proceedings. In fact, the president made clear in the case of *A (A Child: Female Genital Mutilation: Asylum)* [2019][179] that the family court can conduct its own risk assessment of FGM regardless of the decisions made by the Home Secretary or the immigration tribunal.

---

[175] ibid [9].
[176] ibid.
[177] ibid.
[178] On reviewing judgments given in FGMPO cases it makes one question whether family courts approach applications for FGMPOs consistently.
[179] *A (Child: FGM: Asylum)* (n 149).

Seemingly, the family court's approach in this case, namely for FGMPOs to be made *after* the determination of the immigration courts and once the family has been served with a removal notice, contradicts other court decision. In June 2018, the author appeared in the High Court of the Family Division before a High Court judge on behalf of a mother who sought an urgent *ex parte* FGMPO on behalf of her daughter. The family, including the child, had been issued with removal directions and she was due to be removed from England to Nigeria the following day. The mother claimed that there was a risk of FGM to the child in Nigeria. The High Court judge refused the application on the basis that the application was an attempt to appeal against decisions made in the immigration court and by the Home Secretary and if this was a serious issue of concern, the application for an FGMPO would have been made long before removal directions were issued. In this case the application was dismissed and the mother was criticised for not making the application for an FGMPO when she first applied for asylum on the basis that her daughter was at risk of FGM. However, the decision of *A v A (FGMPOs: Immigration Appeals)* [2018] EWHC 1754 (Fam), [2018] 4 WLR 105 held that an application for an FGMPO should only be made when removal directions are in place. The mother followed this guidance and her application was dismissed, despite the fact that the child was due to be removed the next day. The decision of the president in *A (A Child: Female Genital Mutilation: Asylum)* [2019][180] makes clear that it is imperative that family courts conduct their own risk assessment (this issue could be reviewed on appeal) yet in this case the child was not afforded this opportunity. The inconsistent approach in the court's handling of FGMPOs concerning non-British children at risk of FGM is staggering. In the case of *Re A*, the Home Secretary used the instant case as a means of arguing that the family courts must not be used as a device to sway immigration tribunals' decisions. The Court of Appeal held in *Re A (A Child) (Rev 1)* [2020] EWCA Civ 731:

1. The Secretary of State seeks to derive some support for her position from the decision of Holman J sitting in the family court in *A v A (FGMPOs: Immigration Appeals)* [2018] EWHC 1754 (Fam), [2018] 4 WLR 105, where an application for a FGM protection order was refused and at [7] the court held that the 'making of a genital mutilation order in this case might be seen as impacting upon or influencing' the determination of the appeal tribunal. The judge added at [8] that he was hesitant

---

[180] ibid.

to do anything that 'might be seen as impacting on, or influencing, the discretionary decision [to be taken by] the immigration appeal tribunal'.

2. The context of the observations of a judge experienced in both jurisdictions needs to be considered carefully. *A v A* involved an application that was made urgently and prematurely by a mother not by or with the support of a local authority acting in the performance of its safeguarding responsibilities. What the decision demonstrates is not an application of the principle of comity as between the family court and the immigration and asylum tribunal but rather the careful avoidance of what would otherwise have been a tactical attempt to use the family court to interfere in the jurisdiction of the immigration and asylum tribunal.

The Court of Appeal's comments are concerning. The Court of Appeal reiterate that the parent's application for an FGMPO in *A v A* was not supported by the local authority, which as becomes more apparent in later cases, the courts seem reluctant to make FGMPOs in cases where a child does not have immigration status unless supported by the local authority. There is also an implicit suggestion that applications for FGMPOs could be used as a 'tactical attempt' to 'interfere in the jurisdiction of the immigration and asylum tribunal'. This cautious approach has resulted in children without secure immigration status who are at risk of FGM being afforded less protection than British citizens.

Judge Refuses FGMPO where the Child's Immigration Claims Have Failed

In the case of *HM v DM* [2020] EWHC 1117 (Fam), the mother made an application for urgent FGMPOs on behalf of her daughter. The mother reports that she underwent FGM when she was born by her uncle who was the respondent to this application.[181] The mother also reported that her parents supported FGM.[182] The mother claims that when she was sixteen, she was forced to marry her husband who was around forty years old at the time and he was abusive towards her.[183] She gave birth to twins, a boy and a girl, in Nigeria and the girl was cut at three months old.[184] The applicant came to the UK on a six-month medical visa without her children and when in the UK she decided not to return to

---

[181] *HM v DM* [2020] EWHC 1117 (Fam) [3].
[182] ibid.
[183] ibid [4].
[184] ibid.

Nigeria.[185] In response, the mother claims that her husband threatened to 'pour acid and to kill her, were she ever to return to that country'.[186] The mother had two children in the UK by different fathers. The children were reported to be at risk of FGM in Nigeria due to historical threats made by her uncle.[187]

The court noted that the risk of FGM is in Nigeria—not in the UK—due to her uncle being in Nigeria.[188] Whilst the mother's asylum claim appears to have failed, there is no 'deportation order in place' for her or her children which does not suggest an imminent risk of removal to Nigeria.[189] The court noted that there was limited evidence available about the family's immigration status. The court held, 'The court must have before it evidence that establishes a risk of female genital mutilation to the requisite standard, namely, on the balance of probabilities, before it grants such an order.'[190] However, the test under section 1(2) of schedule 2 of the FGM Act 2003 does not state that there must be a risk of FGM on the balance of probabilities in order for an FGMPO to be granted. Instead, the test is broad, 'In deciding whether to exercise its powers under this paragraph and, if so, in what manner, the court must have regard to all the circumstances, including the need to secure the health, safety and well-being of the girl to be protected.' In order for the court to be satisfied that the test is met, the court would need evidence that the uncle is coming to England or the mother will be sent to Nigeria with her children.[191] The court refused the application rather than adjourning the case and giving directions for further evidence.[192] The decision shows again the wide discretion that family court judges have when deciding whether to make FGMPOs.

The Family Court Cannot Prohibit the Home Secretary from Deporting a Girl at Risk of FGM and the Family Court Is Not Bound to Follow the Immigration Tribunal's Assessment of Risk of FGM

In a precedent-setting case in *Re A (A Child: Female Genital Mutilation: Asylum* [2019] EWHC 2475, the president of the Family Division concluded that the

---

[185] ibid [6].
[186] ibid.
[187] ibid [7].
[188] ibid [12].
[189] ibid.
[190] ibid [14].
[191] ibid [15].
[192] ibid.

family court cannot restrain the Home Secretary's immigration powers and it cannot prohibit the Home Secretary from removing a girl or woman at risk of FGM under an FGMPO. In this long-running case, the Home Secretary and the immigration courts refused the mother's asylum claim on the basis that it was unlikely that her daughter would be cut on return to Sudan or Bahrain.[193] In contrast, the family court concluded that there is a high risk of FGM if the girl is removed from the UK. However, the family court has no power to change the decision of the Home Secretary or prevent the removal of the girl from the UK. FGMPOs are unable to protect a girl or woman from FGM when they do not have secure immigration status and the Home Secretary decides to remove them to their country of heritage. The decision is analysed in further detail to highlight the key legal principles in similar cases.

The parents of the child subject to proceedings are of Sudanese heritage but they hold Bahraini citizenship. The mother was subject to Type III FGM as a child in Sudan. Her two sisters died as a result of FGM and the practice continues in her family. The mother has a daughter who was age ten at the time of the application and four sons. The mother believes that the father and her eldest son are detained in a Bahraini prison and thus they were not involved in the case.[194] The mother applied for asylum on behalf of her children claiming that amongst other concerns, her daughter would be cut if they were returned to Sudan or Bahrain. The local authority had been involved with the family due to concerns about FGM.[195] The National FGM Centre had completed a report on the family during the asylum claim process in which they confirmed that if the child was removed from the country, she would be at high risk of FGM and it recommended that an FGMPO is applied for in the family court.[196] The asylum claim was refused and the mother's appeal rights were exhausted, meaning that she had no further mechanism to challenge the immigration decision through the courts.[197]

The family received a removal notice confirming that the Home Secretary intended to remove them on a flight to Bahrain imminently. The local authority applied for an urgent FGMPO due to concerns that the girl would be at high risk of FGM on removal from England and Wales. An urgent hearing was listed at which point the family court made an FGMPO and prohibited the

---

[193] A (Child: FGM: Asylum) (n 149).
[194] ibid [2].
[195] ibid [4].
[196] ibid.
[197] ibid [3].

Home Secretary from removing the child from the jurisdiction of England and Wales.[198] The court recorded in the order that 'this application is not a device to circumvent any immigration orders as such application has been brought by the Local Authority on the advice of Barnardo's who are respected and recognised, for their expertise in relation to Female Genital Mutilation'.[199] In this case, the local authority was the applicant and therefore deemed credible. The unhelpful implication is that women and girls are not deemed credible without third-party corroboration. Applications for FGMPOs are usually made by the parents of the girl. Often third parties such as the police or local authorities refuse to apply for FGMPOs to protect a girl or woman from FGM because the risk is abroad, which follows the logic in the decision of *A v A* [2018].[200] However, local authorities are required to take active steps to ensure that the child is protected from FGM.[201] Immigration determinations are confidential and therefore not normally disclosed to local authorities, which highlights the difficulty of local authorities ensuring that vulnerable children without immigration status are safeguarded.[202]

The case was re-listed for a return hearing, at which point the Home Secretary applied to intervene. The Home Secretary submitted that it was not bound by the FGMPO and the court did not have the power to prohibit the Home Secretary from removing the child from the jurisdiction. It also argued that the family court is bound by the immigration court's assessment of risk of FGM. The matter was eventually transferred to the president of the Family Division to consider a number of legal issues in further detail.[203]

The president concluded that the family court did not have the power to restrain the exercise of the Home Secretary's immigration powers in relation to

---

[198] ibid [6].

[199] ibid.

[200] *A v A* (n 148).

[201] *A (Child: FGM: Asylum)* (n 149) [57]–[58]. Para 57: 'A local authority has duties to safeguard and promote the welfare of children in its area who are in need under CA 1989, s 17(1) and s 47(1) and (3) [in England] and the Social Services and Well-being (Wales) Act 2014, s 21 [in Wales]. If, on investigation, the authority determines that a FGM protection order is necessary, it will issue an application.'

[202] ibid [21].

[203] The president determined: '(a) Whether a judge of the Family Division and/or the Family Court can lawfully injunct or restrain the exercise of the Secretary of State for the Home Department's immigration powers in relation to a mother and child by making an FGM protection order.'

> (b) The role of the Family Division in assessing the risk of a child being subjected to female genital mutilation (FGM) in circumstances where the risk has been assessed by the Immigration and Asylum Tribunal and dismissed as a basis for asylum with all appeal rights exhausted.
> (c) The duty on the local authority in meeting its statutory obligations under the FGM Act 2003 in these circumstances.

the child[204] or to make an injunction against the Home Secretary.[205] The president highlighted case law confirming the family court cannot curtail the Home Secretary's immigration powers. In *Re A (Care Proceedings: Asylum Seekers)* [2003] EWHC 1086 (Fam), [2003] 2 FLR 921, Munby J (as he then was) considered an application for the continuation of care proceedings with the avowed aim of thwarting the Home Secretary's decision to deport the parents and children and concluded that:[206]

> 48. ... a judge of the Family Division can no more than a judge of the County Court or a Family Proceedings Court make an order which has the effect of depriving the Secretary of State of his power to remove a child or any other party to the proceedings.

Counsel for the mother in the FGMPO case attempted to distinguish the case law in respect of other child welfare concerns from FGM cases. The mother submitted that the family court has jurisdiction to injunct the Home Secretary under schedule 2 of the FGM Act 2003 and to continue the order until the family court has evaluated risk.[207] It was argued that the family court has exclusive jurisdiction to make FGMPOs and the executive conferred upon the court wide-ranging powers, for example, paragraph 1(3) of

---

(d) Whether the FGM protection order (dated 1 October 2018) should be continued or discharged'. ibid [8]

[204] ibid [47]–[52]. Also, see relevant case law, *R v Secretary of State for Home Department ex parte T* [1995] 1 FLR 292; *Re A (Care Proceedings: Asylum Seekers)* [2003] EWHC 1086 (Fam); *Re Mohamed Arif (An Infant)* [1968] Ch 643; *Re F (A Minor) (Immigration: Wardship)* [1990] Fam 125; *Re A (Care Proceedings: Asylum Seekers)* [2003] EWHC 1086 (Fam), [2003] 2 FLR 921; *Re W (A Minor) (Wardship: Jurisdiction)* [1985] AC 791.

[205] See, Sir James Munby's judgments in *Re (Anton) v Secretary of State for the Home Department* [2004] EWHC 2730/2731 and in *GD (Ghana) v Secretary of State for the Home Department* [2017] EWCA Civ 1126. In *Re (Anton)*, Sir James Munby held:

33 ... A judge of the Family Division cannot in the exercise of his family jurisdiction grant an injunction to restrain the Secretary of State removing from the jurisdiction a child who is subject to immigration control—even if the child is a ward of court. The wardship judge cannot restrain the exercise by the Secretary of State for the Home Department of his power to remove or deport a child who is subject to immigration control ...

34 This does not mean that the family court cannot make a residence order in respect of a child who is subject to immigration control or cannot make such a child a ward of court. Nor does it mean that the family court cannot make a care order in respect of such a child. What it does mean, however, and this is the important point, is that neither the existence of a care order, nor the existence of a residence order, nor even the fact that the child is a ward of court, can limit or confine the exercise by the Secretary of State of his powers in relation to a child who is subject to immigration control.

[206] *A (Child: FGM: Asylum)* (n 149) [18].
[207] ibid [23].

schedule 2 of the Act states that an order may contain 'such prohibitions, restrictions or requirements ... as the court considers appropriate for the purposes of the order'. There is no explicit statutory bar in the FGM Act 2003 from making an order against the Home Secretary.[208] Furthermore, a firm distinction can be drawn between FGMPOs, which invoke Article 3 ECHR, and an order pursuant to the Children Act 1989 and wardship orders, which concern the child's welfare rather than breach of Article 3 ECHR.[209] Previous case law concerns welfare-based authorities rather than Article 3 ECHR authorities. Under Article 3 ECHR there is a positive duty on the state to undertake risk assessments.[210] The court rejected the mother's submissions and concluded that there is no express exception in legislation to the effect that there is an exception to the blanket prohibition on the family court granting orders against the Home Secretary where there is a risk of Article 3 ECHR.[211] Parliament would need to have included an express provision for an exception under schedule 2 of the FGM Act 2003.[212] Whilst the family court cannot make an injunction against the Home Secretary, it does have the power to invite the Home Secretary to agree not to remove the child until the conclusion of the FGMPO proceedings and the Home Secretary could grant the family discretionary leave whilst the proceedings are ongoing.[213]

The court then went onto determine the role of the family court when the immigration tribunal has already assessed risk of FGM. The family court concluded that the family court and the immigration court assess the risk of FGM differently and therefore each jurisdiction should conduct their own risk assessment of FGM.[214] The court held that the family court in assessing risk under schedule 2 of the FGM Act 2003 does not need to 'start' with the immigration tribunal's assessment of the credibility of the parties and risk of

---

[208] ibid [24].
[209] ibid [29].
[210] ibid [30].
[211] ibid [48].
[212] ibid [50].
[213] In the case of *Ciliz v The Netherlands*—29192/95 [2000] ECHR 365 a father seeking an order providing him with contact with his son was awarded trial contact meetings with him by a court but was detained, removed, and denied re-entry to the Netherlands before those meetings took place. The Strasbourg court held that his expulsion denying him the possibility of the trial meetings with his son prejudged the outcome of the contact proceedings and denied the father meaningful further involvement in those proceedings. In *MS (Ivory Coast) v Secretary of State for the Home Department* [2007] EWCA Civ 133 at [24], [27], and [75] the Court of Appeal held that where family proceedings are under consideration in the case of a party who has no leave to remain or is facing removal, a period of discretionary leave should be granted to enable that person to remain lawfully in the UK and participate in those proceedings.
[214] On this issue King LJ granted permission to appeal to the Court of Appeal.

FGM.[215] The risk assessment undertaken by the family court and immigration tribunals is distinct. The family court has a duty to form its own assessment, unencumbered by having to give priority to the outcome of the immigration jurisdiction.[216] For example, in the family court, the child has the benefit of separate representation through a children's guardian and there is a higher degree of scrutiny as to fact-finding exercises by the family courts.[217] In *Re H (A Child)* [2016] EWCA Civ 988 the court set out that the family and immigration court's assessment of risk of FGM is not comparable:

> 25. In approaching an asylum/humanitarian protection claim, the Home Office looks to see whether the person concerned has a well- founded fear of persecution or is at real risk of serious harm for a non-Convention reason. The approach to risk is not the same as that taken in a family case. In a family case, establishing risk is a two-stage process. First, the court considers what facts are established on the balance of probabilities; then it proceeds to consider whether those facts give rise to a risk of harm, see *Re J (Children)* [2013] UKSC 9. In contrast, in an asylum/humanitarian protection claim, the material presented by the claimant is looked at as a whole with a view to determining whether there is a well- founded fear of persecution or substantial grounds for believing that a person would face a real risk of serious harm, a reasonable degree of likelihood of serious harm being what is required. There is no comparable process of searching for facts which are established on the balance of probabilities.

The Home Secretary argued that the family courts must respect the decision of the immigration tribunal in respect of risk of FGM in the country of return when deciding whether to make an FGMPO.[218] For example, if the immigration tribunal found no risk of FGM, the family court, seized of an FGMPO, would take the immigration tribunal's decision as its starting point.[219] Only in exceptional and rare circumstances should the family courts take

---

[215] *A (Child: FGM: Asylum)* (n 149) [55]–[56].
[216] ibid [56]. 'The family court has a duty by FGMA 2003, Schedule 2, paragraph 1(2) to 'have regard to all the circumstances' and, to discharge that duty, the court must consider all the relevant available evidence before deciding any facts on the balance of probability and then moving on to assess the risk and the need for an FGM protection order. Although the family court will necessarily take note of any FTT risk assessment, the exercise undertaken by a FTT is not a compatible process with that required in the family court. It is not therefore possible for an FTT assessment to be taken as the starting point or default position in the family court.'
[217] ibid [32].
[218] ibid [34].
[219] ibid.

a different view to the immigration tribunal's decision.[220] The family court disagreed with the approach advocated by the Home Secretary.[221] Indeed, it would be wrong for a family court to adopt adverse credibility findings made against a mother by an immigration court when the child who is at risk of FGM was not the claimant. In this case, the mother claimed asylum on behalf of her daughter and the immigration court made findings that the mother (not her daughter) was not credible.[222] If the family court were to adopt the immigration court's adverse credibility findings about the mother as its starting point, this would be contrary to the family court's paramount consideration being the child. Similarly, if the family court made findings about risk of FGM, the immigration courts would not be bound by these findings, thus it would be incomprehensible for the family court to be bound by the immigration court's findings.

If the family court found a high risk of FGM, which conflicts with the findings of the immigration court, the family could make a new claim and invite the Home Secretary to reconsider its decision.[223] However, the Home Secretary might refuse to change its decision and grant the family leave to remain in the UK. Furthermore, the onus of applying to the Home Secretary for the reconsideration of their decision is left to a vulnerable parent who might not be aware of the process for making further representations leaving girls

---

[220] ibid.

[221] Similarly, if the family court made findings about the risk of FGM, the Home Secretary and the immigration courts would not be bound by these findings, thus it would be wrong for the family court to be bound by the immigration courts findings.

[222] Children have a fundamental right to claim asylum in their own names rather than relying upon their parent's application. UK Visas and Immigration guidance further notes concerning Rule 349 (at 6.1, p 15) that para 349 of the Immigration Rules states that family members dependent on the principal mother's asylum claim, may claim asylum in their own right and their applications will be considered individually irrespective of the outcome of the principal mother's claim. Family members may lodge their own asylum claim at any time during their stay in the UK.

UK Visas and Immigration 'Dependents and Former Dependents' (Guidance) (2014) <https://www.gov.uk/government/publications/dependants-and-former-dependants-asylum-policy-instruction> accessed 7 March 2021

[223] A (Child: FGM: Asylum) (n 149) [37]–[38], [51] of the judgment. See Part 12: Procedure and Rights of Appeal, para 353: Fresh Claims, the Immigration Rules https://www.gov.uk/guidance/immigration-rules/immigration-rules-part-12-procedure-and-rights-of-appeal accessed 19 May 2021. '353. When a human rights or protection claim has been refused or withdrawn or treated as withdrawn under paragraph 333C of these Rules and any appeal relating to that claim is no longer pending, the decision maker will consider any further submissions and, if rejected, will then determine whether they amount to a fresh claim. The submissions will amount to a fresh claim if they are significantly different from the material that has previously been considered. The submissions will only be significantly different if the content:

    (i) had not already been considered; and
    (ii) taken together with the previously considered material, created a realistic prospect of success, notwithstanding its rejection.

This paragraph does not apply to claims made overseas.'

unprotected, which could fall short of the state's obligation under Article 3 ECHR.[224]

The president's decision gave guidance to the family courts when dealing with applications for FGMPOs in respect of girls and women without immigration status. The most significant part of the president's decision was the determination that the family court can undertake its own risk assessment of FGM even when the immigration courts have found a low risk or no risk of FGM.

The Home Secretary appealed the decision of the president and leave to appeal was granted on the papers but refused at a substantive oral hearing.[225] The Home Secretary argued that the family court must take the immigrational court's assessment of the risk of FGM as its starting point on the basis of comity and proportionality.[226] The appeal raised an important issue concerning the relationship and overlap between the immigration and family jurisdictions in undertaking risk assessments of FGM. The Court of Appeal upheld the decision of the president for the following reasons: proceedings in the immigration tribunals are adversarial and bind the parties to that appeal (the mother and the Home Secretary) and no-one else;[227] the statutory language is unambiguous, plain, and mandatory that the family court *must* have regard to *all* of the circumstances;[228] and there are clear Family Procedure Rules 2010 on the admission of evidence and expert evidence and there is no need for an additional test.[229] The Home Secretary also relied on the principle of 'proportionality' on the basis that two sets of litigation could take place in the immigration tribunals and the family courts involving the same factual issues which is a 'waste of public expenditure'. However, the Court of Appeal held that the decision-making process is materially different in both jurisdictions. In the family court, a child 'will be separately represented' and will have her own voice.[230]

The family court conducted its own risk assessment at a later hearing.[231] It found that risk of FGM is not static and that it is sensitive to change as new evidence of risk emerges.[232] Anthropologist, Professor Bradley, was instructed as an expert witness and warned that all types of FGM are harmful regardless of the type of FGM performed.[233] FGM is highly prevalent in Sudan, 86.6–97.7%,

---

[224] *A (Child: FGM: Asylum)* (n 149) [42], [52].
[225] *A (A Child) (Rev 1)* [2020] EWCA Civ 731.
[226] ibid [25], [26].
[227] ibid [27].
[228] ibid [28].
[229] ibid [29].
[230] ibid [40].
[231] *A (A Child) (FGMPO Application)* (n 149).
[232] ibid [13].
[233] ibid [20].

and within the Sudanese community in Bahrain.[234] The family court held that 'FGM signified a woman's subservience and obedience to men'.[235] A psychiatrist was instructed as an expert witness to assess the mother's mental health. The psychiatrist found that the mother was suffering from post-traumatic stress disorder, anxiety, and depression and she required the assistance of an intermediary, which was not available to her when she gave evidence in the immigration court.[236] The psychiatrist noted that depression can impact upon recall of information and questioning can re-traumatise her and she was at risk of suicide if returned.[237] The children's guardian stated that the negative impact on the mother's mental health if the family were to be removed would render her less able to provide protection to the child.[238] The court instructed a Bahraini legal expert who confirmed that it is possible for the family to have their citizenship stripped if they are failed asylum seekers.[239] Whilst FGM is criminalised in Bahrain, there are no NGOs actively campaigning against FGM, thus the mother would have limited support.[240] In some parts of Sudan, FGM is criminalised but there had, at that time, not been one conviction.[241] Any court orders made in England and Wales would unlikely have any effect in Bahrain or Sudan.[242] The court also had the benefit of hearing evidence from a social worker at the National FGM Centre and the child's appointed social worker, all of whom confirmed a high risk of FGM on return to Bahrain or Sudan.[243]

The court made findings that the wider family will decide whether the child is cut and the decision does not rest with one person.[244] This conflicts with the immigration court's finding that the mother will be able to protect her daughter from FGM. The child speaks no Arabic and has limited knowledge of her African heritage and no knowledge of FGM; she has lived in the UK since the age of three and will struggle to protect herself.[245] The risk of FGM increases into adulthood, particularly marriage.[246] None of these issues were considered by the immigration court. The court held that whilst the mother may have told

234 ibid [26].
235 ibid [21].
236 ibid [23], [32].
237 ibid [32], [35].
238 ibid [36].
239 ibid [31].
240 ibid [41].
241 ibid.
242 ibid [42], [47].
243 ibid [25].
244 ibid [29].
245 ibid [29], [36], [58]–[59].
246 ibid [29].

lies in respect of some issues, it does not follow that she has lied about every-thing.[247] The court highlighted that there is a language barrier and miscom-munication can occur through errors of translation,[248] which the immigration court probably failed to consider. Unlike in the immigration tribunal where the mother was found not to be credible, the family court found that the mother is credible, 'I do not find the mother inconsistent or unreliable'.[249] Two separate jurisdictions made entirely different findings about the mother's credibility. In 2017, she was found incredible by the immigration court and in 2020, she was found credible by the family court.

The court made an FGMPO to protect the child from a high risk of FGM but noted that the mother is unlikely to be in a position to ensure the order is adhered to due to her vulnerabilities and the wider family pressure and the order would have no real effect in Bahrain or Sudan.[250] Whilst the family court decided that there is a high risk of FGM, the family court has no power to pre-vent the removal of the girl from England and Wales. The divergent decision-making in immigration and family courts is staggering. The case of *Re A* took the family court over twelve months to conclude, whereas it took the immigra-tion court only half a day to assess the risk of FGM. The inquisitorial nature of family court proceedings involving children is more rigorous and robust than immigration proceedings. The concern of immigration courts is that children are being deported to high prevalence countries where they might be cut.

Judge Refuses to Appoint a Children's Guardian and Order Expert Assessments Where the Family Have No Immigration Status

In the case of *AB v AN and another* [2020] EWHC 2048 (Fam),[251] the mother applied for an FGMPO against her husband and the paternal grandmother to restrain them from removing the protected person, her daughter, from the UK and performing FGM on her in Nigeria. The mother sought an FGMPO and later applied for the appointment of a children's guardian to represent the child and three experts to assess the risk of FGM to the child: an independent social worker, an in-country expert in Nigeria, and a psychiatrist to assess the mother.

---

[247] ibid [23].
[248] ibid [24].
[249] ibid [52].
[250] ibid [60]–[61].
[251] Hereafter *AB & AN and another*.

The mother made an asylum claim before her daughter arrived in the UK and her application was refused. The mother alleged that her daughter was at risk of FGM in Nigeria and family members had been injured or killed trying to protect the child. The mother reported that she was a victim of FGM at age five and her sister died from FGM. The mother alleged that the father and his family intend to subject the child to FGM.[252] Her claim for asylum was refused and adverse credibility findings were made against her by the immigration court.

In July 2019, the child's father brought the child to the UK to live with the mother. The mother made a new asylum claim on the basis that her daughter was now in the UK and she would be at risk of FGM if she was returned to Nigeria. However, her asylum claim was refused.[253] The mother applied for an FGMPO which the court refused to grant because there was no risk that the child would be removed to Nigeria as the Home Secretary had not implemented removal directions.[254] The court ordered that the respondents are served with the applications and they confirmed in writing that they intended to play no role in the case but that they supported FGM.[255] The local authority apparently encouraged the mother to apply for an FGMPO but then failed to support her application at court.[256] The court stressed that this case can be distinguished from *Re A* and *Re X* on the basis that the local authority has not made the application for an FGMPO in this case.[257] If local authorities fail to safeguard the child, parents have no alternative but to apply for an FGMPO. When parents apply for an FGMPO without local authority support, the application is perceived as a means of using the family courts as a device or ploy to obtain immigration status. An application for an FGMPO by a local authority lends the parents much-needed credibility in such circumstances.

The court refused to grant the child an FGMPO and it refused the mother's applications for the appointment of a children's guardian and expert assessment of risk of FGM.[258] The court made the Home Secretary an intervener to ensure that the court had all the relevant documents and a 'range of submissions'.[259] The Home Secretary took a robust position in firmly opposing all of the applications.[260] The court takes a surprising leap in attempting to impose a threshold that must be met in order for an FGMPO to be granted even

---

[252] ibid [8].
[253] ibid [6].
[254] ibid [7].
[255] ibid [8].
[256] ibid [13].
[257] ibid [18], [32], [40].
[258] ibid [19].
[259] ibid [26].
[260] ibid [26], [27], [42].

though schedule 2 of the FGM Act 2003 is clear that there is no threshold of risk that must be proved for an FGMPO to be made. Apparently, the evidence must reach a threshold of showing 'a real risk' of FGM before an order can be granted, which suggests a high threshold.[261]

The court expresses an extraordinary view in finding that the motivation for the making of an application for an FGMPO is to support the mother's asylum claim.[262] This finding was made at an interim hearing without hearing evidence. The court states that, 'it is my view obvious from the history of this matter that at least part of the purpose of seeking an FGMPO is for the Applicant to be able to produce it to the SSHD as part of her case against removal from the UK.[263] The court stated that, 'the assessment of the risk of FGM here turns very largely if not wholly on the Applicant's evidence as to the likely conduct of the Father's family and her ability to protect EO [the child].[264] The criteria for appointing a children's guardian was, in my opinion, plainly met (the criteria is set out in the judgment).[265] The Court of Appeal in Re A held that a child will be separately represented in family proceedings.[266] In Re X, the child was also separately represented.[267] The court finds that there is no conflict between the position of the mother and the child because their interests 'are identical.[268] If the mother is found not to be telling the truth then there is 'no basis for granting an FGMPO' and the case entirely turns on whether the mother is telling the truth.[269] In Re A it was noted that a guardian should be appointed because the child needed a separate voice from a parent, especially when the parent's credibility was tarnished and when the parent has a vested interest in obtaining an FGMPO. Even if the parent is found not to be credible, the child might still be at risk of FGM.

The court refused the instruction of independent experts on the basis that litigation must be 'proportionate.[270] The court found that Home Office Country Information Notes could instead be used even though such Notes are produced for the 'purposes of immigration control,[271] which highlights the judge's primary focus in this application—immigration control rather than child protection. The court even refused the application for a psychiatric

---

[261] ibid [20].
[262] ibid [21].
[263] ibid [21].
[264] ibid [21].
[265] Para 7 of Practice Direction 16.4 of the Family Procedure Rules 2020.
[266] A (A Child) (Rev 1) [2020] EWCA Civ 731 [25], [40].
[267] ibid [25].
[268] ibid [31].
[269] ibid [31], [35].
[270] ibid [41].
[271] ibid [42], [43].

assessment of the mother despite GP evidence about anxiety and depression.[272] It is entirely unclear how the court is to assess whether a single mother suffering with anxiety and depression can protect a child from the risk of FGM in Nigeria. Instead, the court finds that the evidence will again turn on whether the mother is credible and her mental health is not 'determinative', which is completely at odds with the Part 25 test of necessity. The court addressed the case in a similar manner to asylum claims. This case highlights the inconsistent decision-making in FGMPO proceedings, which could potentially leave girls at risk of FGM. It also shows a divergent approach towards children without immigration status in contrast to children who are British citizens. Permission to appeal was refused by the Court of Appeal.

Conclusion

There have been more FGMPOs sought than the numbers of criminal prosecutions for FGM in over thirty years since anti-FGM legislation came into force. FGMPOs have helped to protect women and girls from the risk of FGM. The number of orders applied for continues to increase. However, there is a lacuna in the research addressing the impact, if any, that FGMPOs are having upon the protection of women and girls at risk of FGM.[273] Having analysed the published judgments in FGMPO cases, it seems likely that FGMPOs have been successful in protecting women and girls from FGM but that they could have been more widely used than at present. In addition, there remain barriers to the implementation of FGMPOs which need to be addressed with further policy responses, as addressed below.

The courts have adopted a cautionary approach in FGM cases concerning British children. The courts fully investigate the risk of FGM and the risks are reduced by putting safeguards in place. There are a range of key themes that emerge from the published judgments. The central concern is the risk of FGM abroad, which is alleviated by risk assessments and a travel ban imposed by the family courts. Whilst travel bans interfere with a child's and family's Article 8 right to a private and family life, the ban is often proportionate given the risks that are posed by FGM. Medical assessments are becoming increasingly more commonplace to prove a girl's or woman's cut or uncut status.

---

[272] ibid [44]–[49].
[273] See, J Home and others, 'A Review of the Law Surrounding Female Genital Mutilation Protection Orders' (2020) 28(7) British Journal of Midwifery 418.

The real cause for concern is the family courts' reluctance to order FGMPOs involving girls who are habitually resident in England and Wales but who do not have immigration status. The issue usually involves the risk of FGM in the country of heritage. In these cases, the family courts continue to take a cautious and conflicting approach: some family courts order FGMPOs and conduct their own risk assessment, whilst other judges dismiss applications for FGMPOs due to concerns that the family court is used to circumvent the immigration process. In my view, the family courts should adopt the following approach in such cases: first, an application for an FGMPO should be made at the earliest convenience, ideally prior to removal directions imposed by the Home Secretary, to ensure that the family court has ample time to hear the case and make directions to properly assess the risk of FGM to the girl (regardless of the immigration court's findings or otherwise). Second, the local authority should be directed to assess the risk of FGM or pay for a risk assessment because they have a fundamental duty to safeguard children and they cannot simply escape their duties because the risk of FGM is overseas.

It is important to highlight that ethnic minority women and girls often struggle to access the law, particularly laws designed to tackle violence against women and girls. Women and girls from migrant communities might not have access to recourse to public funds and they might only have limited knowledge about the law and therefore are unable to seek support. Women and girls whose first language is not English might experience language barriers. Women with insecure immigration status may suffer in silence because they fear that seeking help could result in their deportation from the UK. It is a well-known fact that insecure immigration status increases girls' and women's vulnerability to gender-based violence.[274] These concerns might also readily apply to cases in which an FGMPO might be applied for. Such barriers can result in necessary orders not being applied for because of the obstacles that women and girls experience. It is unlikely that they will have the required resources to apply for FGMPOs to protect themselves. The majority of FGMPO applications are made by local authorities or the police or family members. However, parents who do make applications for FGMPOs to protect their daughters from FGM abroad are often viewed with suspicion, with courts making a preliminary and often unfair assessment that the application is a device to circumvent immigration proceedings.

---

[274] See, F Gerry and others, 'Widespread Concerns Still Exist in Relation to the Discrimination towards Women and Girls and FGM' (2021) Archives of Disease in Childhood.

A further barrier to applying for FGMPOs is access to legal aid. An individual applying for an FGMPO is not automatically entitled to legal aid. Legal aid is government-paid legal advice and representation. To qualify for legal aid, the individual must meet the stringent means and merits test. The application process can take over six weeks. If the case is an emergency, individuals might not have the benefit of legal representation because their application will probably not have been processed in time.[275] Gerry, Proudman, and others argue that it is time for an FGM Commissioner in the UK to address legal and policy responses to FGM and ensure that they are consistent and working towards the aim of eradicating FGM rather than undermining that aim.[276] A central person who is responsible for overseeing the multi-faceted responses and diverse sectors involved in FGM would be invaluable.

Whilst there are recommendations for change to FGMPOs to make them more effective, they are a novel legal remedy that now has a proven track record of success in protecting women and girls from the risk of FGM in England and Wales and abroad. Serious consideration should be given to rolling out FGMPOs in other European jurisdictions, which would assist in raising awareness of FGM and it would provide a specific legal remedy to prevent FGM. In addition, FGMPOs ordered in the UK could then be enforced in other jurisdictions which also implemented FGMPOs.

---

[275] As a family law barrister, I have come across a number of cases in which clients have had to wait over six weeks for the legal aid agency to grant them legal aid to allow them to apply for an FGMPO with legal representation. The time is excessive and does not allow for emergency situations. The delay in processing legal aid applications also causes clients stress and anxiety in the process.

[276] AG Rowland and others 2021, 'The time is right to introduce an independent commissioner', (2021) 29(1) British Journal of Midwifery 50. Also see, F Gerry and others, 'Why It Is Time for an FGM Commissioner—Practical Responses to Feminised Issues' (2020) Family Law Journal.

Epilogue

I raise my voice and call on others to join me in empowering communities, which themselves are eager for change. We can end FGM within
a generation, bringing us closer to a world where the human rights of
every woman, child and adolescent are fully respected, their health is
protected and they can contribute more to our common future.

Former United Nations Secretary-General Ban Ki-Moon[1]

FGM is a violation of the dignity and integrity of girls' and women's bodies—
and it must be eliminated—this book asks what impact the law has had on
ending the practice. Most discussions about anti-FGM laws show an ambivalence towards the law changing the prevalence of the practice. Whilst FGM
was criminalised in 1985, the first conviction for FGM was not until 2019,
which shows that the law has been ineffective in prosecuting and convicting
perpetrators. Despite changes to laws and policies—in criminal law—and the
introduction of FGM protection orders (FGMPOs) in family law—it is likely
that FGM continues to be performed underground outside of the purview of
law enforcement agents. Measuring the efficacy of the law is challenging for
any social scientist, especially in relation to a practice which is shrouded in
secrecy and performed by minority communities. Early critics of anti-FGM
laws suggested that the law would generate hostility and resistance and thus
the continuation of FGM. The persistence of FGM might suggest continuities
in cultural practices and communities' resistance to abandoning FGM. At the
forefront of this book was the need to understand the reasons and motivations
for performing FGM from the perspective of women who have experienced
the practice or live in communities where FGM is prevalent.

[1] Maggie O'Kane, 'Ban Ki-Moon Calls on Men across the World to Campaign to End FGM' *Guardian*,
(London, 6 February 2016).

Female Genital Mutilation. Charlotte Proudman, Oxford University Press. © Charlotte Proudman 2022.
DOI: 10.1093/oso/9780198864608.003.0007

Women have been placed at the forefront of the practice;[2] FGM is still perceived as a 'woman's issue'. FGM remains a taboo and intimate issue that is rarely discussed within FGM-performing communities. Interview participants and court cases reaffirmed the prevailing view that women control the practice of FGM. Women's attitudes towards FGM depended on a variety of demographic features ranging from age, class, cultural ties, and their families' beliefs about FGM. Whilst the prevailing public sentiment towards FGM is that it is child abuse, there were strong variations in women's attitudes towards FGM, with some sympathising or defending the practice as well as outright rejecting FGM. To encourage the abandonment of FGM, the law needs to accompany extensive education initiatives at a grassroots level. For example, concerns were identified that many women are unaware that all types of FGM are prohibited, including for adult women. Whilst women mainly supported a criminal offence of FGM when performed on children, most women were divided about the prohibition of FGM for adult women. At present, it is a criminal offence for FGM to be performed on adult women. Women's testimonies were divided about whether family and community pressures to conform to engrained cultural practices undermine women's consent to FGM and even if so, some women argued they still ought to be permitted to conform to patriarchal practices. However, it is important to analyse why women make choices that stem from social and cultural influences.[3]

This book explored the key motivations for FGM, including the control of girls' and women's sexuality, preservation of a cultural practice, and religious beliefs. Testimonies from women show that the practice is motivated by the regulation and control of a woman's body and sexuality that undermines her freedom, equality, and dignity. Regardless of women's acts of resistance as accommodators or resisters of FGM, the practice forms part of a patriarchal power structure which legitimises the need to ensure women's virginity, marriageability, fidelity as well as the control of their reproduction. The fear that severe consequences could unfold if girls and women transgressed the norm of FGM serves to maintain the practice by force. The consequences of non-conformity are severe, including ostracisation and isolation, which are examples of

---

[2] Men's voices are absent in the conversation about FGM. Locating male interview participants was a near impossible task. It is far from clear that FGM is controlled solely by women to the exclusion of men. The practice is framed as a means of controlling a woman's and girl's sexuality, thus men have an important role as the drivers of the practice.

[3] For a discussion about the impact of social influences on women's body choices see, Sandra Lee Bartky, 'Foucault, Femininity, and the Modernization of Patriarchal Power' in Lee Quinby and Irene Diamond (eds), *Feminism and Foucault: Reflections on Resistance* (Northeastern University Press 1997) 25.

violent social sanctions imposed on women. As such, the notion that women *choose* to undergo FGM in a context of familial and community pressure arguably undermines or even vitiates their free and full consent.[4] Whilst some women opposed the notion that FGM causes their body irreparable damage, other women argued that the practice has caused them psychological and physical trauma such as flashbacks. When there is a risk that a non-medical procedure can cause significant harm, the state has a duty to ensure that the practice is eradicated.

FGM needs to be understood using a feminist and critical race framework. FGM is a unique offence; the law is designed by the political elite who have no experience or knowledge of FGM and it is projected upon marginalised migrant communities. Women of colour's lived realities of FGM stemmed from unique, intimate, and personal experiences, which can be analysed from a feminist and critical race standpoint, whilst their experiences of the law often relate to systematic and institutional inequality as a result of their gender, race, and class. The multiple layers of discrimination that women experience heighten their vulnerability and experience of FGM and the law.[5] Women's testimonies highlighted that they were cautious about anti-FGM laws because it could provide a means for law enforcement agents to *legitimise* the ongoing surveillance of migrant communities who already feel under attack. Women linked anti-FGM laws to broader structures of oppression within the criminal justice system, such as experiencing racist and sexist treatment or the perpetuation of stereotypes of migrant communities as child abusers, which deters them from accessing support. Rather than relying on law enforcement agents, grassroots level initiatives run by women from FGM-performing communities could encourage women to abandon FGM.

The majority of professionals who were interviewed took a strong stance towards FGM and opposed the practice. Law enforcement officers tended to support anti-FGM laws whilst recognising the limitations of the law engendering changes in attitudes and beliefs towards FGM. Professionals who worked closely with FGM-performing communities, including medical practitioners and NGO workers, often sympathised with the practice and questioned the

---

[4] Isabelle R Gunning, 'Arrogant Perception, World-Travelling and Multicultural Feminism: The Case of Female Genital Surgeries' (1991) 23 Columbia Human Rights Law Review 189 (hereafter Gunning, 'Arrogant Perception'); Clare Chambers, *Sex, Culture, and Justice: The Limits of Choice* (Penn State Press 2008).

[5] For a discussion about intersectional inequality and feminism see, Jennifer C Nash, 'Re-thinking Intersectionality' (2008) 89(1) Feminist Review 1; Yakin Ertürk, '15 Years of the United Nations Special Rapporteur on Violence against Women, its Causes and Consequences (1994—2009)—A Critical Review' (United Nations 2009) (hereafter Ertürk, '15 Years').

impact of the law on ending FGM. The variation in professionals' responses to the practice suggest that there is no mainstreamed response to FGM cases or suspected cases. Education about the legal remedies for FGM is imperative. It remains unclear whether professionals are complying with their duties under section 5B of the FGM Act 2003 to report cases of FGM performed on girls to the police. However, it is essential that professionals who have a duty to report FGM cases to the police are adequately trained in FGM to ensure they are properly equipped with knowledge and understanding about FGM. Gill, Cox, and Wier concluded that the voices of victims and practitioners must be considered in the creation of future priority services.[6] At present, these voices are marginalised when they should be at the forefront of policy and legal changes.

Describing FGM as child abuse is not without criticism, as many women rejected being defined as child abusers and instead argued that many parents perform FGM to safeguard their children from living a life uncut, which could result in social ostracization, amongst other sanctions.[7] Women's descriptions of FGM affirm the widely held view that the practice is abusive, especially when inflicted on children. However, it appears disproportionate to apply the label of 'child abuser' to parents who have not had any educational training in FGM and have been socialised to conceptualise FGM as a normal practice. The label of child abuse has largely two effects amongst others: it can assist in encouraging professionals to acknowledge the seriousness of FGM; and it can have the counter effect of rousing tensions and hostilities within FGM-performing communities who already feel marginalised, and as a consequence they might resist the label and reinforce the practice underground. In order to eliminate FGM, which is the ultimate objective, education and consciousness-raising work needs to be undertaken within communities. Labelling and stigmatising communities as child abusers is unlikely to achieve this objective.

This book suggests that the impact of anti-FGM laws is complicated; such laws can have unintended consequences. The interview participants' testimonies show that communities appear determined to continue FGM by

---

[6] Aisha Gill, Pamela Cox, and Ruth Wier, 'Shaping Priority Services for UK Victims of Honour-Based Violence/Abuse, Forced Marriage, and Female Genital Mutilation' (2018) 57(4) Howard Journal of Crime and Justice 576.

[7] To understand this contrary view, see, Kay Boulware-Miller, 'Female Circumcision: Challenges to the Practice as a Human Rights Violation' (1985) 8 Harvard Women's Law Journal 155; Isabelle R Gunning 'Women and Traditional Practices: Female Genital Surgery' in Kelly D Askin and Dorean Koenig (eds), *Women and International Human Rights Law*, Vol 1 (Transnational Publishers999); Richard A Shweder, 'What about "Female Genital Mutilation"? And Why Understanding Culture Matters in the First Place' (2000) 129(4) Daedalus 209; Moira Dustin and Anne Phillips, 'Whose Agenda Is It? Abuses of Women and Abuses of "Culture" in Britain' (2008) 8(3) Ethnicities 405 (hereafter Dustin and Phillips, 'Agenda').

changing the dynamics of the practice, making it more difficult to detect thereby evading the law; for example, the type of FGM has changed from Type III to Type IV FGM, which is difficult to detect by medical professionals. Women's resistance to anti-FGM initiatives might also stem from perceptions that the law targets and stigmatises women of colour and FGM-performing communities. Rather than the law garnering support from within communities and changing attitudes towards FGM, it can easily have the counter effect, as communities reject anti-FGM laws that are perceived as neo-colonial.

Resistance towards anti-FGM laws appears to be reinforced by the normalisation of cosmetic surgery on women's genitalia, which some women argue mirrors FGM. The permissibility of female genital cosmetic surgery (FGCS), whilst prohibiting FGM, creates double standards and ignites anger and hostility. The legal double standard is an obstacle to the end-FGM movement and is a form of racist discrimination against FGM-performing communities. Whilst so-called Western women and girls can undergo FGCS in private cosmetic clinics, women of colour are discriminated against and refused surgery on their genitalia which is akin to FGCS. In other instances, FGCS has been used as an avenue for women to undergo FGM under the guise of cosmetic surgery. The permissibility of FGCS serves as an advocacy tool for FGM-performing communities to argue against the criminalisation of FGM for adult women. This political objective contrasts with Western feminists who take an analogue approach and compare the practices but with a different purpose. Applying a feminist framework, I conclude that FGM and FGCS exist on a continuum of violence against women. Both practices are performed to ensure that a woman's body looks and functions in accordance with harmful, patriarchal cultural norms and values. FGM and FGCS show that the control of women's sexuality persists on a global scale and is not confined to FGM-performing communities.[8] Patriarchal cultures, whether in the West or in minority communities, pressurise women to conform to body ideals which are often unattainable. Women experience cultural pressures of varying degrees to undergo genital surgery. Some women experience pressure from media advertisements to have a 'designer vagina', while other women seek FGM to ensure social status in their community and marriageability. If a woman fails to comply with body norms, she could be subject to social sanction such as body shaming or social stigma if her labia does not conform to ideal body images—or—they could be subject to

---

[8] Germaine Greer, *The Whole Woman* (Doubleday 1999); Simone Weil Davis, 'Loose Lips Sink Ships' (2002) 28(1) Feminist Studies 7; Kathy Davis, 'Responses to W. Njambi's "Dualisms and Female Bodies in Representations of African Female Circumcision: A Feminist Critique": Between Moral Outrage and Cultural Relativism' (2004) 5(3) Feminist Theory 305.

familial isolation if they refuse to undergo FGM. Both practices stem from cultural pressures of different degrees. Drawing on a feminist analysis, I argue that FGCS should be reconceptualised and defined as harmful to women, thus both FGCS and FGM would then be prohibited for *all* adult women.

FGM is largely defined as a cultural practice which is embedded in traditional understandings of norms and values over generations.[9] However, defining FGM as a cultural practice is fraught with conflicts and tensions and ultimately prevents FGM from being eradicated. The former United Nations Special Rapporteur on Violence against Women argued that 'culture-based identity politics' has posed 'one of the most serious challenges to women's human rights'.[10] Violence against European and American women is not seen as cultural but instead an aberration of the individual man, while violence against African, Arab, and Asian women is viewed as intrinsic to their culture and identity, which is linked to racism.[11] The behaviour of cultural groups is perceived as more culturally determined than that of the dominant culture because the powerful West is seen as having no culture but the universal culture of civilization.[12] Black and Asian activists have campaigned for honour killings and forced marriage to be viewed as a form of violence rather than examples of culturally specific practices.[13] This could prevent the link between gender-based violence and culture, which can unintentionally feed racist narratives. Scholars struggle to achieve a balance between the impact of culture and tradition on violence and how patriarchy operates differently in diverse cultures.[14] Rather than viewing FGM as rooted in culture, scholars argue that it should be viewed as a patriarchal traditional custom in the context of colonialism and economic exploitation of marginalised communities.[15]

---

[9] Sympathising with FGM as a legitimate practice in non-Western cultures is subject to criticism from the former United Nations Special Rapporteur on Violence against Women, Radhika Coomaraswamy, who argued that women have a lack of influence in defining culture and traditions in male-dominated communities: Radhika Coomaraswamy, 'Integration of the Human Rights of Women and the Gender Perspective: Violence Against Women' (Report of the Special Rapporteur on Violence Against Women, its Causes and Consequences, Ms Radhika Coomaraswamy, submitted in accordance with Commission on Human Rights resolution 2001/49: cultural practices in the family that are violent towards women, United Nations Economic and Social Council 2002) (hereafter Coomaraswamy, 'Violence against Women').

[10] Ertürk, '15 Years' (n 5) 39.

[11] Moira Dustin, 'Female Genital Mutilation/Cutting in the UK: Challenging the Inconsistencies' (2010) 17(1) European Journal of Women's Studies 7.

[12] Natalie J Sokoloff and Ida Dupont, 'Domestic Violence at the Intersections of Race, Class, and Gender Challenges and Contributions to Understanding Violence against Marginalized Women in Diverse Communities' (2005) 11(1) Violence against Women 38 (hereafter Sokoloff and Dupont, 'Domestic Violence').

[13] Erica Burman, 'Engendering Culture in Psychology' (2005) 15(4) Theory & Psychology 527.

[14] Sokoloff and Dupont, 'Domestic Violence' (n 12).

[15] ibid.

Whilst it is important to address the cultural roots of FGM, framing it as a cultural form of violence against women and girls specific to migrant communities hinders rather than helps the movement. The testimonies of women and professionals showed that viewing FGM using a singular lens of culture is reductive because it leads to the public condemning the practice as a barbaric cultural custom. Adopting hyperbole language of cruelty and barbarism has the unintended consequence of communities resisting anti-FGM initiatives and continuing FGM underground. FGM has avoided scrutiny from some professionals since 1985 when FGM was initially criminalised because it was seen as a 'cultural practice' that deserves tolerance and respect.[16] Professionals' testimonies showed that some feared intervening in FGM cases due to concerns they might be branded racist, otherwise known as 'race anxiety'.[17] Professionals' failure to intervene in FGM cases can result in so-called cultural issues associated with violence being silenced and marginalised and girls left without protection and legal redress.[18] Recognising the challenges of eliminating FGM when it is defined as a cultural practice, FGM has been reframed as child abuse and a form of violence against women and girls.

Scholars often contend that the human rights approach emphasising law and punishment in eliminating violence against women and girls is ineffective and emphasis should instead be placed on education, community, and health initiatives.[19] However, the law can have a significant impact on changing the normalisation of gender-based violence over time, incrementally. There were examples in the testimonies that women had abandoned the practice or changed the dynamics of FGM due to fears of criminal sanctions, which shows that the law has an impact on the practice and may even act as a deterrent. However, there were examples of the practice continuing as a means of resisting the law. A top-down approach of law enforcement is rarely successful. Increased state responsibility with grassroots-led initiatives targeting health and education programmes combined with effective legislation is likely to have a greater impact on changing ingrained cultural practices. The law cannot change communities' attitudes and beliefs without grassroots-led initiatives. When attempting to eliminate FGM through legislation, the law must account for the discrimination that women experience when accessing the criminal

---

[16] Coomaraswamy, 'Violence against Women' (n 9).
[17] Erica Burman, 'From Difference to Intersectionality: Challenges and Resources' (2003) 6(4) European Journal of Psychotherapy & Counselling 293.
[18] Dustin and Phillips, 'Agenda' (n 7).
[19] For a discussion of this approach in the context of FGM see, Gunning, 'Arrogant Perception' (n 4); Coomaraswamy, 'Violence against Women' (n 9).

justice system and how this operates as a barrier to women seeking support. The law has not been designed from an intersectional perspective, as it fails to recognise women's unique identities and different experiences of FGM. The law approaches FGM as a monolithic issue and essentialises women.

The government must invest funding in community initiatives to challenge the practice over a long duration across the country. Regulated professions, including the police, health, education, and social services, require mandatory training about FGM and anti-FGM laws to ensure they are aware of how to deal with cases of FGM and to avoid fears of 'race anxiety' arising. The discourse and language used by the media and the government when discussing FGM needs to be carefully monitored to ensure the issues are not sensationalised and communities are not labelled and stigmatised as barbaric and child abusers. The impact of such rhetoric can have the adverse effect of reinforcing rather than eliminating FGM.

Further research exploring the impact of women's experiences of FGM and the law when women do not have secure immigration status needs to be explored further. While some women are successful in gaining asylum on the grounds of FGM, other women's claims and appeals are unsuccessful. Globalisation is likely to result in increasing numbers of women seeking refugee status in Britain on the grounds of FGM. With no social security, basic service provision systems, and an anti-immigration sentiment, women's experiences of leaving situations where they face FGM to access safety and support in Britain need to be explored.[20] The barriers to the law functioning effectively as identified in this study could be remedied with a national action plan led by the government. With anti-immigration rhetoric increasing in England, there is less political will to support migrant communities with practical and effective measures to protect vulnerable girls. Instead, there has been a move towards a right-wing discourse that uses FGM as a means of labelling migrant communities as barbaric. Understanding FGM requires examining the practice from an intersectional perspective and removing reductive links to race, culture, religion, and immigration status from anti-FGM discourse.

FGMPOs, a family law remedy, offer the protection and support that women and girls need without punitive sanctions being imposed unless the orders

---

[20] A research study undertaken by anti-FGM NGOs and academics found that migrant women from FGM-performing communities in the UK were deeply concerned by the absence of support for women who have undergone FGM, explaining that it is too hard to open up to their GP, social services, or the police about FGM due to the shame they felt, and instead would have preferred accessing specific services for FGM; Kate Norman, Seblework Belay Gegzabher, and Naana Otoo-Oyortey ' "Between Two Cultures": A Rapid PEER Study Exploring Migrant Communities' Views on Female Genital Mutilation in Essex and Norfolk, UK' FORWARD & National FGM Centre Report (2016).

are breached. These novel legal remedies offer hope that the law can prevent violence against women and girls whilst not marginalising communities. The success of FGMPOs might result in the orders being rolled out in other jurisdictions. The impact of FGMPOs needs to be explored further with interviews with individuals who have been through the court process as protected persons, applicants, and respondents in the process. Understanding women's experiences and the gaps in the law can assist in making the law reflective of women's lived realities, providing them with much-needed legal redress.

A number of policy and legal recommendations emerge from the testimonies. There needs to be an amendment to existing legislation to prevent the existence of the current loophole of FGCS. At present FGCS is permitted on the basis that genital surgery is necessary for a woman's physical or mental health, which is an exemption to anti-FGM legislation. To prevent the double standard, I propose removing section 1(2)(a) and section 1(5) of the FGM Act 2003, which would then prohibit FGM from being performed on grounds of physical or mental health. To remove the current perception that the law infantilises women and regards them as children, there could be a simple amendment to the wording of the FGM Act 2003 which currently refers to 'girls'. A simple change to the language of the Act to state 'girl and woman' reflects the meaning and purpose of the legislation. I suggest further research is undertaken to address whether section 5B of the FGM Act 2003 ought to be amended to provide for criminal sanctions if frontline professionals fail to notify the police of cases of FGM. At present, it appears that professionals are not reporting cases of FGM. Criminal sanctions might encourage compliance. There needs to be an international commitment to criminalising FGM across the globe to prevent loopholes that allow women and girls to be taken from England and cut abroad. For example, FGM is medicalised in Indonesia and performed in government-run hospitals in other parts of the world.[21]

This book is the start of what I hope will emerge as further research about FGM and the law in the UK. The story about the persistence of FGM in Britain and resistance to anti-FGM laws requires further research over an extended period of time, mapping the evolution of behaviours and laws from the 1980s. This hypothesis should be examined in further detail with research about the communication of anti-FGM laws at a grassroots level and the negotiation of the practice within families and communities from the early 1980s to the

---

[21] Radhika Coomaraswamy, 'Identity Within: Cultural Relativism, Minority Rights and the Empowerment of Women' (2002) 34 George Washington International Law Review 483; Coomaraswamy, 'Violence Against Women' (n 9).

present day. But to engage in such research it needs grounding in women's personal experiences and men's understanding about FGM and the law. Whilst further research is required, this book has deepened understandings about a sensitive and intimate practice, allowing access to the complex meanings tied to FGM and an understanding of the way the law is negotiated. These insights can dramatically change our understandings of women's lived realities from marginalised backgrounds.

Appendices

Appendix I: Table of Focus Groups with Women Participants

Focus group no	Location	No of participants	Country of heritage	Interpreter
FG1	Leicester	11	Somalia	Yes
FG2	London	11	Somalia	Yes

Appendix II: Table of Women Participants

Participant no	County of origin if known	Type of FGM if known	Employment [relevant if questioned about professional experience]
P1	Somalia	I	NGO worker
P2	Zimbabwe	IV	NGO worker
P3	Gambia	III	NA
P4	Kenya, Massai Tribe	I	NA
P5	Somalia	Unknown	NA
P6	Nigeria	Not undergone FGM	NA
P7	Somalia	Unknown	NA
P8	Somalia	Not undergone FGM	NA
P9	Mali	Unknown	Midwife
P10	Sierra Leone	II	Social worker
P11	Unknown	Unknown	NGO worker
P12	Somalia	III	Teacher
P13	Somalia	III	Nurse

Appendix III: Table of Male Participants

Participant no	County of origin if known
P14	Ghana
P15	Nigeria

Appendix IV: Table of Professional Participants

Participant no	Organisation as noted in interview tag	Role	Gender
P16	Department of Health	Civil servant working to amend and enforce legislation.	F
P17	Home Office	Civil servant working to amend and enforce legislation.	F
P18	Department for International Development	Civil servant working with NGOs internationally to eliminate FGM.	F
P19	Department for Education	Civil servant working to amend and enforce legislation.	M
P20	Local authority in the North of England	Established an FGM forum collaborating with professionals working with communities to share information.	F
P21	Member of the House of Lords	Government ministerial role when the Prohibition of Female Circumcision Act 1985 was implemented. Role involved scrutinising legislation.	M
P22	Member of the House of Lords	Shadow ministerial role when the Serious Crime Act 2015 was implemented. Role involved amending legislation.	F
P23	Member of the House of Lords	Scrutinised the Serious Crime Act 2015 and lobbied the government to introduce an offence of encouraging FGM in 2015, which was not successful.	F
P24	Member of the House of Lords	Government ministerial role when the Prohibition of Female Circumcision Act 1985 was implemented. Role involved scrutinising legislation.	F
P25	Member of the House of Lords	Involved in the implementation of the Prohibition of Female Circumcision Act 1985. In addition, P25 was a British representative for the UN status of women 1982 to 1988.	F
P26	Member of the House of Lords	Involved in scrutinising the Prohibition of Female Circumcision Act 1985 and the Female Genital Mutilation Act 2003.	F
P27	Member of the House of Lords	Anti-FGM campaigner who timetabled debates about FGM in the House of Lords.	M
P28	Member of Parliament	Instrumental in proposing and ensuring the implementation of the Female Genital Mutilation Act 2003.	F
P29	London Assembly Member	Anti-FGM campaigner since 1980 and former midwife who worked closely with FGM-performing community members.	F

Appendix IV: Continued

Participant no	Organisation as noted in interview tag	Role	Gender
P30	Member of Parliament	Member of the Public Bill Committee when the Serious Crime Act 2015 was implemented.	M
P31	Member of Parliament	Former Home Office minister, which involved improving the government response to FGM.	M
P32	National Health Service (NHS)	Midwife working with women affected by FGM and women and girls at risk of the practice.	F
P33	NHS	Midwife working with women affected by FGM and women and girls at risk of the practice.	F
P34	NGO	Works for an NGO specialising in FGM and provides support to FGM-performing communities.	F
P35	NHS	Midwife working with women affected by FGM and women and girls at risk of the practice.	F
P36	NHS	Midwife working with women affected by FGM and women and girls at risk of the practice and working with FGM national clinical group.	F
P37	General Medical Council	Advisor in standards and ethics team assisting medical professionals working with women and girls who have undergone FGM or are at risk of FGM.	F
P38	NHS and Member of the House of Lords	Involved in scrutinising the Prohibition of Female Circumcision Act 1985 and worked with women and girls affected by FGM as a former doctor.	M
P39	NHS	Obstetrician and gynaecologist working with girls and women affected by FGM.	F
P40	NHS	Obstetrician and gynaecologist working with girls and women affected by FGM.	F
P41	NHS	Consultant paediatrician in child protection clinic working with girls affected by FGM.	F
P42	NHS	Obstetrician and gynaecologist working with girls and women affected by FGM.	F
P43	NHS	Consultant obstetrician and gynaecologist working with girls and women affected by FGM.	F
P45	Mosque in Cambridge	Imam advising on Islamic scripture relating to FGM.	M

(Continued)

Appendix IV: Continued

Participant no	Organisation as noted in interview tag	Role	Gender
P46	Chambers in London	Leading criminal barrister involved in the first and only FGM prosecution.	M
P47	Chambers in London and Ministry of Justice	Leading criminal barrister and member of the judiciary with experience of FGM.	M
P48	Chambers in London	Senior criminal barrister involved in the first and only FGM prosecution.	F
P49	Chambers in the North of England	Leading family law barrister involved in a family law case of FGM.	M
P50	Chambers in the North of England	Senior family law barrister involved in a family law case of FGM.	M
P51	Chambers in the North of England	Leading family law barrister involved in a family law case of FGM.	M
P52	Ministry of Justice	Member of the judiciary with experience of FGM.	F
P53	Chambers in London	Senior family law barrister involved in a family law case of FGM.	M
P54	Law firm in France	Senior lawyer in France with extensive experience prosecuting parents and cutters in cases of FGM.	F
P56	Local Authority in London	Children's safeguarding and development officer working with the voluntary community and faith sector ensuring they have child safeguarding policies relating to FGM.	F
P57	NSPCC	Policy advisor with experience of FGM cases.	F
P58	Consultant for NGOs	Working with NGO organisations to research FGM and launch anti-FGM programmes internationally.	F
P59	NGO	Working with FGM-performing communities to encourage them to abandon FGM.	F
P60	NGO	Working with FGM-performing communities to encourage them to abandon FGM.	F
P61	NGO	Working with FGM-performing communities to encourage them to abandon FGM.	F
P62	NGO	Feminist activist and advocate focusing on women's rights violations.	F
P63	NGO	Working with women and girls from FGM-performing communities to encourage them to abandon FGM.	F

Appendix IV: Continued

Participant no	Organisation as noted in interview tag	Role	Gender
P64	NGO	Working with women and girls from FGM-performing communities to encourage them to abandon FGM.	F
P65	NGO	Working with faith leaders to encourage them to advocate for eliminating FGM.	F
P66	Undisclosed Police Constabulary	Police officer involved in investigating cases of FGM and referring cases to the Crown Prosecution Service.	M
P67	Undisclosed Police and Crime Commissioner	Working for the Police and Crime Commissioner and assisting in advising the police regarding FGM cases.	F
P68	Crown Prosecution Service	Advises on prosecuting cases including FGM cases.	F
P69	Crown Prosecution Service	Advises on prosecuting cases including FGM cases.	M
P70	Crown Prosecution Service	Advises on prosecuting cases including FGM cases.	F
P71	Crown Prosecution Service	Advises on prosecuting cases including FGM cases.	M
P72	Private Health Clinic	Cosmetic surgeon who has worked with women who have undergone FGM.	M
P73	Private Health Clinic	Cosmetic surgeon who has worked with women who have undergone FGM.	M
P74	British Association for Social Workers	Advises on how social workers should deal with cases of FGM.	M
P75	Social worker at undisclosed local authority	Deals with cases of FGM where girls are at risk of the practice.	F
P76	Undisclosed school	Head teacher of a primary school working with girls affected by FGM.	F
P77	Undisclosed school	Head teacher of a primary school working with girls affected by FGM.	F
P78	Undisclosed school	Teacher at a primary school working with girls affected by FGM.	F
P79	Undisclosed school	Head teacher of a primary school working with girls affected by FGM.	F

Bibliography

== '"Genital Mutilation" Doctor Struck off after Undercover Press Sting' *BBC News* (30 May 2014) <http://www.bbc.co.uk/news/uk-england-birmingham-27641431> accessed 7 March 2021

== 'Doctor is Cleared After UK's FGM Prosecution Amid Claims of "show trial"' *Evening Standard* (London, 5 February 2015) <https://www.standard.co.uk/news/crime/doctor-cleared-after-uks-first-fgm-prosecution-amid-claims-of-a-show-trial-10024336.html> accessed 5 March 2021

== 'FGM: Social Workers Should Not Take on the Role of the Police' British Association of Social Workers (11 February 2015) <https://www.basw.co.uk/media/news/2015/feb/fgm-social-workers-should-not-take-role-police> accessed 7 March 2021

== 'First Person to Be Convicted for Female Genital Mutilation in the UK Jailed' *Newstalk* (8 March 2019) <https://www.newstalk.com/news/woman-jailed-female-genital-mutilation-835605> accessed 5 March 2021

== 'Improve Reporting of Female Genital Mutilation, MPs Tell Doctors' The British Medical Journal (18 March 2015) <https://www.bmj.com/content/350/bmj.h1467/rapid-responses accessed 7 March 2021.

== 'Letter: Dawoodi Bohra Women of Detroit Speak Up' *Detroit News* <https://eu.detroitnews.com/story/opinion/2018/12/12/letter-dawoodi-bohra-women-detroit-speak-up/2278119002/> accessed 7 March 2021

== 'An Agonising Choice. After 30 Years of Attempts to Eradicate A Barbaric Practice, It Continues. Time to Try a New Approach' *Economist* (18 June 2016)

Abdalla RHD, *Sisters in Affliction: Circumcision and Infibulation of Women in Africa* (Zed Press 1982)

Abdalla SM and Galea S, 'Is Female Genital Mutilation/Cutting Associated with Adverse Mental Health Consequences? A Systematic Review of the Evidence' (2019) 4(4) The British Medical Journal Global Health e001553

Abdelshahid A, Smith K, and Habane K, '"Do No Harm": Lived Experiences and Impacts of FGM Safeguarding Policies and Procedures, Bristol Study' FORWARD UK (2021) <https://www.forwarduk.org.uk/wp-content/uploads/2021/02/FORWARD-UKs-FGM-Safeguarding-Research-Report-Bristol-Study-2021.pdf> accessed 6 March 2021

Abu-Sahlieh SAA, 'To Mutilate in the Name of Jehovah or Allah: Legitimization of Male and Female Circumcision' (1994) 13 Medicine and Law 575

Abusharaf RM, *Female Circumcision: Multicultural Perspectives* (University of Pennsylvania Press 2013)

Ahmadu F, 'Rites and Wrongs: An Insider/Outsider Reflects on Power and Excision' in Shell-Duncan B and Hernlund Y, *Female 'Circumcision' In Africa: Dimensions of the Practice and Debates* (Lynne Rienner Publishers 2000)

Akers S, 'Female Genital Mutilation-Cultural or Criminal' (1994) 6(1) Tolley's Journal of Child Law 27

Ali A and others, 'Exploring Young People's Interpretations of Female Genital Mutilation in The UK Using a Community-Based Participatory Research Approach' (2020) 20(1) BMC Public Health 1

Ali S and others, 'Female Genital Mutilation (FGM) in UK Children: A Review of a Dedicated Paediatric Service for FGM' (2020) 105(11) Archives of Disease in Childhood 1075

Allen C, Isakjee A, and Young ÖÖ, '"Maybe We Are Hated": The Experience and Impact of Anti-Muslim Hate on British Muslim Women' (2013) University of Birmingham: Institute of Applied Social Studies, School of Social Policy <https://www.tellmamauk.org/wp-cont ent/uploads/2013/11/maybewearehated.pdf> accessed 7 March 2021

Amasanti ML, Imcha M, and Momoh C, 'Compassionate and Proactive Interventions by Health Workers in the United Kingdom: A Better Approach to Prevent and Respond to Female Genital Mutilation?' (2016) 13(3) PLOS Medicine 1

American Association of Pediatrics, 'Policy Statement: Ritual Genital Cutting of Female Minors, American Academy of Pediatrics' (2010) 125(5) Pediatrics 1088

Ammons LL, 'Mules, Madonnas, Babies, Bathwater, Racial Imagery and Stereotypes: The African-American Woman and the Battered Woman Syndrome' (1995) 5 Wisconsin Law Review 1003

Anantnarayan L, Diler S, and Menon N, 'The Clitoral Hood: A Contested Site: Khafd or Female Genital Mutilation/Cutting (FGM/C) in India' WeSpeakOut & Nari Samata Manch (2018)

Arora KS and Jacobs AJ, 'Female Genital Alteration: A Compromise Solution' (2016) 42(3) Journal of Medical Ethics 148

Ashworth A and Zedner L, *Preventive Justice* (Oxford University Press 2014)

Ashworth A and Zedner L, 'Defending the Criminal Law: Reflections on the Changing Character of Crime, Procedure, and Sanctions' (2015) 2(1) Criminal Law and Philosophy 21

Asma El Dareer, *Woman, Why Do You Weep? Circumcision and Its Consequences* (Zed Press 1982)

Assaad MB, 'Female Circumcision in Egypt: Social Implications, Current Research, and Prospects for Change' [1980] Studies in Family Planning 3

Avalos LR, 'Female Genital Mutilation and Designer Vaginas in Britain: Crafting an Effective Legal and Policy Framework' (2015) 48(3) Vanderbilt Journal of Transnational Law 621

Bader D, 'Picturing Female Circumcision and Female Genital Cosmetic Surgery: A Visual Framing Analysis of Swiss Newspapers, 1983–2015' (2019) 19(8) Feminist Media Studies 1159

Bader D and Mottier V, 'Femonationalism and Populist Politics: The Case of the Swiss Ban on Female Genital Mutilation' (2020) Nations and Nationalism

Baillot H and others, 'Tackling Female Genital Mutilation in Scotland: A Scottish Model of Intervention' (Scottish Refugee Council 2014)

Baillot H and others, 'Addressing Female Genital Mutilation in Europe: A Scoping Review of Approaches to Participation, Prevention, Protection, and Provision of Services' (2018) 17(1) International Journal for Equity in Health 21

Baker Brown I, 'On the Curability of Certain Forms of Insanity, Epilepsy, Catalepsy, and Hysteria' (1866) 1(278) The British Medical Journal 438

Bangham S, 'Re E (Children) Female Genital Mutilation Protection Orders) [2015] EWHC 2275 (Fam)' (*Family Law*, 29 July 2015) <http://www.familylaw.co.uk/news_and_comm ent/re-e-children-female-genital-mutilation-protection-orders-2015-ewhc-2275-fam#. Vvp52MdBDdk> accessed 5 March 2021

Bar Human Rights Committee, 'Report of the Bar Human Rights Committee of England and Wales to the Parliamentary Inquiry into Female Genital Mutilation' (2014) <https://www.barhumanrights.org.uk/wp-content/uploads/2015/07/FGM-report.pdf> accessed 6 March 2021

Barbera ML, 'Multicentred Feminism: Revisiting the "Female Genital Mutilation"' (2009) Discourse

Barker-Benfield B, 'Sexual Surgery in Late-Nineteenth-Century America' (1975) 5(2) International Journal of Health Services 279

Barker-Benfield GJ, *The Horrors of the Half-Known Life: Male Attitudes toward Women and Sexuality in 19th. Century America* (Routledge 2004)

Bartky SL, 'Foucault, Femininity, and the Modernization of Patriarchal Power' in Quinby L and Diamond I (eds), *Feminism and Foucault: Reflections on Resistance* (Northeastern University Press 1997) 25

Bassili Assaad M, 'Female Circumcision in Egypt: Social Implications, Current Research, and Prospects for Change' (1980) Studies in Family Planning 3

Bedri N and Bradley T, 'Mapping the Complexities and Highlighting the Dangers: The Global Drive to End FGM in the UK and Sudan.' (2017) 17(1) Progress in Development Studies 24

Bennett G, 'Bristol Dad Accused of Having Daughter "Cut" in Female Genital Mutilation Procedure Found NOT Guilty' *BristolLive* (Bristol, 22 February 2022) <https://www.bristolpost.co.uk/news/bristol-news/live-bristol-dad-trial-child-1232470> accessed 5 March 2021

Bentham M, 'FGM Parents "Are Having Girls Cut at Younger Age"' *Evening Standard* (London, 27 March 2014)

Bentham M, '"Baby FGM" Court Case Thrown Out Due to Lack of Proof' *Evening Standard* (London, 18 January 2016) <https://www.standard.co.uk/news/crime/baby-fgm-court-case-thrown-out-due-to-lack-of-proof-a3159056.html> accessed 7 March 2021

Bentham M, 'Doctor Cleared Over FGM Says Women Should Be Free to Have Intimate Surgery' *Evening Standard* (London, 28 February 2017) <https://www.standard.co.uk/news/health/doctor-cleared-over-fgm-says-women-should-be-free-to-have-intimate-surgery-a3477941.html> accessed 4 March 2021

Berer M, 'Labia Reduction for Non-Therapeutic Reasons vs. Female Genital Mutilation: Contradictions in Law and Practice in Britain' (2010) 18(35) Reproductive Health Matters 106

Berer M, 'The History and Role of the Criminal Law in Anti-FGM Campaigns: Is the Criminal Law What Is Needed, at Least in Countries Like Great Britain?' (2015) 23(46) Reproductive Health Matters 145

Berer M, 'Prosecution of Female Genital Mutilation in the United Kingdom: Injustice at the Intersection of Good Public Health Intentions and the Criminal Law' (2019) 19(4) Medical Law International 258

Bewley S, 'Disingenuous Lack of Interests in Labiaplasty Debate' (2015) 122(3) British Journal of Obstetrics and Gynaecology 444

Bibbings L and Alldridge P 'Sexual Expression, Body Alteration, and the Defence of Consent' (1993) 20(3) Journal of Law and Society 356

Bibbings LS, 'Female Circumcision: Mutilation or Modification' in Bridgeman J and Mills S (eds), *Law and Body Politics: Regulating the Female Body* (Dartmouth 1995)

Bilge S, 'Beyond Subordination vs. Resistance: An Intersectional Approach to the Agency of Veiled Muslim Women' (2010) 31(1) Journal of Intercultural Studies 9

Bindel J, 'An Unpunished Crime: The Lack of Prosecutions for Female Genital Mutilation in the UK' (2014) New Culture Forum

Boddy J, 'Womb as Oasis: The Symbolic Context of Pharaonic Circumcision in Rural Northern Sudan' (1982) 9(4) American Ethnologist 682

Boddy J, *Wombs and Alien Spirits. Women, Men, and the Zar Cult in Northern Sudan* (The University of Wisconsin Press 1989)

Boulware-Miller K, 'Female Circumcision: Challenges to the Practice as a Human Rights Violation' (1985) 8 Harvard Women's Law Journal 155

Boyle EH, Songora F, and Foss G, 'International Discourse and Local Politics: Anti-Female-Genital-Cutting Laws in Egypt, Tanzania, and the United States' (2001) 48(4) Social Problems 524

Bradley T, *Women, Violence and Tradition: Taking FGM and Other Practices to a Secular State* (Zed Books Ltd 2011)

Bramwell R, 'Invisible Labia: The Representation of Female External Genitals in Women's Magazines' (2002) 17(2) Sexual and Relationship Therapy 187

Braun V, '"THE WOMEN ARE DOING IT FOR THEMSELVES." The Rhetoric of Choice and Agency around Female Genital "Cosmetic Surgery"' (2009) 24(60) Australian Feminist Studies 233

Brems E, 'Enemies or Allies? Feminism and Cultural Relativism as Dissident Voices in Human Rights Discourse' (1997) 19(1) Human Rights Quarterly 136

Brennan K, 'The Influence of Cultural Relativism on International Human Rights Law: Female Circumcision as a Case Study' (1988) 7 Law & Inequality 367

Brown E and Porter C, 'The Tackling FGM Initiative: Evaluation of the Second Phase (2013–2016)' (Options Consultancy Services Limited, London 2016)

Bryman A, *Social Research Methods* (Oxford University Press 2012)

Bunch C, 'Women's Rights as Human Rights: Toward a Re-vision of Human Rights' (1990) 12(4) Human Rights Quarterly 486

Burman E, 'From Difference to Intersectionality: Challenges and Resources' (2003) 6(4) European Journal of Psychotherapy & Counselling 293

Burman E, 'Engendering Culture in Psychology' (2005) 15(4) Theory & Psychology 527

Burman E, Smailes SL, and Chantler K, '"Culture" as a Barrier to Service Provision and Delivery: Domestic Violence Services for Minoritized Women' (2004) 24(3) Critical Social Policy 332

Burrage H, *Eradicating Female Genital Mutilation: A UK Perspective* (Routledge 2016)

Burrage H, *Female Mutilation: A Global Journey behind the Curtains of the Horrifying Worldwide Practice of Female Genital Mutilation* (New Holland Publishers 2016)

Cerny Smith R, 'Female Circumcision: Bringing Women's Perspectives into the International Debate' (1991) 65 Southern California Law Review 2449

Chambers C, *Sex, Culture, and Justice: The Limits of Choice* (Penn State Press 2008)

Chase SE, *Ambiguous Empowerment: The Work Narratives of Women School Superintendents* (University of Massachusetts Press 1995)

Christou TA and Fowles S, 'Failure to Protect Girls from Female Genital Mutilation' (2015) 79(5) The Journal of Criminal Law 344

Coker D, 'Crime Control and Feminist Law Reform in Domestic Violence Law: A Critical Review' (2001) 4(2) Buffalo Criminal Law Review 801

Coleman DL, 'The Seattle Compromise: Multicultural Sensitivity and Americanization' (1998) 47 Duke Law Journal 717

Collinson A and Furst J, 'FGM "Increasingly Performed on UK Babies"' *BBC News* (London, 4 February 2020)

Conroy RM, 'Female Genital Mutilation: Whose Problem, Whose Solution?: Tackle "Cosmetic" Genital Surgery in Rich Countries before Criticising Traditional Practices Elsewhere' (2006) 333(7559) The British Medical Journal 106

Cook RJ and Dickens BM, 'Special Commentary on the Issue of Reinfibulation' (2010) 109(2) International Journal of Gynecology & Obstetrics 97

Coomaraswamy R, 'Identity Within: Cultural Relativism, Minority Rights and the Empowerment of Women' (2002) 34 George Washington International Law Review 483

Coomaraswamy R, 'Integration of the Human Rights of Women and the Gender Perspective: Violence against Women' (Report of the Special Rapporteur on Violence against Women, its Causes and Consequences, Ms Radhika Coomaraswamy, submitted in accordance with Commission on Human Rights resolution 2001/49: cultural practices in the family that are violent towards women, United Nations Economic and Social Council 2002)

Creighton SM and Hodes D, 'Female Genital Mutilation: What Every Paediatrician Should Know' (2016) 101(3) Archives of Disease in Childhood 267

Creighton SM and Liao LM, 'Requests for Cosmetic Genitoplasty: How Should Healthcare Providers Respond?' (2007) 334(7603) The British Medical Journal 1090

Creighton SM and Liao LM, Female Genital Cosmetic Surgery: Solution to What Problem? (Cambridge University Press 2019)

Creighton SM and others, 'Multidisciplinary Approach to the Management of Children with Female Genital Mutilation (FGM) or Suspected FGM: Service Description and Case Series' (2016) 6(2) The British Medical Journal 1

Creighton SM and others, 'An Exploration of Attitudes towards Female Genital Mutilation (FGM) in Men and Women Accessing FGM Clinical Services in London: A Pilot Study' (2018) 38(7) Journal of Obstetrics and Gynaecology 1005

Creighton SM and others, 'Tackling Female Genital Mutilation in the UK' (2019) 15 The British Medical Journal 364

Creighton SM and others 'Female Genital Mutilation (FGM) in UK Children: A Review of a Dedicated Paediatric Service For FGM' (2020) Archives of Disease in Childhood

Crenshaw K, 'Mapping the Margins: Intersectionality, Identity Politics, and Violence against Women of Color' (1991) 43(6) Stanford Law Review 1241

Crown Prosecution Service, 'Violence against Women and Girls Crime Report 2017–2018' (CPS 2017–18)

Crown Prosecution Service, 'Violence against Women and Girls Crime Report 2018–2019' (CPS 2018–19).

Daly M, Gyn/Ecology: The Metaethics of Radical Feminism (Beacon Press 1990)

Davis A, 'New Campaign to End Female Genital Mutilation in Africa' Evening Standard (London, 9 October 2014) <https://www.standard.co.uk/news/london/new-campaign-to-end-female-genital-mutilation-in-africa-9784134.html> accessed 4 March 2021

Davis K, 'Responses to W. Njambi's "Dualisms and Female Bodies in Representations of African Female Circumcision: A Feminist Critique": Between Moral Outrage and Cultural Relativism' (2004) 5(3) Feminist Theory 305

Dawoodi Bohra Women's Association for Religious Freedom website: <https://dbwrf.org/#homesection> accessed 7 March 2021

Dearden L, 'FGM Conviction: Mother of Girls, 3, Becomes First Person Found Guilty of Female Genital Mutilation in UK' Independent (London, 1 February 2019) <https://www.independent.co.uk/news/uk/crime/fgm-first-uk-conviction-mother-three-year-old-female-genital-mutilation-witchcraft-london-a8758641.html> accessed 5 March 2021

DeVault ML and Gross G, 'Feminist Interviewing: Experience, Talk, and Knowledge' in Hesse-Biber S (ed), *Handbook of Feminist Research* (Sage Publications 2007)

DFID, 'Ending FGM: UK Aid Makes Largest Ever Investment' (DFID in the News, 23 November 2018) <https://dfidnews.blog.gov.uk/2018/11/23/end-fgm-female-genital-mutilation-uk-aid-makes-largest-ever-investment/> accessed 4 March 2021

Dixon S and others, 'Female Genital Mutilation in the UK—Where Are We, Where Do We Go Next? Involving Communities in Setting The Research Agenda' (2018) 4(1) Research Involvement and Engagement 1

Dixon S, Hinton L, and Ziebland S, 'Supporting Patients with Female Genital Mutilation in Primary Care: A Qualitative Study Exploring the Perspectives of GPs Working in England' (2020) 70(699) British Journal of General Practice 749

Dixon S, Shacklock J, and Leach J, 'Tackling Female Genital Mutilation in the UK: Female Genital Mutilation: Barriers to Accessing Care' (2019) The British Medical Journal 364

Donnelly J,. 'Cultural Relativism and Universal Human Rights' (1984) Human Rights Quarterly 400

Dorkenoo E, *Cutting the Rose: Female Genital Mutilation: The Practice and its Prevention* (Minority Rights Group 1994)

Duits L and Van Zoonen L, 'Headscarves and Porno-Chic: Disciplining Girls' Bodies in the European Multicultural Society' (2006) 13(2) European Journal of Women's Studies 103

Dustin M, 'Female Genital Mutilation/Cutting in the UK: Challenging the Inconsistencies' (2010) 17(1) European Journal of Women's Studies 7

Dustin M, 'Culture or Masculinity? Understanding Gender-Based Violence in the UK' (2016) 24(1) Journal of Poverty and Social Justice 51

Dustin M and Phillips A, 'Whose Agenda Is It? Abuses of Women and Abuses of "Culture" in Britain' (2008) 8(3) Ethnicities 405

Earp BD, 'Does Female Genital Mutilation Have Health Benefits? The Problem with Medicalizing Morality' Quillette (15 August 2017) <https://quillette.com/2017/08/15/female-genital-mutilation-health-benefits-problem-medicalizing-morality/> accessed 7 March 2021

Edwards R, 'Connecting Method and Epistemology: A White Woman Interviewing Black Women' (1990) 13(5) Women's Studies International Forum 477

Ekaney N and Proudman C, 'FGM and the Serious Crime Act 2015' (Family Law Week, 15 July 2015) <https://www.familylawweek.co.uk/site.aspx?i=ed145848> accessed 4 March 2021

El Dareer A, *Woman, Why Do You Weep? Circumcision and its Consequences* (Zed Press 1982)

El Saadawi N, *The Hidden Face of Eve: Women in the Arab World* (Zed Books 2007)

Engle K, 'Female Subjects of Public International Law: Human Rights and the Exotic Other Female' (1991) 26 New England Law Review 1509

Ertürk Y, '15 Years of the United Nations Special Rapporteur on Violence against Women, its Causes and Consequences (1994–2009)—A Critical Review' (United Nations 2009)

Finch J, '"It's Great to Have Someone to Talk to": Ethics and Politics of Interviewing Women' in Hammersley M, *Social Research, Philosophy, Politics and Practice* (Sage 1993)

Finlay F, Baverstock A, and Marcer H, 'G134 A Debate on Female Genital Mutilation, Cosmetic Genital Surgery and Genital Piercings' (2016) 101(1) The British Medical Journal

Foster C and Kelly B, 'Should Female Genital Cosmetic Surgery and Genital Piercing be Regarded Ethically and Legally as Female Genital Mutilation?' (2012) 119(4) British Journal of Obstetrics and Gynaecology 389

Gaffney-Rhys R, 'The Development of the Law Relating to Forced Marriage: Does the Law Reflect the Interests of the Victim?' (2014) 16(4) Crime Prevention & Community Safety 269

Gaffney-Rhys R, 'From the Offences Against the Person Act 1861 to the Serious Crime Act 2015—The Development of the Law Relating to Female Genital Mutilation in England and Wales' (2017) 39(4) Journal of Social Welfare and Family Law 417

Gaffney-Rhys R, 'Female Genital Mutilation: The Law in England and Wales Viewed from a Human Rights Perspective' (2020) 24(4) The International Journal of Human Rights 457

Gallin AJ, 'The Cultural Defense: Undermining the Policies Against Domestic Violence' (1993) 35 Boston College Law Review 723

Garland D, *The Culture of Control: Crime and Social Order in Contemporary Society* (University of Chicago Press 2001)

Gegzabheb SB, Norman K, and Otoo-Oyortey N, ' "Between Two Cultures": A Rapid PEER Study Exploring Migrant Communities' Views on Female Genital Mutilation in Essex and Norfolk, UK' FORWARD & National FGM Centre Report (2016)

Gerry F, Proudman C, Rowland A, Home J, and Walton K, 'Why It Is time for an FGM Commissioner—Practical Responses to Feminised Issues' (2020) Family Law Journal

Gerry F, Proudman C, Ali H, Home J, and Rowland AG, 'Widespread Concerns Still Exist in Relation to the Discrimination towards Women and Girls and FGM' (2021) Archives of Disease in Childhood

Gill A, Cox P, and Wier R, 'Shaping Priority Services for UK Victims of Honour-Based Violence/Abuse, Forced Marriage, and Female Genital Mutilation' (2018) 57(4) Howard Journal of Crime and Justice 576

Gillespie R, 'Women, the Body and Brand Extension in Medicine: Cosmetic Surgery and the Paradox of Choice' (1997) 24(4) Women & Health 69

Gordon H, 'Female Genital Mutilation: A Clinician's Experience' in Momoh C (ed), *Female Genital Mutilation* (Radcliffe Publishing 2005)

Greer G, *The Whole Woman* (Doubleday 1999)

Grewal I, 'On the New Global Feminism and the Family of Nations: Dilemmas of Transnational Feminist Practice' in Shohat E, *Talking Visions: Multicultural Feminism in a Transnational Age* (MIT Press 1998)

Gunning I, 'Arrogant Perception, World-Travelling and Multicultural Feminism: The Case of Female Genital Surgeries' (1991) 23 Columbia Human Rights Law Review 189

Gunning I, 'Uneasy Alliances and Solid Sisterhood: A Response to Professor Obiora's Bridges and Barricades' (1997) 47 Case Western Reserve Law Review 445

Gunning I, 'Women and Traditional Practices: Female Genital Surgery' in Askin KD and Koenig DM, *Women and International Human Rights Law* (Transnational Publishers 1999)

Haddad YY, 'The Post-9/11 Hijab as Icon' (2007) 68(3) Sociology of Religion 253

Hennink M, 'Language and Communication in Cross-Cultural Qualitative Research' (2008) 34 Doing Cross-Cultural Research 21

Hesse-Biber S, 'Feminist Research: Exploring, Interrogating, and Transforming the Interconnections of Epistemology, Methodology, and Method' in Hesse-Biber S (ed), *Handbook of Feminist Research* (Sage Publications 2012)

Hicks EK, *Infibulation: Female Mutilation in Islamic Northeastern Africa* (Transaction Publishers 1996)

Home J, Rowland A, Gerry F, Proudman C, and Walton K, 'A Review of the Law Surrounding Female Genital Mutilation Protection Orders' (2020) 28(7) British Journal of Midwifery 418

Home Affairs Committee, 'Female Genital Mutilation: The Case for a National Action Plan' (second report) <https://publications.parliament.uk/pa/cm201415/cmselect/cmhaff/201/20102.htm> accessed 6 March 2021

Home Office, 'Female Genital Mutilation' (Collection) <https://www.gov.uk/government/collections/female-genital-mutilation> accessed 6 March 2021

Home Office, 'Girl Summit 2014' (Archived) <https://www.gov.uk/government/topical-events/girl-summit-2014> accessed 4 March 2021

Home Office, 'Gender Issues in the Asylum Claim' (2018) <https://assets.publishing.service.gov.uk/government/uploads/system/uploads/attachment_data/file/699703/gender-issues-in-the-asylum-claim-v3.pdf> accessed 7 March 2021

Home Office and Border Force, 'Operation Limelight: Instructions to Police and Border Force Staff' (Guidance) (24 January 2020) <https://www.gov.uk/government/publications/operation-limelight-instructions-to-police-and-border-force-staff> accessed 7 March 2021

Hooks B, *Ain't I a Woman* (South End Press 1981)

Hosken FP, *The Hosken Report: Genital and Sexual Mutilation of Females* (Women's International Network News 1979)

House of Commons Home Affairs Committee, 'House of Commons Home Affairs Committee: Female Genital Mutilation: Abuse Unchecked' (Ninth Report of Session 2016–17) (2016)

House of Lords Debate 23 March 2000, vol 611, cols 402–04 <https://api.parliament.uk/historic-hansard/lords/2000/mar/23/female-circumcision#S5LV0611P0_20000323_HOL_38> accessed 4 March 2021

Hussein E, 'Women's Experiences, Perceptions and Attitudes of Female Genital Mutilation: The Bristol PEER Study' FORWARD (2010)

Izett S and Toubia N, *Learning About Social Change. A Research and Evaluation Guidebook Using Female Circumcision as a Case Study* (RAINBO 1999)

Jeffreys S, *Beauty and Misogyny* (Routledge 2005)

Johnsdotter S and Essén B, 'Deinfibulation Contextualized: Delicacies of Shared Decision-Making in the Clinic' (2020) Archives of Sexual Behavior 1

Johnson-Bailey J, 'The Ties that Bind and the Shackles that Separate: Race, Gender, Class, And Color in a Research Process' (1999) 12(6) International Journal of Qualitative Studies in Education 659

Jones C, 'Interview: Muna Hassan: "One of Us Mentioned Vaginas and Michael Gove Went Really Red!"' *Guardian* (London, 14 December 2014) <https://www.theguardian.com/world/2014/dec/14/muna-hassan-faces-of-2014-one-of-us-mentioned-vaginas-and-michael-gove-went-really-red> accessed 4 March 2021

Kandala NB and Komba PN, 'Compatibility between National FGMs and International Human Rights Law' in *Female Genital Mutilation around the World: Analysis of Medical Aspects, Law and Practice* (Springer 2018)

Kaoma Mwenda K, 'Labia Elongation under African Customary Law: A Violation of Women's Rights?' (2006) 10(4) The International Journal of Human Rights 341

Karlsen S and others, 'When Safeguarding Becomes Stigmatising: A Report on the Impact of FGM-Safeguarding Procedures on People with a Somali Heritage Living in Bristol' University of Bristol (2019)

Kelly L, *Surviving Sexual Violence* (John Wiley & Sons 2013)

Khiabany G and Williamson M, 'Veiled Bodies—Naked Racism: Culture, Politics and Race in the Sun' (2008) 50(2) Race & Class 69

King SC, 'The Sociologist and the Community Developer: Autonomy and Role Conflict in Qualitative Research' (1981) 1(2) Sociological Spectrum 185

Kline M, 'Race, Racism, and Feminist Legal Theory' (1989) 12 Harvard Women's Law Journal 115

Korieh C, '"Other" Bodies: Western Feminism, Race, and Representation in Female Circumcision Discourse' in Nnaemeka O (ed), *Female Circumcision and the Politics of Knowledge: African Women in Imperialist Discourses* (Praegar 2005)

Koso-Thomas O, *The Circumcision of Women: A Strategy for Eradication* (Zed Books 1987)

Kwateng-Kluvitse A, 'Female Genital Mutilation and Child Protection' in Momoh C (ed) *Female Genital Mutilation* (Radcliffe Publishing 2005)

Kymlicka W, Lernestedt C, and Matravers M, *Criminal Law and Cultural Diversity* (Oxford University Press 2014)

La Barbera MC, 'Ban without Prosecution, Conviction without Punishment, and Circumcision without Cutting: A Critical Appraisal of Anti-FGM Laws in Europe' (2017) 17(1) Global Jurist

Lacey N, *Unspeakable Subjects: Feminist Essays in Legal and Social Theory* (Bloomsbury Publishing 1998)

Lacey N, 'Community, Culture and Criminalisation' in Cruft R, Kramer MH, and Reiff MR, *Crime, Punishment, and Responsibility: The Jurisprudence of Antony Duff* (Oxford University Press 2011)Lakshmi A, Diler S, Menon N, WeSpeakOut, and Manch NS, *The Clitoral Hood A Contested Site Khafd or Female Genital Mutilation/Cutting (FGM/C) in India* (2018) http://www.wespeakout.org/site/assets/files/1439/fgmc_study_results_jan_2018.pdf accessed 17 May 2021

Larsson M and others, 'An Exploration of Attitudes towards Female Genital Mutilation (FGM) in Men and Women Accessing FGM Clinical Services in London: A Pilot Study' (2018) 38(7) Journal of Obstetrics and Gynaecology

Lewis H, 'Between Irua and "Female Genital Mutilation": Feminist Human Rights Discourse and the Cultural Divide' (1995) 8(1) Harvard Human Rights Journal 1

Lewis JM and Dias D, 'Feminism, Morality, and Human Rights: Assessing the Effectiveness of the United Kingdom's FGM Act β' in Iyioha IO (ed), *Women's Health and the Limits of Law* (Routledge 2019)

Leye E, 'Strategies for FGM Prevention in Europe' in Momoh C (ed), *Female Genital Mutilation* (Radcliffe Publishing 2005)Leye E and Deblonde J, 'Legislation in Europe Regarding Female Genital Mutilation and the Implementation of the Law in Belgium, France, Spain, Sweden and the UK' International Centre for Reproductive Health (ICRH) (2004)

Leye E and others, 'An Analysis of the Implementation of Laws with Regard to Female Genital Mutilation in Europe' (2007) 47(1) Crime, Law and Social Change 1

Leye E and others, 'Debating Medicalization of Female Genital Mutilation/Cutting (FGM/C): Learning from (Policy) Experiences Across Countries' (2019) 16(1) Reproductive Health 158

Leye E and Sabbe A, 'Responding to Female Genital Mutilation in Europe. Striking the Right Balance between Prosecution and Prevention. A Review of Legislation' International Centre for Reproductive Health (2009)

Lightfoot-Klein H, *Prisoners of Ritual: An Odyssey into Female Genital Circumcision in Africa* (Haworth Press 1989)

Lightfoot-Klein H and Shaw E, 'Special Needs of Ritually Circumcised Women Patients' (1991) 20(2) Journal of Obstetric, Gynecologic, & Neonatal Nursing 102

Litchfield J, 'The French Way: A Better Approach to Fighting FGM?' *Independent* (London, 15 December 2013)

Lloyd J and others, 'Female Genital Appearance: "Normality" Unfolds' (2005) 112(5) British Journal of Obstetrics and Gynaecology 643

Longman C and Bradley T, *Interrogating Harmful Cultural Practices: Gender, Culture and Coercion* (Routledge 2016)

Macfarlane A, 'Misleading Use of FGM Statistics Compounds Concerns about their Reliability' (Letter) (2019) The British Medical Journal 364

Macfarlane AJ and Dorkenoo E, 'Female Genital Mutilation in England and Wales: Updated Statistical Estimates of the Numbers of Affected Women Living in England and Wales and Girls at Risk: Interim Report on Provisional Estimates' City University London (2014)

Mackie G, 'Female Genital Cutting: The Beginning of the End' in Rienner L (ed), *Female 'Circumcision' in Africa: Culture, Controversy, and Change* (Lynne Rienner Publishers 2000)

MacKinnon CA, *Toward A Feminist Theory of The State* (Harvard University Press 1989)

Mahmood S, *Politics of Piety: The Islamic Revival and The Feminist Subject* (Princeton University Press 2011)

Malik Y and others, 'Mandatory Reporting of Female Genital Mutilation in Children in the UK' (2018) 26(6) British Journal of Midwifery 377

Malmström MF, 'The Production of Sexual Mutilation among Muslim Women in Cairo' (2013) 3(2) Global Discourse 306

Malmström MF, *The Politics of Female Circumcision in Egypt: Gender, Sexuality and the Construction of Identity* (IB Tauris 2016)

Marranci M, 'Multiculturalism, Islam and the Clash of Civilisations Theory: Rethinking Islamophobia' (2004) 5(1) Culture and Religion 105

Martinez Perez G, Tmoas Aznar C, and Bagnol B, 'Labia Minora Elongation and its Implications on the Health of Women: A Systematic Review' (2014) 26(3) International Journal of Sexual Health 155

Maynard M and Winn J, 'Women, Violence and Male Power' in Robinson V and Richardson D (eds), *Introducing Women's Studies* (Macmillan 1997)

Megafu U, 'Female Ritual Circumcision in Africa an Investigation of the Presumed Benefits among Ibos of Nigeria' (1983) 60(11) East African Medical Journal 793

Menjívar C and Salcido O, 'Immigrant Women and Domestic Violence: Common Experiences in Different Countries' (2002) 16(6) Gender & Society 898

Mestre i Mestre RMM and Johnsdotter S, 'Court Cases, Cultural Expertise, and "Female Genital Mutilation" in Europe' (2019) Cultural Expertise and Socio-Legal Studies (Studies in Law, Politics, and Society Series) 78

Meyers DT, 'Feminism and Women's Autonomy: The Challenge of Female Genital Cutting' 31(5) Metaphilosophy (2000) 281

Miller J and Glassner B, 'The "Inside" and the "Outside": Finding Realities in Interviews in Silverman D (ed), *Qualitative Research* (Sage Publications 2004)

Mills E, 'UK Midwives' Knowledge and Understanding of Female Genital Mutilation' (2018) 28(4) MIDIRS Midwifery Digest 491

Minister of Justice, 'Family Court Statistics Quarterly, England and Wales, July to September 2019' (UK Ministry of Justice, 13 December 2019)

Moen EW, 'What Does "Control Over Our Bodies" Really Mean?' (1979) International 2(2) Journal of Women's Studies 129

Mohammed GF, Hassan MM, and Eyada MM, 'Female Genital Mutilation/Cutting: Will it Continue?' (2014) 11(11) The Journal of Sexual Medicine 2756

Mohammad S, 'Legislative Action to Eradicate FGM in the UK' in Comfort Momoh (ed), *Female Genital Mutilation* (Radcliffe Publishing 2005)

Momoh C, *Female Genital Mutilation* (Radcliffe Publishing 2005)

Morison LA and others 'How Experiences and Attitudes Relating to Female Circumcision Vary According to Age on Arrival In Britain: A Study among Young Somalis in London' (2004) 9(1) Ethnicity & Health 75

Morris S, 'UK FGM Trial: Father Says Failed Case Put Intolerable Pressure on Him' *Guardian* (London, 23 February 2019) <https://www.theguardian.com/society/2018/feb/23/uk-fgm-trial-father-failed-case-intolerable-pressure> accessed 4 March 2021

Mugo MG, 'Elitist Anti-Circumcision Discourse as Mutilating and Anti-Feminist' (1997) 47 The Case Western Reserve Law Review 461

Murray V, 'Women's Legal Landmarks: Celebrating the History of Women and Law in the UK and Ireland' [book review] (2019) 53(3) The Law Teacher 395

Narayan U, *Dislocating Cultures: Identities, Traditions, and Third-World Feminisms* (Routledge 1997)

Nash JC, 'Re-Thinking Intersectionality' (2008) 89(1) Feminist Review 1

Ngarũiya Njambi W, 'Irua Ria Atumia and Anticolonial Struggles among the Gĩkũyũ of Kenya: A Counternarrative on "Female Genital Mutilation"' in Oyěwùmí O (ed), *Gender Epistemologies in Africa* (Palgrave Macmillan 2011)

NHS Digital, 'Female Genital Mutilation Datasets: The Female Genital Mutilation (FGM) Enhanced Dataset' (28 November 2019) <https://digital.nhs.uk/data-and-informat ion/clinical-audits-and-registries/female-genital-mutilation-datasets> accessed 7 March 2021

Nnaemeka O (ed), *Female Circumcision and the Politics of Knowledge: African Women in Imperialist Discourses* (Praeger 2005)

Norman K and others, 'FGM is Always with Us: Experiences, Perceptions, Beliefs of Women Affected by Female Genital Mutilation in London: Results from a PEER Study' Options Consultancy Services Ltd (2009)

NSPCC, 'Female Genital Mutilation (FGM)' <https://www.nspcc.org.uk/what-is-child-abuse/types-of-abuse/female-genital-mutilation-fgm/> accessed 7 March 2021

O'Donnell NA and others, 'G142 Female Genital Mutilation (FGM) Surveillance in Under 16 Years Olds in the UK and Ireland' (2018) 103(1) The British Medical Journal

O'Kane M, 'Ban Ki-moon Calls on Men across the World to Campaign to End FGM' *Guardian* (London, 6 February 2016)

O' Neill S and others, 'Men Have a Role to Play but They Don't Play It": A Mixed Methods Study Exploring Men's Involvement in Female Genital Mutilation in Belgium, the Netherlands and the United Kingdom' Full Report, Men Speak Out Project (2016)

Oakley A and Roberts H, 'Interviewing Women: A Contradiction in Terms' in Roberts H (ed), *Doing Feminist Research* (Routledge & Kegan Paul Plc 1997)

Obermeyer CM, 'Female Genital Surgeries: The Known, the Unknown, and the Unknowable' (1999) 13(1) Medical Anthropology Quarterly 79

Obermeyer CM, 'The Consequences of Female Circumcision for Health and Sexuality: An Update on the Evidence' (2005) 7(5) Culture, Health & Sexuality 443

Obiora LA, 'Bridges and Barricades: Rethinking Polemics and Intransigence in the Campaign against Female Circumcision' (1997) 47 Case Western Reserve Law Review 275

Obiora LA, 'The Anti-Female Circumcision Campaign Deficit' in Nnaemeka O (ed), *Female Circumcision and The Politics of Knowledge: African Women in Imperialist Discourses* (Praeger 2005)

Obiora LA, 'A Refuge from Tradition and the Refuge of Tradition: On Anticircumcision Paradigms' in Shell-Duncan B and Hernlund Y (eds), *Transcultural Bodies: Female Genital Cutting in Global Context* (Rutgers University Press 2007)

Ogbu MA, 'Comment on Obiora's Bridges and Barricades' (1997) 47 Case Western Reserve Law Review 411

Okin SM, *Is Multiculturalism Bad for Women?* (Princeton University Press 1999)

Otoo-Oyortey N, 'Challenges to Ending Female Genital Mutilation in the UK' (2020) 4(1) Nature Human Behaviour 2

Pearce AJ and Bewley S, 'Medicalization of Female Genital Mutilation. Harm Reduction or Unethical?' (2014) 24(1) Obstetrics, Gynaecology & Reproductive Medicine 29

Pedwell C, 'Theorizing "African" Female Genital Cutting and "Western" Body Modifications: A Critique of the Continuum and Analogue Approaches' (2007) 86(1) Feminist Review 45

Pedwell C, 'Sometimes What's Not Said Is Just as Important as What Is: Transnational Feminist Encounters' in Davis K and Evans M (eds), *Transatlantic Conversations: Feminism as Travelling Theory. The Feminist Imagination—Europe and Beyond* (Ashgate Publishing Limited 2011)

Plugge E and others 'The Prevention of Female Genital Mutilation in England: What Can Be Done?' (2019) 41(3) Journal of Public Health 261

Prohibition of Female Circumcision Bill, HL Deb 18 June 1985, vol 465, cols 207–24 <https://api.parliament.uk/historic-hansard/lords/1985/jun/18/prohibition-of-female-circumcision-bill> accessed 4 March 2021

Proudman C, 'In the Matter of B and G (Children) (No 2) [2015] EWFC 3' (*Family Law Week*, 2015) <https://www.familylawweek.co.uk/site.aspx?i=ed142550> accessed 5 March 2021

Proudman CR, 'The Criminalisation of Forced Marriage' (2012) 42 Family Law 460

Proudman C and Ekaney K, "Reviewing the Law on Travels Bans in FGM Cases" (2019) 49(11) Family law Journal 1305

Rahman A and Toubia N, *Female Genital Mutilation: A Guide to Laws and Policies Worldwide* (Zed Books 2000)

Reinharz S, *Feminist Methods in Social Research* (Oxford University Press 1992)

Rhodes PJ, 'Race-of-Interviewer Effects: A Brief Comment' (1994) 28(2) Sociology 547

Rogers J, *Law's Cut on the Body of Human Rights: Female Circumcision, Torture, and Scarred Flesh* (Routledge 2013)

Rogers JB, 'The First Case Addressing Female Genital Mutilation in Australia: Where Is the Harm?' (2016) 41(4) Alternative Law Journal 235

Rowland AG and others, 'The Time is Right to Introduce an Independent Commissioner' (2021) 29(1) British Journal of Midwifery 50

Royal College of Nursing, 'Female Genital Mutilation: An RCN Resource for Nursing and Midwifery Practice' (Fourth edition) (Royal College of Nursing 2019)

Royal College of Obstetricians & Gynaecologists, 'Ethical Opinion Paper: Ethical Considerations in Relation to Female Genital Cosmetic Surgery (FGCS)' (RCOG Ethics Committee 2013)

Salmon D, Olander E, and Abzhaparova A, 'A Qualitative Study Examining UK Female Genital Mutilation Health Campaigns from the Perspective of Affected Communities' (2020) 187 Public Health 84

Samuel Z, *Female Genital Mutilation (FGM): Law and Practice* (Jordan Publishing 2017)

Savane MA, 'Why Are We Against the International Campaign' (1978) International Child Welfare 40

Scott JW, *The Politics of the Veil* (Princeton University Press 2009)

Scutt JA (ed), *Women, Law and Culture: Conformity, Contradiction and Conflict* (Springer 2016)

Serour GI, 'The Issue of Reinfibulation' (2010) 109(2) International Journal of Gynecology & Obstetrics 93

Shahvisi A, 'Female Genital Alteration in the UK' in Kuehlmeyer K, Klingler C, and Huxtable R (eds), *Ethical, Legal and Social Aspects of Healthcare for Migrants: Perspectives from the UK and Germany* (Routledge 2018)

Shandall AA, 'Circumcision and Infibulation of Females: A General Consideration of the Problem and a Clinical Study of the Complications in Sudanese Women' (1967) 5(4) Sudan Medical Journal 178

Sheldon S and Wilkinson S, 'Female Genital Mutilation and Cosmetic Surgery: Regulating Non-Therapeutic Body Modification' (1998) 12(4) Bioethics 263

Shell-Duncan B, 'The Medicalization of Female "Circumcision": Harm Reduction or Promotion of a Dangerous Practice?' (2001) 52(7) Social Science & Medicine 1013

Shell-Duncan B and Hernlund Y, *Female 'Circumcision' in Africa: Dimensions of the Practice and Debates* (Lynne Rienner Publishers 2000)

Shweder RA, 'What About "Female Genital Mutilation"? And Why Understanding Culture Matters in the First Place' (2000) 129(4) Daedalus 209

Shweder RA, 'Moral Realism without the Ethnocentrism: Is it Just a List of Empty Truisms?' in Sajo A, *Human Rights with Modesty: The Problem of Universalism* (Martinus Nijhoff Publishers 2004)

Sokoloff NJ and Dupont I, 'Domestic Violence at the Intersections of Race, Class, and Gender Challenges and Contributions to Understanding Violence against Marginalized Women in Diverse Communities' (2005) 11(1) Violence against Women 38

Spender D, *Men's Studies Modified: The Impact of Feminism on the Academic Disciplines* (Pergamon Press 1981)

Spillett R, 'Ugandan Mother Becomes First Person in Britain to Be Convicted of FGM for Mutilating her Daughter, Three, as her Bizarre Witchcraft Kit, Including a Cow's TONGUE and Frozen Limes, is Revealed' *Daily Mail* (London, 1 February 2019) <https://www.dailymail.co.uk/news/article-6656933/Mother-three-year-old-girl-person-guilty-FGM-Britain.html> accessed 5 March 2021

Stonehouse R, 'UK Somalis "Racially Profiled" Over FGM" *BBC News* (12 January 2020)

Sullivan DA, *Cosmetic Surgery: The Cutting Edge of Commercial Medicine in America* (Rutgers University Press 2001)

Summers H and Ratcliffe R, 'Mother of Three-Year-Old Is First Person Convicted of FGM in UK' *Guardian* (London 1 February 2019) <https://www.theguardian.com/society/2019/feb/01/fgm-mother-of-three-year-old-first-person-convicted-in-uk> accessed 5 March 2021

Temple B and Edwards R, 'Interpreters/Translators and Cross-Language Research: Reflexivity and Border Crossings' (2002) 1(2) International Journal of Qualitative Methods 12

The Secretary of State for the Department of Health, 'THE GOVERNMENT RESPONSE TO THE NINTH REPORT FROM THE HOME AFFAIRS SELECT COMMITTEE SESSION 2016–17 HC 390: Female Genital Mutilation: Abuse Unchecked' (2016)

Thiam A, *Black Sisters, Speak Out: Feminism and Oppression in Black Africa* (Pluto Press 1986)

Tietjens Meyers D, 'Feminism and Women's Autonomy: The Challenge of Female Genital Cutting' (2000) 31(5) Metaphilosophy 281

Topping A, 'UK Solicitor Cleared of Forcing Daughter to Undergo FGM' *Guardian* (London, 22 March 2018) <https://www.theguardian.com/society/2018/mar/22/uk-solicitor-acquitted-forcing-daughter-fgm-female-genital-mutilation> accessed 5 March 2021

Toubia N, 'Female Circumcision as a Public Health Issue' (1994) 331(11) New England Journal of Medicine 712

Toubia N, 'Female Genital Mutilation' in Peters J and Wolper A, *Women's Rights, Human Rights: International Feminist Perspectives* (Psychology Press 1995)

Toubia N, *Female Genital Mutilation: A Call for Global Action* (RAINBO 1995)

Turnbull T, 'Retrials for Genital Mutilation Accused' *Goulburn Post* (Australia, 7 February 2020) <https://www.goulburnpost.com.au/story/6620104/retrials-for-genital-mutilation-accused/> accessed 7 March 2021

Uccellari P, 'Multiple Discrimination: How Law Can Reflect Reality' (2008) 1 The Equal Rights Review 24

UNICEF, World Health Organization, and UNFPA, 'Female Genital Mutilation: A Joint Statement' (1997)

UNICEF, 'Female Genital Mutilation/Cutting: A Statistical Overview and Exploration of the Dynamics of Change' (UNICEF 2013)

UNICEF, 'Female Genital Mutilation/Cutting: A Global Concern' (UNICEF 2016)

US Immigration and Customs Enforcement, 'ICE Leads Effort to Prevent Female Genital Mutilation at Newark Airport' (Newark NJ, 25 June 2018) <https://www.ice.gov/news/releases/ice-leads-effort-prevent-female-genital-mutilation-newark-airport> accessed 7 March 2021

Veale D and Daniels J, 'Cosmetic Clitoridectomy in a 33-Year-Old Woman' (2012) 41(3) Archives of Sexual Behavior 725

Walker A and Parmar P, *Warrior Marks: Female Genital Mutilation and the Sexual Blinding of Women* (Harcourt Brace 1993)

Waughray A, 'Caste Discrimination: A Twenty-First Century Challenge for UK Discrimination Law?' (2009) 72(2) The Modern Law Review 182

We Speak Out, 'Khatna: What is Khatna in the Bohra Community?' <http://www.wespeakout.org/fgm/what-is-khatna/> accessed 7 March 2021

Weil Davis S, 'Loose Lips Sink Ships' (2002) 28(1) Feminist Studies 7

Welchman L and Hossain S, *'Honour': Crimes, Paradigms and Violence against Women* (Zed Books 2005)

Werbner P, 'Folk Devils and Racist Imaginaries in a Global Prism: Islamophobia and Anti-Semitism in the Twenty-First Century' (2013) 36(3) Ethnic and Racial Studies 450

Wilson TD, 'Pharaonic Circumcision under Patriarchy and Breast Augmentation under Phallocentric Capitalism Similarities and Differences' (2002) 8(4) Violence against Women 495

Winter B, 'Women, the Law, and Cultural Relativism in France: The Case of Excision' (1994) 19(4) Signs: Journal of Women in Culture and Society 939

Wise S, 'A Framework for Discussing Ethical Issues in Feminist Research: A Review of the Literature' (1987) 19 Studies in Sexual Politics 47

World Health Organization, 'Types of Female Genital Mutilation' (WHO.int) <https://www.who.int/teams/sexual-and-reproductive-health-and-research/areas-of-work/female-genital-mutilation/types-of-female-genital-mutilation> accessed 3 March 2021

World Health Organization, 'Eliminating Female Genital Mutilation: An Interagency Statement OHCR, UNAIDS, UNDO, UNECA, UNESCO, UNFPA, UNHCR, UNICEF, UNIFEM, WHO' (World Health Organization 2008)

Yegenoglu M, *Colonial Fantasies: Towards a Feminist Reading of Orientalism* (Cambridge University Press 1998)

Zabus CJ, *Between Rites and Rights: Excision in Women's Experiential Texts and Human Contexts* (Stanford University Press 2007)

Index

For the benefit of digital users, indexed terms that span two pages (e.g., 52–53) may, on occasion, appear on only one of those pages.

Note: The terms Somalia and Somali origin have not been indexed as the focus groups of women participants are of Somali origin so these terms appear throughout.